Management, Labour Process and Software Development

Although software developers are often portrayed as central to the information age, engaged in autonomous, responsible work that is generously rewarded, this book reveals a somewhat different reality.

This book makes an important contribution to the debate over the nature of the new economy and the role of knowledge workers within it. Original research from the US, UK, Europe and Australia is used to examine the differences between the image and reality of working in the software industry.

With contributions from an impressive array of academics and specialists, this timely volume will interest a wide variety of readers including students of work and employment studies as well as those who keep up with the concept of the new economy.

Rowena Barrett is Associate Professor, Department of Management and Director of the Family and Small Business Research Unit, Monash University, Australia.

Routledge research in employment relations

Series editors: Rick Delbridge and Edmund Heery

Cardiff Business School

Aspects of the employment relationship are central to numerous courses at both undergraduate and postgraduate level.

Drawing from insights from industrial relations, human resource management and industrial sociology, this series provides an alternative source of research-based materials and texts, reviewing key developments in employment research.

Books published in this series are works of high academic merit, drawn from a wide range of academic studies in the social sciences.

1 **Social Partnership at Work**
Carola M. Frege

2 **Human Resource Management in the Hotel Industry**
Kim Hoque

3 **Redefining Public Sector Unionism:**
UNISON and the future of trade unions
Edited by Mike Terry

4 **Employee Ownership, Participation and Governance**
A study of ESOPs in the UK
Andrew Pendleton

5 **Human Resource Management in Developing Countries**
Pawan S. Budhwar and Yaw A. Debrah

6 **Gender, Diversity and Trade Unions**
International perspectives
Edited by Fiona Colgan and Sue Ledwith

7 **Inside the Factory of the Future**
Work, power and authority in microelectronics
Alan Macinlay and Phil Taylor

8 New Unions, New Workplaces
A study of union resilience in the restructured workplace
Andy Danford, Mike Richardson and Martin Upchurch

9 Partnership and Modernisation in Employment Relations
Edited by Mark Stuart and Miguel Martinez Lucio

10 Partnership at Work
William K. Roche and John F. Geary

11 European Works Councils
Pessimism of the intellect optimism of the will?
Edited by Ian Fitzgerald and John Stirling

12 Employment Relations in Non-Union Firms
Tony Dundon and Derek Rollinson

13 Management, Labour Process and Software Development
Reality bytes
Edited by Rowena Barrett

Also available from Routledge

Rethinking Industrial Relations
Mobilisation, collectivism and long waves
John Kelly

Employee Relations in the Public Services
Themes and issues
Edited by Susan Corby and Geoff White

The Insecure Workforce
Edited by Edmund Heery and John Salmon

Public Service Employment Relations in Europe
Transformation, modernisation or inertia?
Edited by Stephen Bach, Lorenzo Bordogna, Giuseppe Della Rocca and David Winchester

Reward Management
A critical text
Edited by Geoff White and Janet Druker

Working for McDonald's in Europe
The unequal struggle?
Tony Royle

Job Insecurity and Work Intensification
Edited by Brendan Burchell, David Ladipo and Frank Wilkinson

Union Organizing
Campaigning for trade union recognition
Edited by Gregor Gall

Employment Relations in the Hospitality and Tourism Industries
Rosemary Lucas

Management, Labour Process and Software Development

Reality bytes

Edited by Rowena Barrett

Routledge
Taylor & Francis Group
LONDON AND NEW YORK

First published 2005
by Routledge
2 Park Square, Milton Park, Abingdon, Oxon OX14 4RN

Simultaneously published in the USA and Canada
by Routledge
711 Third Ave, New York, NY 10017

Routledge is an imprint of the Taylor & Francis Group

Typeset in Times by Wearset Ltd, Boldon, Tyne and Wear

British Library Cataloguing in Publication Data
A catalogue record for this book is available from the British Library

Library of Congress Cataloging in Publication Data
A catalog record for this book has been requested

ISBN - 978 0 4153 2047 4

Contents

Tables

Contributors

Christopher K. Andrews is currently a PhD student in the Department of Sociology at the University of Maryland. Specializing in social stratification and social psychology, his interests include labour relations, social class, identity processes, and applied social theory. His PhD is on the role of consumers in contemporary capitalist markets.

Chris Baldry is Professor of Human Resource Management in the Department of Management and Organisation at the University of Stirling. His research interests include workplace technological change, occupational health, changes and continuities in the experience of work, and the social construction of workspace. He is editor of *New Technology, Work and Employment.*

Rowena Barrett is an Associate Professor in the Department of Management and Director of the Family and Small Business Research Unit at Monash University. Rowena's research interests centre on work and employment generally although she has a special interest in software development.

Jeff Hyman is Professor of Human Resource Management in the Department of Management Studies at the University of Aberdeen Business School. His main research interests include the future of work, work–life balance and industrial democracy.

Birgitte Johansen was a researcher at Nordlandsforskning, Bodø, Norway working on work-life and organization development projects at the time she worked on this chapter. From spring 2004 she became a PhD student at NTNU, Trondheim participating in the project 'The modern child and the flexible labour market: Institutionalism and individualisation of children in the light of changes in the welfare state'.

Craig D. Lair is a PhD student in the Department of Sociology at the University of Maryland. He studies issues of social theory, political economy and social stratification.

Bart Landry is Professor of Sociology in the Department of Sociology at the University of Maryland. He specializes in stratification, race, gender, and class, family, and technology and society. His current research focuses on software start-ups in the United States and Brazil.

Cliff Lockyer is a senior research fellow at the Fraser of Allander, University of Strathclyde, Glasgow, and was formerly senior lecturer in the Department of Human Resource Management. His current research interests focus on the nature of modern work, and Scottish labour market and policy issues.

Abigail Marks lectures in organizational behaviour at Heriot-Watt University, Edinburgh. She has undertaken research and published within the areas of teamwork, identity, work centrality and values and the construction of professions.

Graeme Philipson is an independent consultant, analyst and writer specializing in high technology in Australia. He has written over 1000 articles and columns on high technology as well as more than 40 published market research reports. He has conducted proprietary market research studies for vendors and computer publications. He is editor of CCH's *Australian Guide to eBusiness*, co-author of *How to Select a Personal Computer*, and author of *Implementing CASE Technology*, *Mainframe Wars*, and *IBM's ESA Strategy*.

Bente Rasmussen is a Professor in Work and Organization, Department of Sociology and Political Science, University of Trondheim and a researcher at SINTEF-IFIM, Trondheim. She has published extensively on the subjects of technology, work and gender, gender and organization.

Dora Scholarios is a Reader in Organisational Behaviour at the Department of Human Resource Management in the University of Strathclyde, Glasgow, Scotland. Her research is on personnel selection and classification, social process perspectives of selection, and the effects of emerging forms of work on career patterns and employee well being.

Dorothea Voss-Dahm joined the Institute for Work and Technology Gelsenkirchen, Germany in 1996. Her main areas of interest are work organization and working time organization in the service sector and the change of employment systems in an international comparative perspective. She has completed several international research projects on employment structures, flexible working and human resources management in retailing and the IT-industry.

Acknowledgements and dedication

This book has been a long time coming building, as it does, on my PhD work which started in 1995. However, it is through the commitment of the contributors to this book, their enthusiasm and willingness to work with me that this book has been created. My thanks to all of them and especially to Jeff Hyman, who gave me the courage to take on this challenge. My extra special thanks goes to my husband, Al Rainnie, for being my biggest fan and supporter and to my son Euan for putting up with me. Finally thank you to the software developers around the country that I have spoken to about your jobs, without you I would still be wondering what it is you do all day and why.

1 Introduction

Myth and reality

Rowena Barrett

Introduction

This book is the result of research conducted in five countries on three continents. While the end result may look like a cohesive and unified whole, it certainly never started out that way. These five studies were conceptualized, developed and conducted independently of one another. Indeed, prior to the September 2001 Work, Employment and Society (WES) conference in Nottingham the collective existence of these independent studies was unknown as were the researchers to one another.

The catalyst for this book was listening to two papers at the WES conference: one by Dorothea Voss-Dahm and the other by Bente Rasmussen and Birgitte Johansen. As I sat through their presentations (which for some reason I had not originally planned to attend) I could have sworn they had spoken to the same software developers I had for my research. Both papers were illustrated by quotes from developers and what I was hearing from developers in Norway and Germany about their work, their commitment, identity and the firms they worked for was pretty much the same – to all intents and purposes it was identical to what I had heard in Melbourne, Australia. I now realize this is not just the case with the three projects in Australia, Norway and Germany as the same can be said about the US and the UK. And not just about the studies reported in this book where there is a common analytical approach. For example in Swart and Kinnie's (2003) article about sharing knowledge in knowledge-intensive firms they cite a senior software developer who shared some responsibility for recruitment in 'SoftWareCo' saying, 'I think of it as inviting someone to a party. You know, sometimes you invite people who you want to come along – not necessarily those who deserve to come along' ('senior software engineer' quoted in Swart and Kinnie 2003: 67).

In my research (this aspect reported in Barrett 2004), while the CEO and founder of Webboyz did not use those exact words he meant the same thing when he explained their approach to recruitment.

> When we recruit people what we look for is not so much what brains they've got or how smart they are or anything like that, it's how passionate are they about this area. Is this something that means more to them than just a job? Is this really where they want their life to be and are they smart enough that if we step back and say 'here's a broad picture of what we want you to do go away and fill in the details yourself', will they do it?
>
> (Webboyz, CEO)

Similarly in the article by Johanna Shih (2004) looking at the pace and rhythm of work in Silicon Valley high tech firms she reports the Vice President of a new start-up saying 'I am looking for a person who is committed to the company, who is committed to the project, who believes that the idea can really take off in the marketplace' ('Chen' quoted in Shih 2004: 234) and this is interpreted as total dedication to the moment, not a long term commitment to the company. 'Chen' goes on to explain how he expects people to work,

> You must be independent and motivated. I always tell my engineers, you are your own managers. There is a pile of work on the table and I don't want to give you the deadline to finish the work because the work is almost infinite at this point in time so why don't you just dive in, and find your own work and deadlines and it's up to you to figure out how to swim.
>
> ('Chen' quoted in Shih 2004: 234)

For me the key issue is, how, given different national cultures and institutional features and arrangements with respect to business and employment, different product and labour markets, firm sizes and cultural and social expectations about work and employment, do you get workers and managers in software firms in different parts of the developed world thinking and behaving in a remarkably similar fashion?

Software work and workers: a labour process analysis

This book is part of the process of trying to understand this phenomenon and therefore it seeks to shed some light on the differences between the image and reality of both software development work and those who undertake this work. The term 'software' first began to appear in the late 1950s (Ceruzzi 1998), while the importance of software as opposed to hardware can be pinned to the late 1960s when it started to become a tradeable commodity (see Philipson this volume).[1] Software is variously defined but is essentially 'a uniquely designed, highly structured set of assertions, instructions and decisions all of which must be negotiated, codified, analysed for consistency and validated for effectiveness in a constantly changing environment' (Weber 1997: 37).[2] It also has the capability to radically alter the location, timing and content of work for other workers as it increasingly shapes the core of multiple systems (Quintas 1994; Zachary 1998).

There has been an ongoing debate between the 'agilists' and 'formalists' about whether developing software is an 'art' (where 'code and fix' or 'hacking'[3] may best describe the software development process) or a 'science' where an engineering discipline can be applied to software development (see for example Quintas 1994; Austin and Devin 2003). These debates are important as they frame the techniques of software development, but by and large they have taken place within the more technical software development literature, both practitioner and academic.

This book, by way of contrast, comes from a non-technical, sociological perspective. It is also driven by the view that the work of developing or producing computer software is generally seen as a new occupation. Software developers are often seen as typical of 'knowledge workers' (Reich 1991; Scarbrough 1999): the small elite of entrepreneurs, scientists, technicians, information technologists, professionals, educators and consultants (Rifkin 1995) or symbolic analysts (Reich 1991) who trade globally in the manipulation of symbols. They are also central figures in Richard Florida's (2002) creative classes and they are the ones who created the Internet which Manual Castells says 'is the fabric of our lives' (Castells 2001: 1). These workers are among those predicted to be the future aristocrats of the labour market (Reich 1991; Castells 1996) given the centrality of knowledge as a commodity and characteristics of the contemporary economy.

However these workers present a challenge to managers: how do you organize work and manage these individuals when their intellectual capacity, creativity and talent is the source of a firm's competitive advantage? While this is an interesting question in general about knowledge work and workers, it is more so when the nature of software development work is not well understood. For example the hype about technology ushering in a 'new economy' and the high drama associated with the IT industry generally, Silicon Valley[4] specifically and the dot.com boom and bust in particular lead to a view, largely promoted in the business press, of software developers earning high wages, working with enlightened managers in modern (funky, open plan) workplaces that have chill-out rooms and other spaces to promote creativity, and being able to come and go from work as they please. At the height of the dot.com boom these sorts of stories abounded. Indeed even the ongoing effects of the fallout from the March 2000 'tech wreck' (the NASDAQ correction in the US) were used to highlight a particular lifestyle: for example one article reported how Australian Internet workers' personal spending had become more circumspect with weekly restaurant bills falling to less than A$150/week (Nicholas 7 August 2001); and another suggested that many of the 'dot.goners' were 'busy partying their silicon cash away in LA or catching a tan on the beaches of Bali or Hawaii, waiting for the next [IT] wave to happen' (Steele 24 July 2001).

The effect of the dot.com boom was that software developers shed the negative connotations associated with the popular image of people working on computers as 'nerds'.[5] They instead joined the ranks of the young, upwardly mobile 'gold-collar professionals'. What also happened, however, was that the hype, and the seemingly rapid technological advances that were made, served to obscure much of what the people developing software actually do from day to day at work and what their managers 'do' in order to get software developed. Peter Cappelli (2001: 94) has argued that 'aside from pay, many IT jobs – but especially computer programming jobs – would qualify as lousy work'. He goes further to argue that employers do not even know which software developers have the best skills (Cappelli 2001: 95).

The purpose of this book is therefore to strip away some of the mystery of how software is developed, how the work is organized and software developers managed and what this means in terms of their identity and commitment to their work and their employment.

A unifying approach

This book is an edited collection in which Beirne, Ramsay and Panteli's (1998: 142) observation that 'the nature of the work performed in producing and operating software should be a matter of great curiosity to labour process analysis' is taken seriously. A dialectical approach is undertaken in this book and the analysis starts with the totality of economic and social relations in the software development sector and takes into consideration all its contradictory constituents in order to conduct a more complete analysis of the labour process of software development. A dialectical approach sees contradiction and change at the heart of society and seeks an explanation for these phenomena. And it is the interaction between structural conditions and agency that provides the explanation in this book.[6]

This is the approach Gideon Kunda (1992) took in his examination of culture and normative control in 'Tech'. He argues 'to understand and evaluate normative control, it is necessary to grasp the underlying experiential transaction that lies at its foundation: not only the ideas and actions of managers, but the response of members' (Kunda 1992: 22). In this book the chapters are based on original research undertaken by academics in Australia, Germany, Norway, the UK and the US to address the software development labour process and the nature of software development work, strategies used to control that labour process and issues of identity, commitment and career.

Such an analysis locates firms within their sector and the sector's trajectory of development (in an historical sense). At the heart of this analysis lies questions of extraction and realization of surplus value as well as the contradictions and tensions for management that arise at different moments in the circuit of capital (Kelly 1998). However, to overcome charges of this analysis being overly structuralist – where 'behaviour is seen as determined by and reacting to structural constraints' (Astley and Van de Ven 1983: 247) – then equal priority is given to how structures constrain and enable action, and in particular how the reality of people's working lives is formed and constrained by the interplay of the labour market and their expectations of work. The issues of identity and commitment are addressed in this book as are the means of management control as, to paraphrase Marx, 'people make their own history but not in circumstances of their own choosing'. In other words, this book is concerned with both the structural forces that lay down broad parameters within which action takes place, as well as how, in confronting those structural forces to varying degrees, actors change both the nature of those forces and themselves.

This is important given the debate over the nature of (and indeed existence of) a 'new economy' and role of knowledge workers within it. Many software development firms exist as marginal players in a dynamic and rapidly evolving industry, which means that management are constantly aware of the potential for sudden death or takeover, while employees' status is equally as temporary and their privileged position in the labour market is relative: events following the NASDAQ correction in March 2000 highlight this fact and brought about a reappraisal of the over-hyped claims of the 'dot.coms'. While immediate job losses were not significant following the burst of the Internet bubble, the drop off in business investment in technology later in 2000, which continued into 2001 and is only beginning to increase in 2004, led to more significant retrenchment activity in larger firms (Joint Venture Silicon Valley Network 2001). Similarly the recent growth in 'off-shoring' or outsourcing some elements of the software development to firms in places such as Bangalore and Hyderabad in India, also highlights the temporary nature of these workers privileged position in the labour market.

A clear-headed and grounded analysis of software development and developers is therefore warranted and the manner in which this book achieves that aim is outlined below.

This book

A more complete analysis of control of the software development labour process must first start with the totality of economic and social relations in the software sector before considering its contradictory constituents. By placing an emphasis on contradiction and change and underpinning this approach with labour process theory, we can reconsider the priority afforded to the control of labour that occurs in many labour process studies. Drawing on Kelly's (1985: 32) argument that 'there is no sound reason for privileging any moment in the circuit [of capital]', the approach taken in this book is not to prioritize internal management and external labour market arrangements over the effect of the product market. An understanding of the nature of control over the labour process of software development requires a consideration of the dialectical dynamics of both structure and agency. In doing so 'subjectivity' – 'a person's ability to make decisions in the context of social constraints' (Grugulis and Knights 2001: 22), and 'self identity' must be taken into account. Consequently a consideration of how software workers' self identity motivates work performance (van Knippenberg 2000), acts as a form of normative control (Kunda 1992) or is confirmed and/or enhanced by their working practices is attempted in this book.

In Chapter 2 Graeme Philipson draws on his extensive experience as an IT analyst and commentator in the Australian media to map a brief history of the software sector from Babbage and his analytical engine to the future information utility capabilities of the Internet. This is done in order to provide a foundation for addressing the software development labour process and the means of control over that labour process. In a narrative history Philipson provides an overview of the development and change in the global IT industry and the implications for software development. This chapter is important as it grounds and locates the material in the later chapters by providing a description of the structures within which software development firms operate and software development occurs.

In the following chapter (Chapter 3) the nature of the software development labour process is addressed. Chris Andrews, Craig Lair and Bart Landry of the University of Maryland in the United States take a long look at the extent to which the software development labour process is patterned on the industrial labour process. They ask whether software firms resemble the producers of industrial commodities or dispensers of services. Finally they question whether software workers are exploited or are the 'aristocracy' of knowledge workers? Andrews *et al.* draw on their study of 31 start-up software firms in the region known as the Dulles Corridor in the Washington, DC/Baltimore metropolitan area. They argue that unlike the situation in the manufacture of material goods, there are no raw materials used in the production of software: conception and execution cannot be totally separated since the production process itself *depends* upon the creativity of workers. While elaborate software development methodologies introduce an element of predictability and structure to the labour process, the process defies standardization because the stages in which the development occurs are so varied across firms. As a result control is more normative than technical as the characteristics of software production and the current competitive environment in which these firms operate militates against manufacturing type controls on software developers.

The matter of means of management control is further elaborated and explored in Chapter 4. Here I take a step back and cover some older ideas about the means of management control of the labour process, in particular I concentrate on the debate in the 1980s between John Storey and Andrew Friedman. I take Storey's (1985) idea that there are levels of control exerted over the labour process and then use a modified version of Friedman's (1977, 1984) direct control and responsible autonomy strategies as 'two directions towards which managers can move, rather than two pre-defined states between which managers can choose' (Friedman 1984: 3), to show how the means of management control can be seen by looking at what employees do all day and how they do it. As such I argue that management uses various strategies both separately and simultaneously to control the labour process depending on the type of software product being developed, the timing in the software product's development lifecycle and the type or nature of the software worker (Barrett 2004). I use a series of semi-structured interviews with software developers and managers in three Australian software firms to explore these ideas. In this chapter the discussion centres on the temporary nature of the relatively privileged labour market position of these workers and this is contrasted with the optimistic, and largely uncritical, view of writers on knowledge workers and symbolic analysts in the information age or new economy.

In Chapter 5, Bente Rasmussen and Birgitte Johansen use two case studies: one of web designers in the advertising industry and another of systems developers in an IT services firm in Norway, to explore the balance between autonomy and management control. They look closely at how new entrepreneurial organizations offer workers professional autonomy as a means of increasing their work effort to meet project deadlines, even if it means unpaid overtime. This unpaid overtime can be a source of frustration for workers who realize their psychological contract (Rousseau 1995) is being violated and they are being treated as labour to be exploited rather than valuable professionals. Rasmussen and Johansen therefore argue that autonomy and control should not be understood as opposite measures taken by management and they show how control over the workers' effort is achieved by offering the workers autonomy and honouring their position as an 'expert workforce'. The case studies in this chapter shows that even if software workers are motivated by professional interest and find work meaningful and exciting, their hard work and long hours are primarily motivated by the economic pressure exerted by new entrepreneurial firms. However, when management are unwilling to listen to worker suggestions for better planning and project management to improve the situation and reduce the unpaid overtime, worker loyalty to the firm fades. If the labour market offers more promising opportunities then workers will leave, or alternatively they will start their own firms or become freelancers. In this chapter Rasmussen and Johansen argue that strategies to control the labour process are in part a response to product market conditions, while the labour market strategies of the web workers can be understood by the local labour market situation and the (resulting) human resource strategies of the firms.

In Chapter 6 Dorothea Voss-Dahm uses data from seven German IT companies to elaborate on another aspect of the means of management control. In this chapter the time dimension of project based work is explored, as is its importance to achieving the ideal of work humanization, which is significant in the German context. While in chapter 3 Andrews *et al.* argue that the software development labour process resists exact temporal management, in this chapter Voss-Dahm examines the extent to which a balance can be successfully struck between the interests of individual workers and the temporal demands of the labour process. Voss-Dahm argues that room for manoeuvre or an individual's ability to assert their own interests depends on the individual's position in the labour process. This chapter shows that while high skill workers in the IT industry enjoy considerable freedom to determine the start and finish of their working day, there are questions about the real level of autonomy for workers associated with this time sovereignty. Voss-Dahm makes the case that the existence of working time sovereignty for employees actually intensifies performance levels by strengthening management access to employees' productive capacities as employees are required to manage their own working time, which is a resource to be deployed in the labour process.

In the next two chapters the focus of the analysis of the different means of management control moves to examine the issues of identity and commitment of software workers. These are important issues which are underpinned by the notion of professionalism. While on the one hand the debate about whether software developers have achieved the status of 'professionals' is unimportant given Scarbrough's (1999: 8) comment that 'although professional groups themselves continue to wield a significant degree of power, there is little doubt about the decline of professionalism as a paradigmatic model for organizing knowledge'. On the other hand it is important given that the ascription of professional status to an occupational group implies a sense of entitlement to special privilege and respect, and legitimates that group's 'right' to autonomy and high social reward (Meiksins 1985). At the same time, however, it also implies that there is an ever present prospect of de-professionalization. While there are clear advantages to membership of a professional group, the privileges involved have to be constantly defended against those who would take them away (Meiksins 1985).

Abigail Marks and Cliff Lockyer take up this issue in Chapter 7, which emerges from a desire to investigate the process used by knowledge workers to protect their expertise and related rewards.[7] Marks and Lockyer's interest is with the concept of identity and in particular they concentrate on 'the most poignant identities for individuals': membership of a profession. They argue that very little is known about the relationship between loyalty, commitment and identification for knowledge workers in general and in particular the construction of professional or occupational identity for software workers. Marks and Lockyer use data collected as part of a three-year project looking at the nature and experience of work in the twenty-first century. They develop case studies of two Scottish-based software firms: one they term a non-professional organization being a software engineering division of a formerly public-owned telecommunications utility and the other they term a professional organization being a large independent Scottish-based software house. Marks and Lockyer's analysis of the case materials shows that the context of software development work is extremely important to understanding the construction of professional identities. Further that the nature of the software development work makes it difficult to place these workers within more traditional explanations that suggest either erosion or preservation of professional identification when working in different types of software organizations.

In Chapter 8 Chris Baldry, Dora Scholarios and Jeff Hyman further explore this issue of commitment using more of the data collected as part of the same research project used by Marks and Lockyer in the previous chapter.[8] Baldry *et al.* argue that given software workers are the 'prototypes of the new knowledge worker' then there is no need to look any further than these workers for the ideal recipients of HRM policies to engender high commitment. Baldry *et al.* seek to explore whether software workers do exemplify highly committed knowledge workers and use quantitative and qualitative data collected in five Scottish software houses to do so. They propose two models of commitment that could apply to software workers: the direct high commitment model where they are primarily committed to their organization and the indirect process model where software workers primarily identify with their profession. Essentially their analysis shows that organizations may be valued by software workers if workers perceive the organization embodies those values which are seen to be prototypical of the professional occupational community. In other words, software workers exert job effort – they work the hours to get a project delivered because that is part of their identity of being a software professional – but this does not necessarily mean they are committed to the particular organization in which they work, just organizations like them.

In Chapter 9 I am left with the task of pulling together the threads and themes from the earlier chapters in the context of how they serve to elaborate and develop elements of the unified framework proposed at the beginning of this chapter. The similarities and differences in the dualisms between structural forces and human agency across countries are considered. The insights in the chapters about how software workers construct their social identity, develop their career, balance aspects of their work with other parts of their life, manage working time constraints and respond to managerial control strategies are drawn together. Finally I examine how fixed and eternal are the conditions that produced this apparently 'new economy' and the implications on this for how people within the industry view their work. In both parts of the chapter I draw on insights from a series of semi-structured interviews I conducted between June 2002 and May 2003 with 14 software developers around Australia.

Notes

1 This period coincides with the beginning of what Friedman (1994; 1999) terms the second phase of the evolution of the information technology field.

2 It has been suggested that the 'half-life' of software is around two to three years compared with seven years for other forms of engineering knowledge (Costlow 2003).

3 The mainstream interpretation of 'hacking' or 'hacker' is usually negative referring to someone who is a 'computer criminal'. A range of authors dispel this interpretation, notably Himanen (2001) more generally and Castells (2001) in the context of the Internet: the hacker ethic is to create and share information and this is exemplified in the Open Source movement (see also Philipson this volume). Computer criminals are best referred to as 'crackers' or 'script kiddies', not hackers.

4 There are numerous books and articles that focus on Silicon Valley, which this one does not. Without doubt Silicon Valley is important, particularly in terms of understanding entrepreneurial regions and as Larsen and Rogers (1984: 273–4) write:

> Silicon Valley represents a special kind of super capitalism – a system resting on continuous technological innovation, entrepreneurial fever and rigorous economic development.... Unfettered market forces pass final judgement on the boom and bust of firms and of individuals. Silicon Valley is high technology capitalism run wild. There is nothing quite like it anywhere else in the world.

The continued growth of the Internet ensures that for the immediate future Silicon Valley's record of success will continue. As a result government's have tried to replicate the success of the region. Some examples include 'Silicon Glen' (central Scotland), 'Silicon Fen' (the Cambridge region of the UK), 'Silicon Bog' (Ireland), 'Silicon Alley' (New York), 'Silicon Wadi' (Israel), Route 128 (around Boston, US), the M4 Corridor (through Berkshire and Buckinghamshire, UK), the Cyberport (Hong Kong), the Multimedia Super Corridor (Malaysia) and more recently in various locations in India. However the image of Silicon Valley as an industrial region based upon competition and cooperation (Saxenian 1994) providing an endless supply of well-paid, high technology jobs is questionable. The media largely focuses on the 'glamour' jobs and associated pay and neglects the darker side of the IT industry. Although there is a large well-paid, professional workforce in Silicon Valley, which is predominantly located around hardware rather than software production (Henton 2000; Kvamme 2000), there is also a larger number of poorly paid workers, either directly or indirectly employed in chip production or service work in local, national and international locations. This workforce is highly segregated by class, race and gender (Siegal 1998).

5 Capretz (2003: 208) argues that 'people stereotype the behaviour of software professionals as introverts working alone in a corner of their office, hating interaction with others, a typical *nerd*' (italics in original).
6 A version of this argument, as it pertains to the analysis of employment relations in small firms, can be seen in Barrett and Rainnie (2002).
7 This chapter is based on data collected as part of an ESRC research project funded under the *Future of Work* initiative (award number L212252006) 'Employment and Working Life beyond the Year 2000: Two Emerging Employment Sectors' (1999–2001). The full research team at Strathclyde, Stirling, Aberdeen and Heriot-Watt Universities is: Peter Bain, Chris Baldry, Nick Bozionelos, Dirk Bunzel, Gregor Gall, Kay Gilbert, Jeff Hyman, Cliff Lockyer, Abigail Marks, Gareth Mulvey, the late Harvie Ramsay, Dora Scholarios, Philip Taylor and Aileen Watson.
8 See previous note.

References

Astley, W. and Van de Ven, A. (1983) 'Central perspectives and debates in organization theory', *Administrative Science Quarterly*, 28: 245–73.

Austin, R. and Devin, L. (2003) 'Beyond requirements: Software making as an art', *IEEE Software*, Jan/Feb: 93–5.

Barrett, R. (2004) 'Working at Webboyz: Life in a small Australian internet firm', *Sociology*, 38, 4: 777–94.

Barrett, R. and Rainnie, A. (2002) 'What's so special about small firms? Developing an integrated approach to analysing small firm industrial relations', *Work Employment and Society*, 16: 415–32.

Beirne, M., Ramsay, H. and Panteli, A. (1998) 'Developments in computing work: Control and contradiction in the software labour process', in P. Thompson and C. Warhurst (eds) *Workplaces of the Future*, Houndsmill, UK: Macmillan Business.

Cappelli, P. (2001) 'Why is it so hard to find information technology workers?', *Organizational Dynamics*, 30, 2: 87–99.

Capretz, L. (2003) 'Personality types in software engineering', *International Journal of Human-Computer Studies*, 58: 207–14.

Castells, M. (1996) *The Rise of the Network Society*, Oxford: Blackwell.

Castells, M. (2001) *The Internet Galaxy: Reflections on the Internet, Business and Society*, Oxford: Oxford University Press.

Ceruzzi, P. (1998) *A History of Modern Computing*, USA: MIT.

Costlow, T. (2003) 'Globalization drives changes in software careers', *IEEE Software*, Nov/Dec: 14–16.

Florida, R. (2002) *The Rise of the Creative Class*, New York: Basic Books.

Friedman, A. (1977) *Industry and Labour: Class Struggle at Work and Monopoly Capitalism*, London: Macmillan.

Friedman, A. (1984) 'Management strategies: Market conditions and the labour process', in F. Stephen (ed.) *Firms Organisation and Labour*, London: Macmillan.

Friedman, A. (1994) 'The information technology field: Using fields and paradigms for analysing technological change', *Human Relations*, 47, 4: 367–92.

Friedman, A. (1999) 'Rhythm and the evolution of information technology', *Technology Analysis and Strategic Management*, 11, 3: 375–90.

Grugulis, I. and Knights, D. (2001) 'Glossary', *International Studies of Management and Organisation*, 30: 12–24.

Henton, D. (2000) 'A profile of the Valley's evolving structure', in C.-M. Lee, W. Miller, M. Hancock and H. Rowen (eds) *The Silicon Valley Edge: A Habitat for Innovation and Entrepreneurship*, Stanford, CA: Stanford University Press.

Himanen, P. (2001) *The Hacker Ethic and the Spirit of the Information Age*, New York: Random House.

Joint Venture Silicon Valley Network (2001) *Next Silicon Valley: Riding the Waves of Innovation. White Paper Dec 2001*, San Jose, CA.

Kelly, J. (1985) 'Management's redesign of work', in D. Knights, H. Willmott and D. Collinson (eds) *Job Redesign: Critical Perspectives on the Labour Process*, Aldershot: Gower.

Kelly, J. (1998) *Rethinking Industrial Relations: Mobilization, Collectivism and Long Waves*, London: Routledge.

Kunda, G. (1992) *Engineering Culture: Control and Commitment in a High-Tech Corporation*, Philadelphia: Temple University Press.

Kvamme, E. (2000) 'Life in Silicon Valley: A first-hand view of the region's growth', in C.-M. Lee, W. Miller, M. Hancock and H. Rowen (eds) *The Silicon Valley Edge: A Habitat for Innovation and Entrepreneurship*, Stanford, CA: Stanford University Press.

Larsen, J. and Rogers, E. (1984) *Silicon Valley Fever: Growth of High-Technology Culture*, London: Unwin.

Meiksins, P. (1985) 'Beyond the boundary question', *New Left Review*, 157: 101–20.

Nicholas, K. (7 August 2001) 'New economy staff lose confidence', *The Australian Financial Review*, 44.

Quintas, P. (1994) 'Programmed innovation? Trajectories of change in software development', *Information Technology and People*, 7, 1: 25–47.

Reich, R. (1991) *The Work of Nations: Preparing Ourselves for 21st Century Capitalism*, New York: Alfred A Knopf.

Rifkin, J. (1995) *The End of Work*, USA: Putnam and Sons.

Rousseau, D. M. (1995) *Psychological Contracts in Organizations*, Thousand Oaks: Sage.

Saxenian, A. (1994) *Regional Advantage: Culture and Competition in Silicon Valley and Route 128*, Boston, Mass.: Harvard University Press.

Scarbrough, H. (1999) 'Knowledge as work: Conflicts in the management of knowledge workers', *Technology Analysis and Strategic Management*, 11: 5–16.

Shih, J. (2004) 'Project time in Silicon Valley', *Qualitative Sociology*, 27, 2: 223–45.

Siegal, L. (1998) 'New chips in old skins: Work and labour in Silicon Valley', in G. Sussman and J. Lent (eds) *Global Productions: Labour and the Making of the 'Information Society'*, New Jersey: Hampton Press.

Steele, S. (24 July 2001) 'Crash breeds consulting collectives', *The Age IT2*, 6.

Storey, J (1985) 'The means of management control', *Sociology*, 19: 193–211.

Swart, J. and Kinnie, N. (2003) 'Sharing knowledge in knowledge-intensive firms', *Human Resource Management Journal*, 13, 2: 60–75.

van Knippenberg, D. (2000) 'Work motivation and performance: A social identity perspective', *Applied Psychology: An International Review*, 49: 357–71.

Weber, H. (1997) (ed.) *The Software Factory Challenge*, Amsterdam: IOS Press.

Zachary, G. (1998) 'Armed truce: Software in the age of teams', *Information Technology and People*, 11: 62–5.

2 A short history of software

Graeme Philipson

Introduction

The two key technologies in computing, hardware and software, exist side by side. Improvements in one drive improvements in the other. But there are key differences between the hardware and the software industries. Hardware design and manufacture is a comparatively costly exercise, with a consequently high cost of entry. Nowadays hardware development is left to large or largish companies whereas many major software advances have been the results of individual effort. Anybody can start a software company, and many of the largest and most successful of them have come from nowhere, the result of one or a few individuals' genius and determination.

However, there are different types of software: applications software, such as financial programs, word processors and spreadsheets, enable the sort of work computers are bought for; systems software, such as operating systems and utilities, sit behind the scenes and make computers work; applications development tools, such as programming languages and query tools, are used in building applications; and some software is a mixture of the above – database management systems (DBMSs), for example, are a combination of applications, systems and applications development software.

The software industry has bred millionaires and not a few billionaires. Its glamour, rate of change, low cost of entry, and the speed at which a good idea can breed commercial success has attracted many of the brightest technical minds and sharpest business brains of two generations. Hardware is important, but in a very real sense the history of information technology (IT) is the history of software. This chapter tells that story.

Software before computers

Babbage and the Analytical Engine

The concept of software was developed in nineteenth-century England by Charles Babbage (1791–1871). The son of a wealthy London banker,

Babbage was a brilliant mathematician and one of the most original thinkers of his day. His privileged background gave him the means to pursue his obsession, which was to build mechanical devices to take the drudgery out of mathematical computation. His last and most magnificent obsession, the Analytical Engine, lays claim to being the world's first computer, if only in concept (Augarten 1985: 44).[1]

By the time of Babbage's birth, mechanical calculators were in common use throughout the world, but they were calculators, not computers – they could not be programmed, nor could Babbage's first conception, which he called the Difference Engine. This remarkable device was designed to produce mathematical tables. It was based on the principle that any differential equation can be reduced to a set of differences between certain numbers, which could in turn be reproduced by mechanical means. The Difference Engine was a far more complex machine than anything previously conceived. It was partially funded by the British government, and partially by Babbage's sizeable inheritance. He laboured on it for nearly 20 years, constantly facing technical problems. But the device was too complex to be made by the machine tools of the day. He persevered, and was eventually able to construct a small piece of it that worked perfectly and could solve second-level differential equations. The whole machine, had it been completed, would have weighed two tonnes and been able to solve differential equations to the sixth level. After battling with money problems, a major dispute with his grasping chief engineer, the death of his wife and two sons, and arguments with the government, the whole project collapsed (Augarten 1985: 48).

Part of the problem was Babbage's perfectionism – he revised the design again and again in a quest to get it absolutely right. By the time he had nearly done so he had lost interest. He had a far grander idea – the Analytical Engine – which never came close to being built. This remarkable device, which exists in thousands of pages of sketches and notes that Babbage made in his later years, was designed to solve any mathematical problem, not just differential equations.

The Analytical Engine was a complex device containing dozens of rods and hundreds of wheels. It contained a mill and a barrel, and an ingress axle and egress axle. Each of these components bears some relationship to the parts of a modern computer. And, most importantly, it could be programmed, by the use of punched cards, an idea Babbage got from the Jacquard loom.

The first programmer was Ada, Countess of Lovelace (1815–52), daughter of the famously dissolute English poet Lord Byron.[2] She met Babbage in 1833 and became fascinated with the man and his work (Augarten 1985: 64). In 1843 she translated from the French a summary of Babbage's ideas which had been written by Luigi Federico Manabrea, an Italian mathematician. At Babbage's request she wrote some 'notes' that ended up being three times longer than Manabrea's original. Ada's notes make fascinating reading.

> The distinctive characteristic of the Analytical Engine ... is the introduction into it of the principle which Jacquard devised for regulating, by means of punched cards, the most complicated patterns in the fabrication of brocaded stuffs ... we may say most aptly that the Analytical Engine weaves algebraical patterns just as the Jacquard-loom weaves flowers and leaves.
>
> (quoted in O'Connor and Robertson 2002)

Her notes included a way for the Analytical Engine to calculate Bernoulli numbers. That description is now regarded as the world's first computer program. Ada's name lives on in the Ada programming language, devised by the US Department of Defense.

Alan Turing and the Turing Machine

Alan Turing was a brilliant English mathematician, a homosexual misfit who committed suicide when outed, and one of the fathers of modern computing. He was one of the driving forces behind Britain's remarkable efforts during the Second World War to break the codes of the German Enigma machines. He is best known for two concepts that bear his name, the Turing Machine and the Turing Test.[3]

He conceived the idea of the Turing Machine (a name later adopted by others) in 1935 while pondering German mathematician David Hilbert's *Entscheidungsproblem* or Decision Problem, which involved the relationship between mathematical symbols and the quantities they represented (Hodges 1985: 80). The Turing machine, as described in his 1936 paper 'On computable numbers, with an application to the Entscheidungsproblem' (Turing 1937), was a theoretical construct, not a physical device. At its heart was an infinitely long piece of paper, comprising an infinite number of boxes, within which mathematical symbols and numbers could be written, read and erased. Any mathematical calculation, no matter how complex, could be performed by a series of actions based on the symbols (Hodges 1985: 100)

The difficult concept, involving number theory and pure mathematics, was extremely influential in early thinking on the nature of computation. When the first electronic computers were built they owed an enormous amount to the idea of the Turing Machine. Turing's 'symbols' were in essence computer functions (add, subtract, multiply, etc.), and his concept of any complex operation being able to be reduced to a series of simple sequential operations is the essence of computer programming.

The birth of electronic computing

The first true electronic computer was the ENIAC (Electronic Numerator, Integrator, Analyzer and Computer). In 1942 a 35-year-old engineer named John W. Mauchly wrote a memo to the US government outlining his ideas for an 'electronic computor' (McCartney 1999: 49). His ideas were ignored at first, but they were soon taken up with alacrity, for they promised to solve one of the military's most pressing problems: the calculation of ballistics tables, which were needed in enormous quantities to help the artillery fire their weapons at the correct angles.

The US government's Ballistics Research Laboratory commissioned a project based on Mauchly's proposal in June 1943. Mauchly led a team of engineers, including a young graduate student called J. Presper Eckert, in the construction of a general purpose computer that could solve any ballistics problem and provide the reams of tables demanded by the military. The machine used vacuum tubes, a development inspired by Mauchly's contacts with John Atanasoff, who used them as switches instead of mechanical relays in a device he had built in the early 1940s (Augarten 1985: 114).[4]

ENIAC differed significantly from all devices that went before it. It was programmable. Its use of stored memory and electronic components, and the decision to make it a general purpose device, marked it as the first true electronic computer. But despite Mauchly and Eckert's best efforts ENIAC, with 17,000 vacuum tubes and weighing over 30 tonnes, was not completed before the end of the war. It ran its first program in November 1945, and proved its worth almost immediately in running some of the first calculations in the development of the H-bomb.[5]

By modern day standards, programming ENIAC was a nightmare. The task was performed by setting switches and knobs, which told different parts of the machine (known as 'accumulators') which mathematical function to perform. ENIAC operators had to plug accumulators together in the proper order, and preparing a program to run could take a month or more (McCartney 1999: 90–4).

ENIAC led to EDVAC (Electronic Discrete Variable Computer), incorporating many of the ideas of John von Neumann, a well-known and respected mathematician who lent a significant amount of credibility to the project (Campbell-Kelly and Aspray 1996: 92). Neumann also brought significant intellectual rigour to the team, and his famous paper 'First Draft of a Report on EDVAC' (von Neumann 1945) properly outlined for the first time exactly what an electronic computer was and how it should work. Von Neumann's report defined five key components to a computer – input and output, memory, and a control unit and arithmetical unit. We still refer to the 'Von Neumann architecture' of today's computers.

When the war was over, Mauchly and Eckert decided to commercialize their invention. They developed a machine called the UNIVAC (Universal Automatic Computer), designed for general purpose business use. But they were better engineers than they were businessmen, and after many false starts their small company was bought by office machine giant Remington Rand in 1950. UNIVAC was not a particularly impressive machine by today's standards (for example it used decimal arithmetic) but nearly

50 machines were sold and the first was installed in the US Census Bureau.[6]

The 1950s was a decade of significant improvements in computing technology. The efforts of Alan Turing and his Bletchley Park codebreakers during the Second World War led to a burgeoning British computer industry. Before his death, after studying von Neumann's EDVAC paper, Turing designed the ACE (Automatic Computing Engine), which led to the Manchester Mark I, technically a far superior machine to ENIAC or EDVAC (Augarten 1984: 148). It was commercialized by Ferranti, one of the companies that later merged to form ICL, the flag bearer of the British computer industry.

The most significant US developments of the 1950s were the Whirlwind and SAGE (Semi Automatic Ground Environment) projects. MIT's Whirlwind was smaller than ENIAC, but it introduced the concepts of real-time computing and magnetic core memory. It was built by a team led by Ken Olsen, who later founded Digital Equipment Corporation, the company that led the minicomputer revolution of the 1970s (Ceruzzi 1999: 140). SAGE was a real-time air defence system built for the US government in the Cold War. The project was accorded top priority, with a virtually unlimited budget. In a momentous decision, the government awarded the contract to a company that had only just decided to enter the computer industry. That company's name was IBM.

SAGE broke new ground on a number of fronts. The first was its sheer size. There were 26 data centres, each with a 250 tonne SAGE mainframe. It was built from a number of modules that could be swapped in and out. It was the world's first computer network, using the world's first fault-tolerant computers and the world's first graphical displays. And it gave IBM a head start in the computer industry that it has retained ever since (Augarten 1985: 204).

By the end of the 1950s there were dozens of players in the computer industry. Remington Rand had become Sperry Rand, and others like RCA, Honeywell, General Electric, Control Data and Burroughs had entered the field. The UK saw the likes of Ferranti and International Computers and Singer, and continental Europe Bull and Siemens and Olivetti. In Japan, a 40-year-old company called Fujitsu moved into computers. The machines they built all ran software, but there was no software industry. Early commercial machines were programmed mechanically, or by the use of machine language. In the early days there was little understanding of the distinction between hardware and software. That was to change with the development of the first programming languages.

Programming languages

The term 'software' did not come into use until 1958. It is probable that it was coined by Princeton University professor John W. Tukey in an article in *The American Mathematical Monthly* in January of that year (Peterson 2000). Originally the term 'computer' was applied to people who worked out mathematical problems. ENIAC was designed to take over the work of hundreds of human 'computers' who were working on ballistics tables. Most of them were women, recruited from the best and brightest college graduates when the men went off to war. Thus, the first computer programmers were, like Ada Lovelace, women.

The most famous and influential of them was Grace Murray Hopper, a mathematician who joined the US naval reserve during the war and who rose to become an Admiral. She died in 1992. In 1951 Hopper joined Eckert and Mauchly's fledgling UNIVAC company to develop an instruction code for the machine. She devised the term 'automatic programming' to describe her work (Campbell-Kelly and Asprey 1996: 187). Hopper also used the word 'compiler' to describe 'a program-making routine, which produces a specific program for a particular problem' (quoted in Cerruzi 1999: 85). Today the term 'compiler' means a program that translates English-like instructions into binary code, but Hopper used the term to describe a way of handling predefined subroutines, such as those hard-wired into the ENIAC. The first compiler in the modern sense of the word was devised for the MIT Whirlwind project in 1954 by J. H. Laning and N. Zierler (Ceruzzi 1999: 86). Hopper became a tireless proselytizer for the concept of automatic programming. Her work led directly to the development of FORTRAN (FORmula TRANslator), the world's first true computer language.

FORTRAN was developed in the mid-1950s by an IBM development team led by a young researcher named John Backus. The first version of FORTRAN was released in 1954. There were many sceptics who believed that it would be impossible to develop a high-level language with anything like the efficiency of machine language or assembler, but Backus argued for FORTRAN on economic grounds. He estimated that half the cost of running a computer centre was the programming staff (Campbell-Kelly and Asprey 1996: 188) and he (rightly) saw in FORTRAN a way of vastly improving programming productivity. FORTRAN enabled people to program computers using simple English-like instructions and mathematical formulas. It led to a number of other languages, the most successful of which was COBOL (Common Business-Oriented Language), initially developed by the US government Committee on Data Systems and Languages (CODASYL) and strongly promoted by Grace Hopper. COBOL and FORTRAN dominated programming until the late 1970s. Other languages, such as ALGOL (Algorithmic Language), PL/1 (Programming Language 1), RPG (Report Program Generator) and BASIC (Beginner's All-purpose Symbolic Instruction Code) also became popular, inspired by the success of FORTRAN and COBOL.

These languages became known as 3GLs (third Generation Languages), so called because they were an evolution from the first and second generations of computer language – machine code and assembler. Some people wrote bits of applications in those more efficient but much more cryptic languages, but the English-like syntax of the 3GLs made them easier to learn and much more popular. These 3GLs brought a discipline and a standardization to program design. They enabled programs to be structured, or ordered in a hierarchical fashion, usually comprising modules with a limited number of entry and exit points. Structured programming led to structured design, comparatively simple methodologies which set out ways in which these modules could be strung together. Soon, the term 'systems analysis' was used to describe the process of collecting information about what a computer system was intended to do, and the codification of that information into a form from which a computer program could be written.

Operating systems

Not only did they not have programming languages, early computers also did not have operating systems. Every function had to be separately programmed, and in the early days there was no distinction between systems and applications software. Programming languages such as FORTRAN and COBOL greatly improved general programming functions, but the task of handling machine-specific functions such as control of peripherals was still left up to individual programmers. Most of the innovative early work on what we now call operating systems was done by individual users (Ceruzzi 1999: 96). One such system, designed at General Motors in 1956, evolved into IBM's well-known JCL (Job Control Language), a basic operating system designed for punch card systems that would tell the computer which cards were data and which were instructions.

The first true operating system is generally agreed to be MAD (Michigan Algorithmic Decoder), developed at the University of Michigan in 1959 (Ceruzzi 1999: 98). MAD was based on the ALGOL 3GL, and was designed to handle the various details of running a computer that were so tedious to code separately. But the concept of the operating system was still largely unknown, until the momentous development of IBM's S/360 (System 360).

The IBM S/360 and OS/360

April 1964 marks the beginning of the modern computer industry, and by extension the software industry. In that month IBM released the S/360, its revolutionary mainframe architecture. The 19 models in the S/360 range comprised the first ever family of computers, the first with a consistent architecture across computers of a different size.[7] They could use the same peripherals and software, making it very easy to move to a larger computer within the range, and to move on to new models as they were released.

In the 1960s developing a family of computers was a revolutionary idea. Previous IBM machines, such as the 1401, were incompatible with other machines in IBM's range. Every time IBM, or anybody else, brought out a new computer, users had to rewrite their entire applications suite and replace most of their peripherals. IBM invested over $US5 billion and 350,000 man-years in the S/360 (Watson 1990: 340). It was the largest R&D project ever undertaken by a commercial organization. It was more than twice as successful as IBM had hoped, and it became virtually the standard operating environment for large corporations and government agencies.

The S/360 evolved into the S/370, and then into the S/390, and then into today's zSeries, with many of its features intact. A piece of software written for the first S/360 will still run on today's zSeries machines. Predictions of the death of the mainframe, common 10 to 15 years ago, have proved wildly inaccurate, and the S/360's successors still power most large transaction processing systems today. But the S/360's success was not preordained. Many within the company argued against it. The machine was rushed into production, and IBM could not handle the demand, its internal accounting and inventory control systems buckling under the strain. IBM's chairman at the time, Thomas J. Watson Jr, recounts the story.

> By some miracle hundreds of medium-sized 360s were delivered on time in 1965. But ... behind the scenes I could see we were losing ground. The quality and performance ... were below the standards we'd set, and we'd actually been skipping some of the most rigorous tests ... everything looked black, black, black. Everybody was pessimistic about the program ... we were delivering the new machines without the crucial software; customers were forced to use temporary programs much more rudimentary than what we'd promised ... with billions of dollars of machines already in our backlog, we were telling people they'd have to wait two or three years for computers they needed ... I panicked.
>
> (Watson 1990: 349)

IBM recovered and the S/360 became the most successful computer in history. It introduced a number of innovations, such as the first transaction processing system and the first use of solid logic technology (SLT), but it was no technical miracle. Its peripherals performed poorly, its processor was slow, its communications capabilities were virtually non-existent. Most importantly, the S/360 introduced the world's first sophisticated operating system, OS/360. This was both the architecture's biggest advance, and also its biggest problem. OS/360 was by far the largest software project ever undertaken, involving hundreds of programmers and more than a million lines of code (Campbell-Kelly and Asprey 1996: 197). In charge of the project was Fred Brooks, who was to become the father of the discipline known as software engineering. Brooks's book on the development of OS/360, *The Mythical Man-Month*, remains one of the all-time classic descriptions of software development.

The task facing Brooks and his team was massive. They had to design an operating system that would work on all S/360 models, and which would enable the machines to run multiple jobs simultaneously, a function known as 'multitasking'. At its peak the OS/360 project had more than 1000 programmers working on it, which led Brooks to his famous conclusion that software cannot be designed by committee, and that there are no necessary economies of scale: 'the bearing of a child takes nine months, no matter how many women are assigned' (Brooks 1995: 17). OS/360 was eventually delivered, years late and millions of dollar over budget. It was never completely error-free, and bugs kept surfacing throughout its life. IBM eventually spent over half a billion US dollars on the project, the biggest single cost of the entire S/360 project (Campbell-Kelly and Asprey 1996: 200). But it was the archetype of the operating system, the precursor of all that have followed it.

With all its problems the S/360 was an architecture, the first the computer industry had ever seen. It excelled nowhere, except as a concept, but it could fit just about everywhere. For the first time upward and downward compatibility was possible and the phrase 'upgrade path' entered the language. With the S/360, IBM also promised compatibility into the future, protecting customers' investment in their applications and peripherals. With the S/360 and OS/360, the operating system became the key distinguishing factor of a computer system. Other companies soon began making 'plug-compatible computers' that would run S/360 software. The best known of these was Amdahl, started by IBM engineer Gene Amdahl, who had led the design team for the S/360. Amdahl released its first IBM-compatible mainframe in 1975.

Software comes of age

Largely as a result of the problems highlighted by the development of OS/360, there was an increased realization in the late 1960s that software development should be regarded as a science, not an art. A seminal conference held in Garmisch, Germany, in October 1968, entitled *Software Engineering* (Naur and Randell 1969), brought together many of the world's leading software designers. The conference was sponsored by NATO, whose member states were desperate to bring some order into software development for the military, the costs of which were spiralling out of control (Cerruzi 1999: 105).

The Garmisch conference marked a major cultural shift in perceptions of what software was and how it should be developed (Campbell-Kelly and Asprey 1996: 201). The term 'software engineering' was used by adherents of the approach that building software was like building a house or a bridge – there were certain structured techniques and formal design methodologies that could be applied to the complexity of writing software. This approach marked the beginnings of 'structured design methodology', which became enormously popular and influential in the 1970s and 1980s.

At around the same time another major development occurred. In December 1968, just two months after the Garmisch conference, IBM made the decision to 'unbundle' its software. The two events are unrelated, but together they constituted a revolution in software and software development. Until 1969 IBM included all its software with the computer: buy (or lease) the computer and the software was thrown in as part of the deal. Hardware was so expensive IBM could afford to give the software away. But in 1968, under pressure from the US government, which was soon to initiate an anti-trust suit against IBM, the company started to charge separately for its systems software (Ceruzzi 1999: 106). The first piece of software to be sold separately was CICS (Customer Information Control System), IBM's widely used transaction processing system.

The effect of IBM's decision was to open up the software market to independent software vendors (ISVs), who could compete against IBM. The changed environment, and the vast increase in the use of computers, led to the emergence of software contractors and service houses. By the mid-1970s, there were hundreds of software suppliers, many of them developing the first software packages – pre-written software that could be purchased off-the-shelf for any number of applications. Most of the new companies were formed to supply software for IBM and compatible mainframes. Such was the growth in computing that even a company of IBM's size was not able to come close to keeping up with demand.

Software was moving from being a cottage industry to mass production. Many companies came into being to supply applications software, such as financial and manufacturing packages. Leading applications software companies that were formed in this era included McCormack and Dodge, MSA and Pansophic. By 1972, only three years after the unbundling decision, there were 81 vendors in the US offering packages in the life insurance industry alone (Campbell-Kelly and Asprey 1996: 204).

There was also a large group of companies formed to supply systems software. Many of these were one-product companies, formed by individuals who had worked out a better way to perform some operating function. This included tape backup, network management, security, and a host of other features that OS/360 and its successors were not able to do well. Systems software companies from this era included SKK, Compuware, Dusquene, Goal Systems, BMC, Candle and many more. Most of them eventually merged with each other. Many were acquired by the largest of them all, Computer Associates, started by Chinese immigrant

Charles Wang in 1976 (Campbell-Kelly and Asprey 1996: 205). However the largest and most successful group of independent software vendors were the database management system (DBMS) suppliers.

Database management systems

The development of programming languages and the standardization of operating systems brought some order to software, but data management remained an important issue. During the 1950s and the early 1960s there was no standardized way of storing and accessing data, and every program had to manage its own. The file structure was often determined by the physical location of the data, which meant users had to know where data was, and how the program worked, before they could retrieve or save information. The mid-1960s saw the first attempts at solving this problem.

In 1963 IBM developed a rudimentary data access system for NASA's Apollo missions called GUAM (Generalized Update Access Method), and in 1964 Charles Bachmann developed a data model at Honeywell which became the basis for IDS (Integrated Data Store), the first true database (Crawford and Ziola 2002). A company called Informatics developed a successful file management system called Mark IV in 1967 (Campbell-Kelly and Asprey 1996: 204) and after IBM unbundled software in 1968, Informatics became the first successful independent software vendor. In the late 1960s IBM developed IMS (Information Management System), still in use today. Boston-based Cullinet, founded by John Cullinane in 1968, bought a data management system called IDMS (Integrated Data Management System) from tyre company BF Goodrich and turned it into a successful mainframe product. In 1969 Germany's Peter Schnell founded a company called Software AG, which developed a hierarchical file management system called Adabas (Advanced DAta BAse System). There were many others. Most used a hierarchical system, where a tree represented data relationships. This model was codified by CODASYL in 1969.

However the biggest revolution in data management came with the concept of the relational database. Like many other developments in the history of computing, it came from IBM. In 1970 IBM researcher E. F. (Ted) Codd[8] wrote a seminal paper called 'A relational model of data for large shared data banks'. It became one of the most famous and influential documents in the history of computing describing how data could be stored in tables of related rows and columns. This became known as an RDBMS (Relational Database Management System). The idea was revolutionary as it enabled standardization of data structures allowing different programs to use the same data, and applications to take their data from different sources. Codd wrote his paper while working in IBM's San Jose Research Laboratory. IBM saw the potential of the idea, and initiated a project called System R to prove the concept in a real application. Codd expanded his ideas, publishing his famous 12 principals for relational databases in 1974.

RDBMSs were a revolution in IT theory and practice. Codd's work made database management a science, and vastly improved the efficiency, reliability and ease of use of computer systems. Relational databases are today the basis of most computer applications – indeed, it is impossible to imagine computing without them. There have always been some, such as Peter Schnell at Software AG and Cincom's Tom Nies, who have doubted the validity of the relational model and pursued other directions, but their models have faded, as the relational model has grown stronger. Codd himself admitted to limits in the capabilities of relational databases, and he became a critic of SQL (Structured Query Language), a standard language for querying RDBMSs which was also developed as part of the IBM System R project. But his was one of the greatest software innovations as it directly led to the foundations of companies like Oracle and Informix, and to the database wars of the 1980s and 1990s.

IBM was not the first to market with an RDBMS. That honour goes to a company called Relational Technology with a product called Ingres. Second was Relational Software with Oracle. Both these companies eventually renamed themselves after their better-known products. Ingres had some modest success before being eventually acquired by Computer Associates, and Oracle, under co-founder Larry Ellison, went on to become one of the largest and most successful companies in the industry (Symonds 2003: 72). IBM's own development was slow. It released SQL/DS in 1981 and DB2, for mainframes, in 1983. Other companies, such as Informix and Sybase, entered the fray, and the DBMS market became one of the most hotly-contested in the software industry.

Today the DBMS market has changed significantly. Most of the big players of ten years ago are gone or irrelevant. IBM and Oracle are the only ones left although they have been joined by Microsoft. Microsoft's Access has seen off its competitors in the PC DBMS market, and it has had great success with its high end SQL/Server DBMS. SQL/Server runs only on Microsoft's Windows operating system, but that has not held it back. Windows has been the big operating system success story of the last ten years, halting Unix in its tracks and destroying most proprietary operating systems (see below).

The rise of the minicomputer

By the mid-1960s computers were in common use in government and industry throughout the world. Owing to the tremendous success of the S/360, IBM was the industry leader, as large as its major competitors combined. Its main competitors were known collectively as the 'Bunch' – a clever acronym for Burroughs, Univac (by this time the company was called Sperry, though it still used Univac as a model name), NCR, Control Data and Honeywell.

IBM and the Bunch sold large and expensive mainframe computers to government departments and large corporations. But some people thought that computers need not be that big, or cost that much. One of these was Ken Olsen, who had worked on the Whirlwind project. In 1957 he started a small company called Digital Equipment Corporation, better known as DEC, in an old wool mill in Boston. DEC's first products were small transistorized modules that could be used to take the place of the vacuum tubes still used by computers of that era. These modules proved very popular, and DEC was soon making so many different types that Olsen decided to build his own computers based around them. The first of these, the PDP-1 (the PDP stood for Programmed Data Processor), was released in 1960. It was followed by the PDP-5 in 1963 and the PDP-8 in 1965 (Augarten 1985: 257).

The PDP-8 ushered in the minicomputer revolution and brought computing to a whole new class of users. It had just 4K of memory, but it was a real computer, and much less expensive ($US18,000) than any other machine on the market. It was an enormous success, especially with scientists and engineers, who finally had a computer they could afford and easily use. In 1970 DEC released the equally successful PDP-11. New technology and economies of scale meant that the prices of DEC's minicomputers kept dropping as quickly as their capabilities improved, and soon DEC had many competitors. One of the most successful, Data General, was founded in 1968 by ex-DEC employees. The Data General Nova, announced in 1969, set new benchmarks for price-performance, and by 1970 over 50 companies were making minicomputers (Augarten 1985: 258), including IBM and the Bunch, but they moved slowly and largely missed the act. IBM did catch up by the end of the 1980s with its AS/400. The big winners were Data General and other start-ups and companies new to the industry like Prime, Hewlett-Packard and Wang. The world's most successful minicomputer, the VAX, was released by DEC in 1977 and is still in use today.[9]

Early computers used vacuum tubes as switches. These were soon replaced by transistors, invented by Bell Labs' William Shockley, John Bardeen and Walter Brattain in 1948. The three received the Nobel prize for their achievement. Transistors worked in solid state – the switching depended on the electrical properties of a piece of crystal – and led to further developments in miniaturization throughout the 1950s and 1960s. The next significant development was the invention of the integrated circuit (IC) by Jack Kilby at Texas Instruments in 1959. ICs combined many transistors onto a single chip of silicon, enabling computer memory, logic circuits and other components to be greatly reduced in size.

Electronics was becoming a big industry. After he left Bell Labs, Shockley started a company to commercialize the transistor. His acerbic personality led to problems with his staff, and eight of them left in 1957 to found Fairchild Semiconductor. Two of those eight, Gordon Moore and Bob

Noyce, in turn founded their own company, Intel, in 1968. All these companies were located in the area just north of San Jose, California, an area dubbed 'Silicon Valley' in a series of articles published in 1971 in *Electronic News* by journalist Don Hoefler (Hoefler 1971).

The next step was the development of the microprocessor, conceived by Intel engineer Marcian Hoff in 1970 (Augarten 1985: 265). Hoff's idea was simple. By putting a few logic circuits onto a single chip, the chip could be programmed to perform different tasks. The first microprocessor, the 4004, was developed as a cheap way of making general purpose calculators, which led directly to the microcomputer revolution of the late 1970s and 1980s.

The birth of the microcomputer

Intel's 4004 microprocessor was not an immediate success. No-one really knew what to do with it, but sales picked up as its flexibility became apparent. In 1972 Intel released a vastly improved version called the 8008, which evolved in 1974 into the 8080. People started to realize that these devices were powerful enough to run small computers.

In July 1974 *Radio-Electronics* magazine announced the Mark 8 as 'your personal minicomputer', designed around the 8008 by Virginia postgraduate student Jonathan Titus (Augarten 1985: 269). Users had to send away for instructions to build it, but thousands did. Its success inspired rival magazine *Popular Electronics* to announce the 'World's first minicomputer kit to rival commercial models' in the January 1975 issue (Roberts and Yates 1975). The device, the Altair 8800, was designed by Ed Roberts, who ran MITS, a small electronic company in Albuquerque. MITS sold Altair kits for less than $US400, at a time when the cheapest DEC PDP-8 cost more than ten times as much. Roberts was swamped with orders, and the microcomputer revolution had begun (Campbell-Kelly and Asprey 1996: 242). One of the Altair's great strengths was its open architecture, which Roberts deliberately designed so others could add to it by developing plug-in cards. Soon hobbyists and small companies all over America began developing Altair cards. But, like the early mainframe computers, the Altair had no software and it was programmed by flicking switches on its front panel.

Paul Allen, a Harvard undergraduate, noticed the Altair story in the magazine. He and his friend Bill Gates had played with computers since their high school days in Seattle. Allen suggested to Gates they write a BASIC interpreter for the Altair. Gates wrote the compiler in six weeks, Allen rang Roberts in Albuquerque and they drove to New Mexico. Gates finished the software in the parking lot before their meeting with Roberts (Freiberger and Swaine 1984: 143). The compiler worked, and Gates and Allen dropped out of Harvard to start a company they called Micro-Soft around the corner from MITS in Albuquerque. Soon after the hyphen was dropped and they moved their small company back to their hometown in the Pacific Northwest.

The Altair spawned a host of imitators. Computer clubs sprang up across the world. The most famous, located in Silicon Valley, was the Homebrew Computer Club. Two of the club's most active members were Steve Wozniak and Steve Jobs, who teamed up to build a little computer called the Apple I, powered by the 6502 microprocessor from a small Silicon Valley company called MOS. The Apple I was moderately successful, so Jobs sold his VW microbus and Wozniak his HP calculator, they borrowed $US5,000 from a friend, and they went into business. Apple soon attracted the attention of venture capitalist Mike Markkula, who believed that microcomputers were The Next Big Thing. He was right.

Apple released the Apple II in the middle of 1977. About the same time commercial designs from Tandy (the TRS-80) and Commodore (the PET) were released. But the Apple II outsold them both, because of its attractive design and its greater ease of use. In 1980 Apple went public, in the most successful float in Wall Street history (Carlton 1997: 10). The Apple II used its own proprietary operating system, called simply Apple DOS, but the most popular microcomputer operating system was called CP/M (Control Program/Microcomputers). CP/M ran on most microcomputers that used Zilog's popular Z80 microprocessor.

The low cost and ease of programming microcomputers spawned a software industry to rival that of the mainframe and minicomputer world. Most early applications were amateurish, but microcomputer software came of age with the invention of the spreadsheet in 1979.

The PC software industry

The first spreadsheet program, called VisiCalc, was released for the Apple II in November 1979. Dan Bricklin had the idea while doing an MBA at Harvard (Freiberger and Swaine 1984: 229) when his professors had described the large blackboards divided into rows and columns which were used for production planning in large companies (Cringely 1992: 65). Bricklin reproduced the idea electronically, using a borrowed Apple II. VisiCalc and its many imitators revolutionized accounting and financial management. Soon large companies were buying Apple IIs by the dozen, just to run VisiCalc. With the release of Mitch Kapor's Lotus 1-2-3 for the IBM PC (see below), the spreadsheet became a standard microcomputer application.

The other key microcomputing application was the word processor. Word processors evolved from typewriters rather than computers, but with the advent of the microcomputer the two technologies merged. The first word processor was IBM's MT/ST (Magnetic Tape/Selectric Typewriter) released in 1964 (Kunde, 1996), which fitted a magnetic tape drive to an IBM Selectric electric typewriter.

In 1972 word processing companies Lexitron and Linolex introduced machines with video displays that allowed text to be composed and edited on-screen. The following year Vydec introduced the first word processor with floppy disk storage. All these early machines and many that came afterwards from companies like Lanier and NBI (which stood for Nothing But Initials) were dedicated word processors – the instructions were hard-wired into the machines.

The first word processing program for microcomputers was Electric Pencil, developed for the MITS Altair by Michael Shrayler in 1976. It was very rudimentary. The first to be commercially successful was Wordstar in 1979, developed by Seymour Rubinstein and Rob Barnaby (Kunde 1996). Wordstar used a number of cryptic commands, but it had all the power of a dedicated word processor. By the time the IBM PC was released in 1981, PCs and word processing machines had all but converged in technology and appearance. It took some time before word processing software caught up with dedicated machines in functionality, but they won the battle in price-performance immediately. All the dedicated word processing companies were out of business by 1990.

Spreadsheets and word processors led the way, but there were many other types of PC applications. PC databases became popular with dBase II and its successors, dBase III and dBase IV, the leading product for most of the decade. The growth of the microcomputer software industry in the 1980s mirrored the growth of mainframe and minicomputer software in the 1970s (see above). Leading companies of the era included WordPerfect, Lotus (acquired by IBM in 1995), Ashton-Tate, Borland and, of course, Microsoft.

The IBM PC and the rise of Microsoft

The success of the Apple II and other early microcomputers persuaded IBM to enter the market. In July 1980 Bill Lowe, head of IBM's entry level systems division, made a presentation to IBM senior management about why Big Blue should make a move. More importantly, he suggested how this could be done. The key to moving quickly was using standard components. This was a major departure for IBM, which normally designed and built everything itself. There was no time for that, argued Lowe. Management agreed, and he was told to go off and do it. The building of the IBM PC was given the name Project Chess, and the machine itself was internally called the Acorn (Campbell-Kelly and Asprey 1996: 255). The machine was ready in less than a year. It was a triumph of outsourcing. The microprocessor was an Intel 8088. Microsoft supplied the operating system and a version of the BASIC programming language. Disk drives (just two low capacity floppies) were from Tandon, printers from Epson, and power supplies from Zenith. Applications software included a word processor and a spreadsheet.

Many in IBM were uncomfortable with the idea that the company should become involved in the personal computer market. One famous internal memo warned that it would be 'an embarrassment' to IBM. The doubters were quickly proved wrong. Within days of the machine's launch on 12 August 1981, IBM was forced to quadruple production. Still they could not keep up with demand. Businesses and people, who were previously wary of microcomputers were reassured by the IBM logo. A brilliant advertising campaign featuring a Charlie Chaplin look-alike hit just the right balance between quirkiness and quality. The machine was no technological marvel, but it worked, and of course it was from IBM.

Big Blue's decision to source the components from other manufacturers had far-reaching, if unintended, consequences. It meant that anybody could copy the design. Hundreds of companies did, and the IBM PC became the industry standard. A huge industry grew up in peripherals and software, and for the first few years the big battle in the computer industry was over 'degrees of compatibility' with IBM. But the decision with the most far-reaching consequences was IBM's decision to license the PC's operating system, rather than buy one or develop one itself. It initially called on a company called Digital Research, developers of the CP/M operating system used on many early microcomputers. But Gary Kildall, Digital Research's idiosyncratic founder, broke the appointment because he was out flying his plane (Freiberger and Swaine 1984: 272). Irritated, IBM turned to another small company in Seattle they had heard had a suitable operating system. That company's name was Microsoft.

The problem was Microsoft did not have an operating system, a fact Bill Gates did not let IBM know. He quickly bought an operating system called QDOS (Quick and Dirty Operating System) from another small company, Seattle Computer Products, for $US30,000. He renamed it MS-DOS and licensed it to IBM. The licensing deal was important: for every IBM PC sold, Microsoft received $US40, and Microsoft, previously just another minor software company, was on its way. The licensed version of MS-DOS IBM used was renamed PC-DOS (Campbell-Kelly and Asprey 1996: 257).[10] After the astounding success of the PC, IBM realized it had made a mistake licensing Microsoft's operating system as this was where the battle for the hearts and minds of users was being fought, so IBM built their own. OS/2 was a vastly superior operating system to MS-DOS. It had a microkernel, which meant it was much better at multitasking, and it was built for the new era of microprocessors that were emerging. Moreover it would operate across architectures and across platforms. In its early days, Microsoft and IBM cooperated on the development of OS/2, but Microsoft withdrew to concentrate on Windows NT (New Technology). Microsoft out-marketed IBM, and OS/2 died. Apple imploded, Microsoft started bundling its applications, and the battle for the desktop became a one-horse race.

A key development in Microsoft's success was its release of Windows 3.11 in 1992. It was the first Microsoft operating system to employ successfully a graphical user interface (GUI) with its now-ubiquitous WIMP (Windows, Icons, Mouse, Pull-down menus) interface. Although Microsoft released earlier versions of Windows, they did not work well and were not widely used (Campbell-Kelly and Asprey 1996: 278). The GUI was popularized by Apple, which introduced a GUI on the Macintosh, first released in 1984. Apple got the idea of the GUI from Xerox, which developed the first GUI in its famous Palo Alto Research Center (PARC) in Silicon Valley in the late 1970s.[11] Xerox PARC developed many of the key inventions in the history of computers, such as computer networking and laser printers, but has itself rarely made money from PARC's innovations. Apple's Steve Jobs visited Xerox PARC in December 1979 and saw a prototype of Xerox's Alto computer, the first to use a GUI. He was inspired to develop the Apple Lisa and then the Macintosh, which was the first commercially successful machine to use a GUI (Carlton 1997: 13).

Getting users in touch with data

As computers became widespread in business the role of programmers, and programming, changed. When computers were first employed on a wide commercial scale in the 1960s, applications development was a comparatively simple, if cumbersome, exercise. Just about everybody wrote their own applications from scratch, using 3GLs like COBOL (see above).

In the late 1970s a new applications development tool came into existence, as demand for increased computer performance began to far outstrip the capabilities of the limited number of 3GL programmers to write and maintain what was wanted. These were so-called 4GLs (fourth Generation Languages) such as Ramis and Focus, which were reporting and query tools that allowed end users to make their own enquiries of corporate information, usually in the IBM mainframe environment. They worked well, but only when coupled with a good database. They were useful in this role, freeing up programmers to develop applications (Philipson 1990: 12). 4GLs produced usable computer code. They were widely used by end users to create applications without going through the IT department.

At the same time PCs were becoming widespread in many corporations, further enhancing the idea of end user computing. 4GLs spread from the mainframe onto PCs. Many of the most popular PC applications, such as the Lotus 1-2-3 spreadsheet and the dBase database products (see above), were in effect 4GLs optimized for particular applications. But most of them produced code that needed to be interpreted each time they ran, which made them a drain on computing resources. Programs written in these early 4GLs typically ran much slower than programs written in 3GLs, just as 3GL programs ran slower than assembly language programs, which in turn ran slower than those written in machine language. This drain on resources caused many companies to re-evaluate their use of 4GLs, and also caused the 4GL suppliers to create more efficient versions of their products, usually by the use of compilers. 4GLs are more accurately called non-procedural languages. They are used to explain what needs to be done, not how it should be done. Non-procedural languages are now used widely, and have been a major factor in the move to increased end user computing. For all the advantages offered by 4GLs, there remained a need for query languages, which was what 4GLs were designed for originally. This need grew with the widespread use of relational databases. SQL (Structured Query Language) has evolved to perform many of the query functions of the early 4GLs. The wheel has turned full circle.

From 4GLs it was a short step to applications generators. Whereas 4GLs produced code in their own specialized languages, applications generators used a user-friendly 4GL-type front end to produce standard 3GL code. Thus, the use of a 4GL was similar to that of an applications generator, and the two types of product competed against each other. But the end result was different. Applications generators had the advantage of producing code which could then be maintained or modified by 3GL programmers unfamiliar with the way in which it was produced.

Applications generators merged with another new technology in the 1980s – CASE (Computer-Aided Software Engineering), which referred to the use of software to write software.[12] Building applications from scratch is never an easy job. CASE promised to simplify this task and instead of a programmer cutting code, they would tell a smart computer program what they wanted done and it would do the work. In its broadest sense, CASE is any computer-based product, tool or application that assists in the software development process. With the realization that software design could be systematized came the inevitable development of standard methodologies, procedures to guide systems analysts through the various stages of software design.[13] These design methodologies were the precursor to CASE, and a precondition to its effective use, guiding analysts and end users through the design process.

The rise and fall of CASE

The promise of CASE was virtually irresistible. Applications development had long been beset by two major difficulties: getting the developments finished on time; and ensuring that the finished software was robust, meaning it was properly documented, internally consistent, and easy to maintain. IBM released a strategy called AD/Cycle, which was like a unified field theory of applications development, an umbrella under which various CASE tools addressing different stages of the applications development life cycle fitted together, allowing developers to mix and match various products to suit their purposes (Philipson 1990: 24). CASE boomed because it would (so the theory went) allow a developer to outline the specifications, from which point the CASE software would automatically generate the code, documented and modular and consistent.

But in practice, however, CASE products demanded a level of discipline that did not come naturally to many developers. They were a great aid to program design, but the real creative work was still left to people, not machines. Many CASE tools were quite advanced, but none of them ever reached the stage where a developer could simply tell them to develop a retail banking system, for example, and wait for all the code to be written. What developers found was that the bigger the system being developed, the more that could go wrong. The complexities were not so much in the computer system as in the organizational structure it was trying to service. CASE did not address those problems. So most large and small organizations stopped developing their own applications, and most of the CASE vendors withered and died. Some stayed in existence, but they changed their focus and moved into other areas.

In the early 1990s there was a shift towards packaged software. Packaged applications became much more flexible than ever before, and it no longer made sense for users to write their own software when something bought off-the-shelf could do it as well, for a fraction of the price. The focus for application development moved to the desktop, where people used products like Microsoft's Visual Basic and Access to build quick and dirty systems allowing them to download corporate data, often out of these packaged software systems, into desktop systems like Excel where they can be easily manipulated. End user access to corporate data drove the applications software industry and a class of software developed in the 1980s called the Decision Support System (DSS), which quickly evolved into the Executive Information System (EIS). These systems took operational and transactional data from corporate databases and reformatted it in such a way that it could easily be understood by end users, for example graphs comparing sales data by region by time.

EISs became necessary because traditional computer systems were not designed to make it easy to extract information being optimized for operational purposes – to record transactions and to compute balances and the like (Power 2003). In the 1990s EISs evolved into a whole new class of PC software, generically called Business Intelligence (BI), which displays information in attractive graphical formats, and allows information from different sources to be easily juxtaposed. Displaying data in multiple dimensions, multidimensionality or online analytical processing (OLAP) underpins this type of software. OLAP tools are often used as front ends to data warehouses, which are systems in which operational data has been downloaded and optimized for such retrieval (Power 2003).

UNIX, Windows and the death of proprietary operating systems

The success of IBM's OS/360 spawned many imitators. Most early minicomputers used proprietary operating systems designed just for that computer, but all of them were mini-architectures capable of being run on different models in the range. Data General had AOS, Digital had VMS, Bull had GCOS, Wang had VS, Hewlett-Packard had MPE. There were dozens more. But Unix, developed in 1969 by Ken Thompson and Dennis Ritchie in AT&T's Bell Labs, gradually replaced them all. Thompson and Ritchie's aim was to build a small and elegant general purpose operating system that would be independent of the hardware platform it ran on. They succeeded and Unix filled a gap at a time manufacturers were developing their own proprietary operating systems (Ceruzzi 1999: 106). Unix prospered, largely because AT&T adopted a policy of giving it away to universities.[14] A generation of programmers learnt about the basics on Unix, taking their expertise with them into the workforce. The inevitable happened and different versions of Unix began to appear, but there remained an identifiable core Unix.

In the 1980s many new hardware suppliers entered the industry, lured by the massive growth in commercial computing and the lower cost of entry afforded by the new breed of microprocessors and cheap off-the-shelf peripherals. The leading vendors stayed with their proprietary operating systems, but most of them could not afford to develop their own. So they used Unix, which was cheap, functional and readily available. Each tweaked Unix to their own specifications, and at one stage there were dozens of different varieties. The momentum grew and in 1984 Hewlett-Packard legitimized Unix and the others followed including IBM with its RS/6000 Unix computer in 1990.

During the early 1990s there were attempts to unify the various strands of Unix. Two major consortiums emerged, Unix International (essentially the AT&T camp) and the so-called Open Software Foundation, which was neither open nor a foundation, having more to do with politics and marketing than software. These groups and other splinter bodies conducted an unedifying fight over standards and directions now loosely referred to as the 'Unix Wars'. However, standards emerged through market forces rather than industry agreement, as the user community coalesced around three major varieties of Unix: those from Sun Microsystems, Hewlett-Packard and IBM.[15]

A unifying force was the growth of Novell's Netware networking operating system, which enjoyed a great boom in the early to mid-1990s as people started to network PCs together in earnest. But Netware was a flash in the pan, now relegated to the dustbin of history along with the other proprietary systems. Netware's demise occurred largely at the hand of Microsoft when they decided to move into operating systems for larger computers with the 1993 release of Windows NT, which unlike others had just one version across all architectures.[16] NT did many of the things Unix and Netware did. While it started out slow and underpowered it gradually improved and was able to compete at the technical level. Users migrated to Windows NT and it looked as if Windows would sweep all before it.

Linux and open source

But in 1992 a Finnish university student named Linus Torvalds developed a version of Unix, called Linux, which used the 'open source' model, meaning any developer can improve the software and submit those improvements to a committee for acceptance. Linux is free despite an army of developers improving it all the time.[17] It represents the antithesis of the proprietary Microsoft development method as well as the Microsoft marketing model. The battle between the two has become religious.

The Linux development process of continuous improvement has now seen it move up the ladder of scalability and respectability, to the point where we are starting to see it in the data centre, and where most software suppliers are now readily supporting it. One of the key reasons for this shift is its endorsement by IBM, the company that understands enterprise computing like no other. IBM picked up on the move to Linux in the late 1990s, and now spends $US1 billion a year on Linux development, mainly in what used to be called in the mainframe world 'RAS' – reliability, availability, scalability – the very things that make an operating system suitable for enterprise computing.

Microsoft and many others see a threat to capitalism in the open source movement.[18] There is little doubt that the open source software movement has anti-capitalist elements. 'Linux is subversive' (Raymond 1995) are the first three words of the Linux manifesto, the well known tract *The Cathedral and the Bazaar*, written by Eric Raymond, the movement's Karl Marx. The title reflects Raymond's idea of open source software development as a medieval bazaar: an untidy agglomeration of merchants and stalls and thronging people, rather than the standard method of building software which is like a stately cathedral, planned in advance and built over time to exacting specifications.

Open source worries the software establishment. In October 2003 Microsoft president Steve Ballmer cut short a holiday in Europe to try to convince the Munich city council to rescind a decision to move to open source. In early 2004 software company SCO, which claims ownership of Unix after a convoluted series of deals in the late 1990s, sued IBM for $US3 million over allegations that Big Blue stole Unix code and put it into Linux. To date this matter is unresolved.[19]

The Internet and the World Wide Web

In the late 1960s the world's biggest computer user was the US Department of Defense. It had many machines of its own, and it used many more at universities and research institutions. Bob Taylor, a manager at ARPA (Advanced Research Projects Agency), proposed that their computers should be connected and he eventually persuaded ARPA to call for tenders. A small company in Boston called BBN wrote a proposal for 'interface message processors for the ARPA network'. They got the job, and BBN's Frank Heart and his team started work, using a new technology called packet switching (Segaller 1998: 45).

Packet switching sends data in discrete packets, rather than all at once. BBN was the first company to implement the technology, but the concept was also picked up by a young man in Hearst's group called Bob Metcalfe, who four years later used it to devise Ethernet, the technology underlying most local area networks (LANs). Metcalfe is famous for Metcalfe's Law – 'the utility of a network expands by the square of the number of users' (Segaller 1998: 283).

On 1 October 1969 the first Internet message was sent from UCLA to Stanford Research Institute. Before the end of the year the University of California at Santa Barbara and the University of Utah were connected in a network called ARPAnet. Growth was slow. A year later the network had expanded to 15 nodes, but it took a further seven years to reach 100. Usage was restricted to academia and the military, and it remained very difficult to use until a networking standard called TCP/IP (Transmission Control Protocol/Internet Protocol) was developed by ARPA in 1982 (Segaller 1998: 111).

Gradually people began calling the new network the Internet. Its most widespread application became email, and things improved substantially in 1983 with the introduction of domain names, like .com and .org. But it was not until Tim Berners-Lee conceived the idea of the World Wide Web in 1989 that it began to resemble the Internet known today.

Berners-Lee, an English scientist working at CERN, the European particle physics laboratory, came up with some simple specifications that made navigation around the Internet much easier. He devised a language called HTML (HyperText Markup Language), and a communications protocol called HTTP (HyperText Transfer Protocol) that used the concept of 'hypertext' to allow people to jump easily between locations on the Internet (Berners-Lee 1999: 36).

But the Internet was still not a place for beginners. Addresses and locations were standardized, but you still had to know where you where going, and you needed a range of different software tools to get there. Enter the browser. The browser was the brainchild of Marc Andreessen, a 21-year-old student at the University of Illinois' National Center for Supercomputing Applications (NCSA). He was working for $US7 an hour cutting code for the NCSA's Unix computers, and became frustrated with how difficult it was to use the Internet. He enlisted the aid of a colleague, Eric Bina, and set out to change that (Segaller 1998: 296). Over three months in the winter of 1992–93 Andreessen and Bina developed the first browser. It ran only on Unix, but it was revolutionary. Their aim was a single piece of software that could navigate through hypertext links with the push of a button or the click of a mouse that could display graphics as well as text, with an attractive and easy to use interface. The result was Mosaic. They completed their first version in February 1993, and in April they released it for widespread use. Immediately there were 10,000 users, and by the end of the year, by which time they had developed Windows and Apple versions, there were over a million users.

An indicator of Mosaic's impact can be seen from the growth in the number of web sites. In January 1993 there were about 50 commercial web sites on the Internet (the US Congress had only authorized commercial usage the previous year). A year later, there were more than 10,000. Amazon.com became the archetype of a new e-Business model, and once Pizza Hut let people order pizzas over the Internet in 1994, things started to happen very quickly (Segaller 1998: 348). Although the browser has developed substantially in the last ten years, it is still recognizably the same piece of software it was ten years ago.[20]

ERP and e-Business

While the Internet was the biggest IT story of the 1990s, the second most important trend was the growth in enterprise resource planning (ERP) systems. ERP basically means the integration of high end applications, usually based around manufacturing or accounting systems. Their development was driven by the need for sophisticated commercial computing applications to talk to each other. For example, feeding purchasing data into the manufacturing system and then for sales information to flow directly to the general ledger.

In the 1980s large organizations wrote their own applications software, hence the CASE boom, but the rise of packaged ERP solutions saw most large organizations using an off-the-shelf ERP system. ERP vendors grew in the 1990s led by the German company SAP, with database company Oracle in second place and others like Peoplesoft and Baan blossoming. Many older manufacturing software companies like JD Edwards also made a successful move into ERP, though others like SSA and QAD had less success in breaking out of their niche.

At the end of the 1990s the ERP market went into a slump, although forecasts of the 'death of ERP' were mistaken. ERP sales declined because many organizations had bought ERP systems during the 1990s in a saturated market. The Y2K scare also brought a lot of activity forward, meaning there was a slowdown after 2000.[21] Another reason for the apparent decline in ERP was the greater publicity given to electronic commerce and customer relationship management (CRM) applications. These were often wrongly referred to as separate applications when in reality they were different aspects of ERP reflecting the increased integration of large scale computer applications.

ERP has now evolved into something variously called e-Business or e-Commerce. e-Business of a kind was possible without the web. In the 1980s a number of different systems were devised to enable commercial transactions via computer. EDI (electronic document interchange) was standardized by the mid-1980s and adopted by a number of organizations, but it was not a widespread success. It relied on closed systems with specialized protocols and on real-time communications – the two computers conducting the transaction had to be connected directly to each other. EDI was successful in specific industries with regularized transactions. EDI's success in these areas meant that its users were ready to embrace the use of a better and cheaper medium a decade later. EDI systems are still in place, carried via the Internet.

e-Business became inevitable as soon as the Internet was freed from its academic and scientific limitations in 1992. Amazon.com and eBay were both formed in 1995, and one of the most amazing booms in history occurred. By 1999 the worldwide e-Business market was worth $US30 billion (Philipson 2002a: 18). The rapid growth of the Internet and e-Business in the late 1990s made many believe that the old rules of business no longer applied. There was much talk of the 'new economy', and many new companies were formed on the basis that the Internet boom would transform overnight the way consumers and businesses behaved. Many of these new dot.com companies were based on unrealistic and unsustainable business models, but a feeding frenzy of investors eager to cash in on the speculative growth of these organizations led to a spectacular stock market boom, which led to an equally spectacular crash.

On 10 March 2000 the NASDAQ index of US technology stocks hit a peak of 5,049, after doubling in the previous year. Two years later it was hovering in the low 1,100s, a drop of more than 75 per cent.[22] In the three years following the top of the boom nearly 5,000 computer companies in the US, and many more internationally, went broke or were acquired. Twenty thousand jobs were lost in Silicon Valley alone. In early 2004 the market capitalization of all the world's computer companies was about 20 per cent what it had been three and half years earlier (Philipson 2003b). After every boom there is a bust. Rarely has this fact been more graphically demonstrated than in the Great Tech Bust of 2001–03. And while the crash led many people to believe erroneously that the promise of the Internet was a fallacy, in fact it was essentially a minor correction after a burst of over-enthusiasm.

The 1990s saw the industry change beyond recognition. Large and proud companies like DEC, Wang, Compaq, Prime, Data General, Amdahl and many others are no more. PCs have become so cheap that they are commodities, and so powerful that no-one takes much notice of their technical specifications. In the new millennium the battleground has moved to where software is being developed, and by whom.

Outsourcing, offshoring and the 'skills shortage'

During the 1990s much attention was paid to outsourcing, or the phenomenon of contracting out all or part of the IT function.[23] The arguments were essentially those of 'make versus buy', familiar to any manufacturing concern. The movement from in-house development to packaged software, described above, was part of this trend. But towards the end of the 1990s and into the new millennium, outsourcing took on a whole new dimension, known as 'offshoring', which described the outsourcing of various business functions, including software development, to other countries. Very often 'other countries' meant India, whose software industry grew enormously in the 1990s. The removal of import restrictions, improved data communications, and the sheer number and quality of Indian software professionals, combined with their very low cost compared with their Western equivalents, made India an attractive software development centre for many Western vendors and users. The substantial immigration of Indian programmers to Western countries, particularly the UK, the US and Australia (Philipson 2002b) caused a major backlash in these countries. Even as Western governments and industry spokespeople were proclaiming an IT skills shortage, employment figures and salaries in the IT industry fell, blamed mainly on IT immigration and offshoring.

What most people missed was a fundamental structural change occurring in the industry as in others, but in this case the shift of IT jobs was from inside user organizations to outside. Outsourcing was an attempt to lower the costs of IT which are largely internal – salaries, data centre management, consumables, etc. Increasing amounts of activity moved from internal (do-it-yourself) to external (product): buying packages rather than writing applications; plugging into the Internet rather than building networks; outsourcing training, programming and help desks.

Vendors are aware of this trend. Over the last 10 years IBM has reinvented itself as a service company. Oracle, itself now a major services company, is pushing to run its clients' applications for them. Compaq bought DEC, and HP bought Compaq, largely for their consultancy capabilities. Web services, the hottest trend of the new millennium, is all about facilitating the outsourcing of business functions. The trend is being accelerated by the increased globalization of the IT industry. Much of the debate over IT skills worldwide has centred around the immigration of cheap labour, but the real action is in the wholesale export of IT jobs to low cost countries. The chief beneficiary of this has been India, because of its sheer size. With over a billion people, and a much higher birthrate, India will overtake China in population this decade, and it has over half a million IT graduates, with over 50,000 more entering the workforce each year. And they all speak English.

The future of software: the information utility

The Internet is a fact of life. It is now almost impossible to do business without it. Most airline tickets are bought over the Internet, email is the standard method of commercial communication, and all media are digital. Mobile phones and other wireless devices are commonplace, removing physical location as a constraint on communication. There is more processing power in the average car than in the largest data centre of the 1970s.

Data communication and voice telephony costs are now so low, bandwidth so broad and the Internet so ubiquitous that applications development centres can be run offshore. An increasing number of the world's call centres are now in India, or the Philippines, or southern Africa. We are now witnessing, on a global scale, the kind of disruption that occurred in the English countryside in the industrial revolution 200 years ago. We have long witnessed the movement of blue-collar jobs to low-cost countries, now we are seeing white-collar jobs move offshore, at an even faster rate. The dark satanic mills of the information millennium are in the suburbs of Bangalore, Shenzhen and St Petersburg. And it is not just IT jobs – it is architects, accountants, engineers, indeed any type of knowledge worker. If the work can be digitized, it can be exported. Microsoft's second largest development centre is in Beijing, and Oracle plans to have 4,000 software designers in India by the end of 2004. Large and small IT shops are moving software development and other functions to India and elsewhere in the world at an increasing rate.

Oracle's Larry Ellison famously said in 2003 that 90 per cent of the software companies in Silicon Valley do not deserve to exist (Philipson 2003b) and Gartner says that half of them will go out of business in the next five years. The software industry, after more than 50 years of fabulous growth, has grown up. It has matured. As its products have commoditized, its margins have reduced. The offerings from one player look much like those from another. In most parts of the industry the number of significant companies has fallen to just three or four.

One company, Microsoft, has a virtual monopoly on desktop software – operating systems and applications. Its abuse of its position has led to legal action by the US Department of Justice, which went after IBM in the 1970s for just the same reason. The IBM case eventually fell apart, not because IBM had not abused its position (it had), but because the industry had changed so much that the circumstances became irrelevant. The same is happening in Microsoft's case. The software giant has been exposed as a serial bully and a master of IBM's old FUD (fear, uncertainty and doubt) tactics, but it is all becoming meaningless. Microsoft's dominance will decline, because of the very market forces it claims to uphold.

The ubiquity of the Internet will ensure that. There are more people online today than there were at the height of the technology bubble. More things are being purchased by consumers over the Internet, and more business-to-business commerce is being done over the Internet, than at any previous time. Software, and the functions it performs are increasingly traded as Web-delivered services. Web services standards, which allow business processes to be shared between organizations, are one of the key software building blocks of the new millennium.

The open source movement, which is already making significant inroads with Linux, is another force of the future. The very concept of intellectual property, be it software, or music, or film, is under threat from the new technology. That will be the battleground of the future. We are moving towards the era of the information utility, with IT delivered on demand via an invisible grid that encircles the globe. It is also called grid computing, or fabric computing, or cluster computing. There is no standard definition of utility computing, but the idea has been around for some time. In the developed world power, water and increasingly telephones are utilities. The Internet is getting there.[24] Indeed, the Internet has done a lot to promote the 'information utility' idea, where all the information a user wants is available right there in front of them. Utility computing suggests that a user can switch on their computer and have as much or as little computing power as they need. Like other utilities, users pay for what they use, plus a standing charge for being connected to the system. Computers are all connected together in a grid, so they all can share the load of every application being run across the entire network.

The idea is attractive and becoming pervasive. Just about every major computer supplier, with the notable exception of Microsoft, is talking about utility computing, although few of them call it that. IBM is heavily promoting what it calls 'on demand computing'. It does not like the term 'utility computing' because it wants to be the provider. It sees the 'utility' idea as being a little impersonal, and suggestive of the idea that users can seamlessly shift from one supplier to another. That is also why not much has been heard from Microsoft. But IBM is talking at length about grid computing. So is Oracle, and many other suppliers. Sun has an initiative called N1. HP has something called the Utility Data Center. And Dell plans to populate the planet with low-cost Intel-based servers that will perform any and every computing task imaginable.

The history of information technology is in many ways the history of improved end-user access and innovation continues to push the boundaries of what is possible. Every major development in computing has had to do with making it easier to get at, manipulate and report on the information contained within the systems. The PC revolution, the rise of networking, the development of the graphical user interface, the growth in distributed computing, the rise of the Internet and e-Business: all are part of this trend. As a result the software industry has changed forever, and more in the last five years than in the previous twenty. As hardware becomes ubiquitous and commoditized, software becomes more pervasive and more important. It is now nearly 60 years since ENIAC's first switches were flicked and the first software program ran. In 60 years time the software used today will look as primitive as the software used on the ENIAC now does.

Notes

1 The ENIAC (Electronic Numerator, Integrator, Analyzer and Computer) is generally agreed to be the first computer.

2 Augusta Ada Byron was born in 1815 and brought up by her mother, who threw Byron out, disgusted by his philandering (O'Connor and Robertson 2002). She was named after Byron's half sister, who had also been his mistress. Her mother was terrified that she would become a poet like her father, so Ada was schooled in mathematics, which was very unusual for a woman in that era. Her life was beset by scandalous love affairs, gambling and heavy drinking: despite her mother's best efforts, she was very much her father's daughter. She considered writing a treatise on the effects of wine and opium, based on her own experiences. She died of cancer in 1852, aged only 37.

3 The Turing Test is used in artificial intelligence. Briefly, it states that if it is impossible for an observer to tell whether questions they are asking are being answered by a computer or a human, and they are in fact being answered by a computer, then, for all practical purposes, it can be assumed that the computer has reached a human level of intelligence.

4 Atanosoff's machine, the ABC, was the first fully electronic calculator.

5 A later version, appropriately named MANIAC, was used exclusively for H-bomb calculations.

6 UNIVAC leapt to the forefront of public consciousness in the 1952 US presidential election when it correctly predicted the results of the election based only on one hour of counted votes.

7 The number 360 was meant to refer to the points on a compass.

8 Ted Codd was born in England in 1923. He studied mathematics and chemistry at Oxford, and was a captain in the Royal Air Force during the Second World War. He moved to the USA after the war, briefly teaching maths at the University of Tennessee before joining IBM in 1949 (Philipson 2003a). His first job at IBM was as a programmer on the SSEC (Selective Sequence Electronic Calculator), one of Big Blue's earliest computers. In the early 1950s he was involved in the development of IBM's STRETCH computer, one of the precursors to today's mainframes. He completed a masters and doctorate in computer science at the University of Michigan in the 1960s, on an IBM scholarship. Ted Codd retired from IBM in 1984. His career is dotted with awards recognizing his achievements. He was made a Fellow of the British Computer Society in 1974, and an IBM Life Fellow in 1976. In 1981 he received the Turing Award, probably the highest accolade in computing. In 1994 he was made a Fellow of the American Academy of Arts and Sciences. He died in 2003 (Philipson 2003a).

9 DEC was acquired by Compaq in 1997 then became part of Hewlett-Packard in 2002.

10 Kildall at Digital Research realized his mistake, and his company developed a rival to MS-DOS called DR-DOS. At the end of the 1980s it was far from certain which computer operating system, and which hardware architecture, would win out. Apple was still strong, and in the IBM PC and compatible world MS-DOS was still dominant, but it faced challenges from Digital Research's DR-DOS and – more significantly – from IBM's OS/2.

11 The genesis of the GUI goes back well before even the establishment of PARC, which opened its doors in 1969. Stanford University's Human Factors Research Center, led by Doug Engelbart, was founded in 1963 to develop better ways of communicating with computers. Engelbart's group developed the first mouse, and in 1968 demonstrated a prototype GUI at the National Computer Conference in San Francisco (Campbell-Kelly and Asprey 1996: 266).

12 CASE has its origins in the 1960s Apollo space program, the most complex

computer-based project of that era when two computer scientists, Margaret Hamilton and Saydeen Zeldin, developed a set of mathematical rules for implementing and testing complex computer systems (Philipson 1990: 14). They later formed a company called Higher Order Software, and their methodology evolved into a product called USE.IT, which was not a commercial success, despite being promoted by software guru James Martin in his influential book *Systems Development Using Provably Correct Concepts*, published in 1979. Martin was at the time one of the industry's leading and most successful theorists, and an important figure in the development of CASE.

13 Many such systems were designed, such as SSADM (Structured Systems Analysis and Design Methodology), which was mandated by the British Government and became very popular in the United Kingdom.

14 By giving Unix away to universities a generation of computer science graduates joined the industry familiar with its arcane workings. But Unix was not perfect – it was difficult to learn and a nightmare for end users. However it prospered as the only alternative to the maze of proprietary systems, even if vendors built their own little proprietary extensions to it to differentiate themselves from their competitors.

15 Other varieties faltered, including Digital's Unix which should have been most successful. Digital, which led the minicomputer revolution and on one of whose machines Unix was originally developed, could never make up its mind about Unix. Its ambivalence become doctrine when founder and CEO Ken Olsen referred to Unix as 'snake oil' (Rifkin and Harrar 1988: 305). Digital was acquired by Compaq in 1999, and the combined company was acquired by Hewlett-Packard in 2002.

16 Zachary (1994; 1998) tells the story of the development of Windows NT whose 'chief lesson is that software systems are wholly human creations' (1998: 63).

17 In an interesting article Postigo (2003) explores this issue of unwaged work in software development in the context of software game 'modders'.

18 There is much more to open source than Linux. All variety of software is available in open source. Web sites such as Sourceforge (www.sourceforge.net) and Freshmeat (www.freshmeat.net) list thousands of open source utilities and applications that anyone can download for free. Open source databases like MySQL and PostgreSQL are widely used around the world, often in production applications, and the Apache web server is more widely used than its commercial competitors. There is even an open source ERP package, called Compiere (www.compiere.com).

19 SCO says that IBM's continued shipment of AIX, IBM's version of Unix, is illegal because it relies on a licence from SCO. IBM says its Unix licence is irrevocable. Novell, which sold Unix to SCO in 1995, says that sale excluded all 'copyrights' and 'patents'. Microsoft has bought a SCO licence, though it does not plan to ship any Unix. The open systems people say SCO does not own Unix anyway. The basis of SCO's argument is that it is now the owner of the intellectual property that is Unix, and that IBM has stolen that intellectual property and incorporated it into Linux, where all can benefit. It has allowed a select group of analysts to view the pieces of code it says were stolen. They agree there are major similarities. But Unix has evolved in such a complex fashion that it is ultimately impossible to tell where the source code comes from. At the time of writing (April 2004) the matter remains unresolved.

20 Much has happened in that time – Andreessen left the NCSA, which to this day downplays his role in history, saying that development was a collective effort. He became one of the founders of Netscape, which briefly became one of the most successful companies in history before Microsoft entered the browser market and started the acrimonious 'browser wars' of the late 1990s, which led directly to Microsoft's legal problems, and also to its unrivalled success. Tim

Berners-Lee, inventor of the World Wide Web, has not been idle in recent years. He is now director of the Word Wide Web Consortium (W3C), the non-profit coordinating body for Web development. His work still involves conceptualising where the Web is headed, and how to get it there. Berners-Lee believes the next big thing will be the 'Semantic Web', which he describes as an extension of the current Web where information is given meaning and where computers can not only process information but understand it (Berners-Lee 1999: 157). The Web as it is currently constituted is optimized for human beings – to allow people easy access to documents. In the Semantic Web, data contained in Web pages will be coded with an extra dimension of information that will enable computers to make sense of it. XML (Extensible Markup Language – an extension of HTML) is a step in that direction, as are emerging Web Services protocols, but the Semantic Web will contain much more meaning. It will enable intelligent software agents to perform many of the searches and conduct many of the transactions that can currently only be undertaken by humans.

21 The Y2K issue, otherwise known as the 'Millennium Bug', came about because of the habit of many programmers writing the date as just the last two digits of the year. That meant that as the years rolled through from 1999 to 2000, the date counters would go back 99 years instead of forward one year. An enormous amount of time and money was spent fixing the problem, which ended up not being much of a problem at all. Whether that was because appropriate remedial action had been taken, or because it was never going to be a problem anyway, will never be known.

22 There are hundreds of print and online articles written about the rise and fall of the Internet. One book of note is *Dot.Con* by John Cassidy (published in the UK in 2002 by Allen Lane: The Penguin Press)

23 These developments led Yourdon to reconsider his original (1992) premise in the classic *The Decline and Fall of the American Programmer* in his later (1996) book *Rise and Resurrection of the American Programmer.*

24 Sun tried to popularize the term 'web tone' a few years ago.

References

Augarten, S. (1984) *Bit by Bit: An Illustrated History of Computers*, London: Unwin Paperbacks.

Berners-Lee, T. (1999) *Weaving the Web*, San Francisco: HarperCollins.

Brooks, F. P. (1975, Anniversary edition 1995) *The Mythical Man-Month: Essays on Software Engineering*, New York: Addison-Wesley.

Campbell-Kelly, M. and Aspray, W. (1996) *Computer: A History of the Information Machine*, New York: HarperCollins.

Carlton, J. (1997) *Apple: The Inside Story of Intrigue, Egomania and Business Blunders*, New York: Random House.

Cassidy, J. (2002) *Dot.Con*, London: Allen Lane, The Penguin Press.

Ceruzzi, P.E. (1999) *A History of Modern Computing*, Cambridge, MA: MIT Press.

Crawford, A. and Ziola, B. (2002) *Oracle for Molecular Informatics*. Online. Available HTTP: <http://www.managedventures.com/images/OraMolInfoBW6.pdf> (Accessed 3 February 2003).

Cringely, R. X. (1992) *Accidental Empires*, London: Viking.

Freiberger, P. and Swaine, M. (1984) *Fire in the Valley: The Making of the Personal Computer*, Berkeley, CA: Osborne/McGraw Hill.

Hodges, A. (1983, Unwin Paperbacks edition 1985) *Alan Turing: The Enigma of Intelligence*, London: Unwin Paperbacks.

Hoefler, D. (1971) 'Silicon Valley USA', *Electronic News*, 11 January 1971.

Kunde, B (1996) *A Brief History of Word Processing (Through 1986)*. Online. Available HTTP: <http://www.stanford.edu/~bkunde/fb-press/articles/wdprhist.html> (Accessed 12 April 2004).

McCartney, S. (1999) *ENIAC: The Triumphs and Tragedies of the World's First Computer*, New York: Walker and Company.

Naur, P. and Randell, B. (1969) *Software Engineering*, Brussels: NATO.

O'Connor, J. J. and Robertson, E. F. (2002) *Augusta Ada King, Countess of Lovelace*. Online. Available HTTP <www-gap.dcs.st-and.ac.uk/~history/Mathematicians/Lovelace.html> (Accessed October 2003).

Peterson, I. (2000) *Software's Origin*. Online. Available HTTP <www.maa.org/mathland/mathtrek_7_31_00.html> (Accessed 20 March 2004).

Philipson, G. (1990) *Implementing CASE Technology*, Charleston, SC: CTR Corporation.

Philipson, G. (2003a) 'Database pioneer dies', *The Sydney Morning Herald* (Next supplement), 20 May 2003: 3.

Philipson, G. (2003b) 'A brief history of computing', *Australian Personal Computer*, December, 84–103.

Philipson, G. (ed) (2002a) *Australian eBusiness Guide*, 2nd edn, Sydney: CCH Australia.

Philipson, G. (2002b) 'Skills glut prompts clampdown on Indian visas', *Butler Group Review*, November: 30.

Postigo, H. (2003) 'From *Pong* to *Plant Quake*: Post-industrial transitions from leisure to work', *Information Communication and Society*, 6, 4: 593–607.

Power, D. J. (2003) *A Brief History of Decision Support Systems*, version 2.8. Online. Available HHTP <http://dssresources.com/history/dsshistory.html> (Accessed 12 March 2004).

Raymond, E. (1995) *The Cathedral and the Bazaar*. Online. Available HTTP <http://catb.org/~esr/> (Accessed 15 October 2003).

Rifkin, G. and Harrar, G. (1988) *The Ultimate Entrepreneur: The Story of Ken Olsen and Digital Equipment Corporation*, Chicago: Contemporary Book.

Roberts, H. E. and Yates, W. (1975) 'Altair 8800 Minicomputer, Part 1', *Popular Electronics*, January, 33–8.

Segaller, S. (1998) *Nerds 2.0.1: A Brief History of the Internet*, New York: TV Books.

Symonds, M. (2003) *Softwar: An Initimate Portrait of Larry Ellison and Oracle*, New York: Simon & Schuster.

Turing, A. (1937) 'On computable numbers, with an application to the Entscheidungsproblem', *Proceedings of the London Mathematical Society*, 2: 42.

von Neumann, J. (1945) *First Draft of a Report on EDVAC*. Reproduced in B. Randall (ed.) *The Origins of Digital Computers*, New York, Springer-Verlag, pp. 355–64.

Watson, T. J. (1990) *Father Son & Co: My Life at IBM and Beyond*, New York: Bantam Books.

Yourdon, E. (1996) *Rise and Resurrection of the American Programmer*, Englewood Cliffs, NJ: Yourdan Press, Prentice Hall.

Zachary, P. (1994) *Showstopper! The Making of Windows NT and the Next Generation at Microsoft*, New York: Free Press.

Zachary, P. (1998) 'Armed truce: Software in the age of teams', *Information Technology and People*, 11, 1: 62–5.

3 The labor process in software startups

Production on a virtual assembly line?

Christopher K. Andrews, Craig D. Lair and Bart Landry

Introduction

The commercialization of software production in the 1990s raises important questions for the sociology of work and for the labor process in particular. To what extent is the labor process in software firms patterned on the industrial labor process? Do software firms resemble the producers of industrial commodities or dispensers of services? Are software workers exploited or are they the 'aristocracy' of knowledge workers? Newspaper reports during the dot.com bubble of extravagant perks, of fun-filled environments, and of stock-option multimillionaires created almost daily, painted pictures sharply at variance with the Marxian image of industrial sweatshops.

Against this backdrop we began a study designed to test the relevance of Marx's theory of capitalism (*Capital*, 1976 [1867]) to the reality of what was being called a 'new economy'?[1] A fresh reading of Braverman's *Labor and Monopoly Capital* (1998 [1974]), convinced us that the labor process would be a good place to start. Critics notwithstanding, Braverman not only revived interest in the labor process, but pushed the envelope beyond the industrial work site. While giving due attention to Scientific Management (Taylor 1967 [1911]) in industry, he also explored the labor process among clerical and white-collar service workers.[2] Reminiscent of Mills' (1951) analysis of the impact of office machines on the clerical workforce, Braverman detailed the further encroachment of Taylorist ideas among clerical workers through office automation and suggested that early computer programmers might suffer the same fate. He even briefly hinted at these issues of the labor process among those we refer to today as 'knowledge workers', including 'the mass employments of draftsmen and technicians, engineers and accountants, nurses and teachers, and the multiplying ranks of supervisors, foremen, and petty managers' (Braverman 1998 [1974]: 282). It was Braverman's reference to 'engineers' and 'early programmers' that especially caught our attention. Would Taylorism find a new home in the very heart of the new economy – the burgeoning software industry?

The Dulles Corridor

The Washington, DC/Baltimore metropolitan area presented itself as a convenient place to pursue this question. This area is one of the six major software production concentrations in the US – along with Silicon Valley, New York City, Boston, Seattle, and the East Bay area of California. With 521 software firms in 1997, DC/Baltimore ranked fourth in the number of software firms in the nation (US Census 1999), while VentureOne.com ranked it fourth in the amount of venture capital (VC) money ($US814.52 million) received by software firms in 2000 (VentureOne.com). The highest concentration of firms is located in a band stretching from Tysons Corner to Reston, in Northern Virginia. Here in the 'Dulles Corridor', named for the nearby Dulles International Airport, are hundreds of small startups and some high-flying firms like AOL and Microstrategy.

Software firms are not limited to this area, however. The nearby Virginia counties of Arlington and Alexandria City, as well as the District of Columbia, are homes to many more. In Maryland, software startups are found in Silver Spring, Rockville, and Baltimore. In 2001, Local Business.com posted a partial list of over 300 firms in the region, with new startups sprouting up almost weekly.

Methodology

Data collection

Our study is exploratory and we took a qualitative approach using semi-structured questionnaires in face-to-face interviews, which we conducted in the summer and fall of 2001. We began with a snowball approach (Babbie 1999) to locate firms, then extended our sampling frame by using web-based lists, newspaper articles, news releases, and by soliciting references from respondents to their friends and acquaintances in other software firms. Our sample includes a total of 30 firms.[3] See Tables 3.1 and 3.2 for a description of the firm's activities and the interviews conducted.

In most firms, we conducted two or three interviews, one with the founder, if present, or with the CEO if the founder was no longer part of the company. We also interviewed one or two programmers in each firm: a project lead (a senior programmer with supervisory function) and another programmer without supervisory responsibility. Our objective was to learn first-hand from founders or CEOs about the origin and development of the startup. Of both programmers and managers we asked questions about various aspects of the labor process; and, on some issues, we asked the same questions of both to check for consistency. By obtaining information

Table 3.1 Profile of software start-ups making software 'products'

Software type	*Management structure*	*Year founded*	*Interviews conducted*
Product	Formal	1993	Founder/CEO, Project manager, Programmer
Product	Formal	1995	Lead programmer
Product	Formal	1995	Co-founder/CEO, Architect
Product	Formal	1997	CEO, Team leader, Programmer
Product	Formal	1998	Co-founder/Executive VP of Research and Development, Business Analyst
Product	Formal	1999	Founder/CEO
Product	Formal	1999	Director of Marketing
Product	Formal	1999	CEO, 2 × Programmers
Product	Formal	2001	Founder, Technical lead, Programmer
Product	Formal	2000 (1980)[a]	CEO, Manager of Product Development, Technical lead
Product	Non-formal	1995	Founder/CTO
Product	Non-formal	1997	CEO, Senior Director of Technology, Programmer
Product	Non-formal	1998	Founder/CEO, Programmer
Product	Non-formal	1998	CEO/Co-founder, COO/Co-founder, Programmer
Product	Non-formal	2000	Founder/CEO, Senior developer, VP of Engineering
Product	Non-formal	2000	Co-founder/President, Programmer
Product	Non-formal	2000	Co-founder/CTO, Programmer

Note

a While this company was originally founded in 1980 through an acquisition it transformed itself into a 'new economy' firm.

from different positions in a firm and from both management and workers we hoped to access different 'layers' and possibly varying accounts of work in these companies.

Sample profile

Tables 3.1 and 3.2 outline some of the 30 firms' characteristics. The firms vary in size: from a one-person firm[4] to companies with hundreds of employees in several locations around the country. The largest firms had offices occupying multiple floors in prestigious locations with their names emblazoned in bold letters on the side of high rise office buildings. A few also had overseas offices in Europe at the time of the interview or had recently closed such offices. Some of the smallest firms functioned with a skeletal staff of two to four full-time individuals and several part-time freelance programmers; and often maintained low overheads by locating in low rent buildings, their quarters sometimes consisted of only two to three rooms. However, size is a problematic variable as most large firms

Table 3.2 Profile of software start-ups making software 'applications'

Software type	*Management structure*	*Year founded*	*Interviews conducted*
Application	Formal	1983	Founder/CEO, Project manager
Application	Formal	1990	Founder/CEO, Project manager, Programmer
Application	Formal	1997	Founder/Chairman, Programmer
Application	Non-formal	1996	Co-founder/President, Co-founder/Creative Director, Interface Designer
Application	Non-formal	1996	Founder/President, CEO
Application	Non-formal	1999	Co-founder/CEO, Co-founder/COO
Application	Non-formal	1999	Founder/CEO
Application	Non-formal	1999	Founder/CEO/Creative Director, Lead programmer, Programmers
Application	Non-formal	2000	Founder/CEO, Lead programmer
Application	Non-formal	2000	Founder/CEO
Application	Non-formal	2001	Director of Development
Application	Non-formal	1997	Founder/CEO
Application	Non-formal	1998	Co-founder/CEO

were downsizing and many smaller firms were struggling to stay afloat during the time we conducted interviews. In this period of flux, personnel numbers would not have been accurate for very long.[5]

Yet intuitively it seemed reasonable to expect that the labor process – as well as other firm dynamics – might vary by firm size. Bigger firms were more capitalized, had larger programming staffs, and more ambitious projects. Given the difficulty of classifying by firm size, we searched for another dimension that might correlate with size. In the end, we opted for a classification by management structure. While a small firm might function smoothly with a founder/CEO, larger firms, we reasoned, could not be effective without a minimum number of managers responsible for the basic functions of overall management (CEO), finance (CFO), technology (CTO) and operations (COO) or marketing and sales. We thus divided our sample between firms with formal (four full-time senior managers) and non-formal (less than four full-time senior managers) management structures. Our sample therefore included 13 formal and 17 non-formal firms.

Firms were further classified by type of software produced (see Tables 3.1 and 3.2). It was clear from our interviews that some startups began with an idea for a product that they were attempting to develop into a marketable commodity; others were responding to the needs of clients. Might not these two types of firms face different production constraints or opportunities, and have different needs and outcomes? This classification yielded a breakdown of our sample into 13 firms that built applications such as databases and web pages, and 17 product firms that worked on such projects as security software and interfaces for wireless communication. However, some application firms converted a successful application into a marketable product, or also turned out products; while a number of the larger product firms combined this activity with a service component.[6]

Most of the 30 firms in our sample were founded after 1994 during the period of the startup boom. A few of the largest companies were previously existing firms that had reinvented themselves with the advent of powerful PCs and the Internet in the second half of the 1990s. From firms that developed software for mainframes and micros, they now became virtual startups focused on the PC market and/or the Internet. Regardless of their origin, these 30 startups were all part of the 'new economy'.

Production on a virtual assembly line?

Software firms are paradoxical. While they produce 'commodities' in the Marxian sense: 'an external object, a thing which through its qualities satisfies human needs of whatever kind' (Marx 1978 [1867]: 125), their commodity is intangible. Software is useless in a 'hardcopy' form of symbols on paper; only in its disembodied digital form can it satisfy human needs. Moreover, while the software labor process requires 'instruments' used by workers to produce the product, no raw materials are needed except the ideas in the programmers' mind. Although ideas may be given the semi-tangible form of words or diagrams on paper, they are not the raw material Marx had in mind.

The labor process of software development differs from that of manufacturing in yet another important way; software workers are knowledge workers rather than manual workers. In this respect, software 'producers' resemble skilled service sector workers – teachers, lawyers, or accountants who work with their mind rather than with their hands. Unlike them, however, software workers produce commodities rather than services. Software firms, therefore, would appear to share characteristics of both industrial and service firms. As a consequence does the production of software resemble the production of tangible goods or the delivery of services or does it represent a new mode of production?

In the following sections we first describe our findings on the labor process in our 30 software startups. We then focus on the question of the similarity or dissimilarity in the labor process of startups compared with the labor process in manufacturing. An underlying issue that is discussed, sometimes directly at other times obliquely, concerns structuration in software firms versus the agency of software workers.[7] This issue has been a preoccupation of neo-Marxist scholars such as Braverman (1998 [1974]), Edwards (1979), and Burawoy (1979), usually discussed as the question of control versus the autonomy of workers in traditional manufacturing. Others, such as Kraft (1977, 1979, 1999), Greenbaum (1979, 1998),

Orlikowski (1988), and Friedman (1989) have focused on these issues in the software programming labor process. Thus our analysis proceeds on two levels, the first being descriptive, with the second unfolding as an analysis of a number of neo-Marxian concepts in the new context of software 'manufacturing'.[8]

The basic model

Despite the images of dot.coms as extremely informal – almost *laissez faire* – the workplaces we studied all had some kind of production process in place. Although we found differences in the details, respondents' comments suggested that the following four basic stages were common practice within the segment of the software development community we studied. These four stages are: Requirements, Design, Development, and Testing. Several respondents referred to these four stages as the standard life-cycle of software development. One of these respondents, a programmer at a large applications firm noted:

> Basically you follow your four standard development steps of a requirements gathering, called discovery and planning, a design phase, a construction/development phase. And then you do, you know, quality assurance and roll out, which we call deployment [which encompasses testing].

Drawing from our interviews across the 30 firms we briefly describe below the four basic stages. Following this, we turn to more elaborate versions of this process found in many companies.

Requirements

Software development generally begins with a discussion of and negotiation over its desired functionalities or capabilities. With custom-built applications, requirements typically entail the company and client coming to a consensus on the end product and its functionalities. This is often an arduous process of negotiation, where software developers attempt to translate clients' 'wish lists' into realistic and feasible projects. Clients were frequently described as not knowing exactly what they wanted or prone to changing their mind as the following statement by a CEO of an applications firm illustrates.

> So you go out and build the system, and you come back with it. And people are like, 'What's this?' And it's like, 'Well, it's the system to collect [the information you wanted]'. 'Well, we don't want to type [that information] in ourselves'. 'Well, you didn't say that'. 'Well, you didn't ask that'.

Once a new product has been successfully launched, requirements in product firms are typically market driven. The desires of existing and prospective customers, competitors' products, and the creativity of technicians may all contribute to the list of features for the next versions. While applications firms shape their work to their specific clients' needs and desires, product firms have the onerous task of anticipating such needs and desires on a broader scale, planning not only the next version of the product but also the future of the company and its niche in the software industry. As a developer in a large product firm remarked, 'Our products need to be customer-driven, not, "I have a great idea. I think it will help sell millions."'

Similar to applications work, however, the requirements document generated by sales or marketing departments in product firms may represent a laundry list of features and functionalities that could take programmers years to develop because of the excessive quantity of 'wants' and/or because of the difficulty of the desired functionalities. As a result, requirements in most firms take the form of a 'round table' discussion where all sides negotiate not only on what is to be built, but also the feasibility of the construction and the priority to be given to the various functionalities of the commodity, 'try[ing] to just nail down what the features are that they need'.

Having reached agreement on these issues, in applications work this process normally ends with the two parties signing an official document specifying what is to be built, as well as the cost of the project and its delivery deadlines. For clients, this ensures that their desires will be fulfilled within the allotted budget of time and money. However, it was repeatedly stressed that this also protects software firms from clients who are known to change their mind and/or ask for additional features and functions. The founders of a small Washington, DC applications firm learned this the hard way, as the client wrangled over the wording in the requirements contract:

> [S]he basically said, 'You've got to re-start.' And we said, 'No, we don't.' And she said, 'The contract here says "You will give us a site that makes us happy". This doesn't make me happy. Therefore, you have to do it again.' And legally, she was right.

In product firms, the requirements document provides a project roadmap, reflecting the vision for a new product or ideas for the next version of an existing product. Thus, the requirements document makes visible the firm's developmental goals for a particular product. In the final analysis, while the requirements document is often an indispensable first step in the development process, it is only the first step and an imperfect one at best.

Design

The design stage moves the proposed project one step closer to reality. While the requirements state what is to be built, the design outlines an overall picture of how such functionalities will be built, and delineates the relationships between various segments or functionalities in the program. It is also a process of figuring out the 'best way' to bring all the parts of the program together given resource, time, and other constraints. The CEO of a large and well established firm described this stage as follows:

> Requirements have to be transmuted into something that actually works so, usually the dialogue is me saying, 'Well, these are the requirements'. And then, 'Now how can we do this?' 'Well, there's six different ways, let's pick one'. Then we argue about which one is best. And then once we've figured out which one is best; best has a vague meaning in terms of best means shortest, least work, least complex, most reliable, most likely to please the customer, so that there's these intangible factors in there. And we switch them around and we try to come up with something that is most reasonable given the constraints we've got.

In a small number of firms the requirements stage was bypassed to get straight into the design and development work as the following example described by a lead programmer in an applications firm shows.

> We have an idea of what the client wants to do. We don't spend a lot of time. We get them a prototype, let them start playing with it, and really the client drives the product here. The client drives the changes.... It's kind of like spend as little time as possible, getting them an initial [prototype]. They start working with it, and they work through us, and then we basically tweak it to the way that they want it and then we release it. That's basically how we work.

Software design in small firms was often a process in which all four or five members participated. Some of the larger firms employed design specialists, such as 'architects', who focused on the bigger picture of the overall software program and design. In some firms these specialists were joined by senior developers. Many of the firms following Rational's development methodology or a derivative of Rational, used UML modeling tools and use case scenarios to aid in the design process. The latter provide, in non-technical terms, a further level of specification of the design document.

Development

At this stage, functionalities are produced in the form of actual computer code. Whether it was a project of a million lines of code or one with a few thousand lines, all required collective efforts and these efforts of teams and/or individuals writing code for select functionalities had to mesh together. Large projects may have several development teams, with each coding for a set of functionalities. For smaller projects – or in smaller firms – the various functionalities might be divided among a number of individuals working alone. Typically software was produced in a group setting with programmers frequently consulting each other.

The development stage usually starts with further design work below the level of the design document. If the design document is a large scale map, then what we call second-level designs are like detailed street-level maps with instructions about distances and turns. Individual programmers and teams do these designs as they are more technical in nature and programmers must sort out the 'nuts-and-bolts' of their portion of the program in the form of logical statements and data flows. Asked about how she translated requirements and design into development, a web page programmer replied, '[T]hat's usually just kind of from what has been defined in writing. We've flushed it out in emails and meetings, but it's pretty much just in the brain in terms of the details'. Being 'in the brain' is a hallmark of software production that distinguished it from industrial production.

Some firms required programmers to draw up several of these second-level designs, from which a manager or project lead could choose. A manager in a prominent product firm explained:

> [Y]ou want them to come up with more than one way of doing something. You don't want them just to say, 'This is the only way that it can be done'. Think about other ways that it can be done, have a healthy conversation, and figure it out. And maybe there'll be a fourth way after talking about those three. . . . [W]e use the term a lot, 'think out of the box', which means don't get stuck inside the box only thinking there's one way to do something. Be creative.

Often, we were told, more time was spent designing the functionality than actual coding. Thus, at this level at least, conception and execution were partially united. We were struck by the fact that, unlike in manufacturing, the production of code was extremely variable. Rather than following a single design resulting in multiple physical products such as a thousand tables that were all exactly alike, programming a single function could be accomplished in a large variety of ways. Five different programmers might typically code the same functionality in different ways and yet all be successful. It is one of the features that characterizes programming as knowledge work in contrast to the physical work of manufacturing. Yet, in both cases workers are engaged in the production of commodities with exchange value.[9]

The union of what we call second-level design with coding at the development stage is strategic: with hundreds, and even thousands, of functionalities it would be difficult for lead programmers to perform this function then hand the designs over to programmers. The pressure to produce code in the shortest time possible makes this approach a rational choice. At the same time the involvement of programmers in second-level designs is also a strategic decision to increase their commitment and personal involvement in software production. Several managers and senior programmers stressed the importance of rank-and-file programmer involvement. An architect at an imaging (product) firm reflected on this point noting:

> We keep talking about this idea of people getting almost alienated. I try and combat that with involving people early on in the process, getting them to design the code that they're going to end up writing. I think that gets people more involved, and they're more closely associated with it and then get passionate about it.

Source code writing commences once the design for a segment of code is approved. Whether this writing is done individually or in teams, code is subsequently merged and combined in a process called a build, which was typically aided by Microsoft software called SourceSafe.[10] Builds are done on a specific schedule, such as weekly, in order to routinely update the development process; or more frequently to meet the demands of clients – who want to see demos – or the prerogatives of managers who want to chart progress. A build determines whether the coding of many developers actually works when meshed. Version control and source code control software facilitate this incremental process helping to keep track of iterations and revised segments of code as well as providing a safeguard against new code that fails to perform as expected. In most firms these sorts of tools were used, suggesting they provided a useful programming function, specifically in the incremental or iterative aspects of software development.

Developing code for a software commodity is not the same as putting the various parts of a chair together – parts that are standardized and tested before mass production. The various segments written at the development stage are living bits of unique code in the process of creation. Since the second-level designs represent one of many approaches that could be taken, the resulting code bears the signature or style of a particular developer. Another developer might have executed the design differently, producing a segment of code that, while largely identical in functionality, looks different, reflecting programmers' different coding styles and preferences. In the end, these various segments of coding must be joined together and function as though written by a single individual. Both builds and testing are necessary to reach this goal. The development stage is therefore a dynamic, living, and ongoing process of creative tension which produces a product that can enable cell phone users to communicate across the city or across the globe, or manage accounts in Fortune 500 companies.

Code writing is also typically accompanied by comments, which are symbols or short remarks set apart within the code. They help users (and other programmers) by providing a short description of certain commands or functions and are extremely useful, as one programmer in an established product firm explained.

> I comment a lot.... [G]enerally I will outline what my code is going to do in comments, before I write the code. And it helps me structure my thoughts and the flow of what I'm doing ... it actually saves me time, I would say. Because if I already have plugged-in comments about what certain pieces of code have to do, what certain methods will have to do, then I can stop that work at any time, come back to it a day or two later, save my comments, and be able to figure out, 'Well, here's my comment on what this section, that I haven't coded yet is supposed to do.' So I can go back and more easily restart and start writing that code out.

Commenting can safeguard the project if individuals leave; a point made by one manager in a large product firm that tried to improve their commenting process.

> Commenting is important ... we would basically juggle people around and say, 'Okay, you worked on this piece last time. This time you're going to work on this, and we're going to have somebody else responsible for what you did'. So there is a certain level of, 'This isn't your thing. And you're not the only one who's going to know how it works'. We used to get that a lot from customers. They're like, 'How does this work?' 'Go ask Joe'. 'Joe's the only one who knows how this works?' 'It's his baby. He's been working on it for three years now'. You look at it, and there's no comments in there whatsoever. What happens when Joe gets hit by a bus? You're really in trouble.

Given the importance of commenting, we were surprised to discover that many firms had not formalized their process. One reason may be because commenting can impose a restraint on programmers, slowing these knowledge workers' mental processes. 'You should comment before you write', one CEO at a large product firm explained, but conceded that 'people just want to start writing, and that's just sort of how it goes'. On the other hand, small firms may simply lack the resources for effective enforcement, as a manager at an incipient product firm noted, 'The standards and things are there. They're not that strictly enforced, because it would take a senior behind everybody's back to involve it. Even the manager of the place is cranking out code all day long'.

Regardless of coding standards, the end result of this stage is a relatively functional piece of code which can go to the next stage for formal testing.

Testing

At this stage of the basic development life-cycle, the code produced is tested for errors or bugs, some of which may reflect minor 'grammatical' errors, while others are more complex and have the potential to crash a system.[11] Each developer is expected to test their code for bugs prior to a build, and the number of bugs in a segment of code is often seen as a sign of the developer's skills and/or commitment to the project. Those repeatedly turning in code with many bugs may eventually be fired. In some firms a testing and quality assurance (Q&A) team also actively tested throughout the process of code production.

Left to themselves, many programmers would eschew this mundane development activity. As one complained, '[Testing is] really monotonous. And it's like you spend all this time just to find one little mistake. "I spent a day looking for that." It's pretty frustrating, like, "Why can't I just find this thing?"' At the same time, debugging is so much a part of programming that it permeated one developer's unconscious moments. 'You can go to bed lots of times, dreaming about code. I have found at least two [bugs in my sleep] . . . I came into the office, and sure enough it was there'.

Some firms use automated debugging software which can automatically detect and 'fix' some of the more common coding errors, although this was no substitute for a watchful, non-automated, eye according to a CEO in an applications firm:

> [Debugging] . . . [d]epends on the environment you're working in, but usually it's just sort of a manual process. In ASP for example, there's different types of bugs, but let's say there is a bug that's a critical error in the code that you've written. I mean it will stop on the line of code that is bad and it will tell you this line of code is bad, and you would go fix it. And then there's logical bugs, where maybe you wrote a loop that doesn't end, or you misspelled a variable name or something like that, and [it's] always still pretty manual to figure that out.

Once coding is complete, there is final testing, accompanied by debugging to produce a reliable product. In larger firms this was typically done by a special testing or Q&A team whose sole function was to test software code. Whether or not the Q&A team engaged in continuous testing throughout the development stage, it undertook the final stage of the development process where the completed software product was tested for bugs, cleaned, and released. While error-free software was the desired result, according to numerous respondents, 'there is no such thing as a bug-free program', and so fixing as many errors as possible within time constraints becomes the practice.

Despite presenting the four stages as a linear sequence of software development, our respondents indicated that these stages often intermingle, co-occur, and/or overlap. While one programmer was writing his/her segment of the program, another may be designing or redesigning, while yet another built their code, adding revisions and new code to the existing overall program. Therefore, while requirements, design, implementation, and testing describe four distinctly different activities, we found that in practice they were not necessarily completely separated or compartmentalized. Obviously, much of this depends upon the type of software being developed, whether it is a product or application, and whether it is the first or a subsequent version. Nevertheless, the process as a whole unfolds in the sequence listed above, although the whole or parts of this basic life-cycle may be repeated several times until the final product was ready. While the majority of our firms adopted this basic methodology, there were important variations in the extent of the adoption and in the formality of that adoption.

In search of the perfect methodology

A few firms built software with fewer stages, while many more went beyond the basic methodology adopting formal and structured methodologies. History goes part of the way toward explaining this, particularly the commercialization of software in the mid-1990s with the widespread adoption of the PC and the introduction of the Internet. During the boom years, many software firms were founded by self-taught developers with little or no formal training in computer languages, management experience, or nascent software development methodologies. Trial and error became the norm. By the late 1990s, however, the more successful firms – driven by the profit imperative and possibly the influence of venture capitalists – were searching for 'best practices' and thus the adoption of elaborations of the basic model.

This search was aided by the elaborate methodologies emerging from software giants like Microsoft and IBM, as well as from the experiences of programming pioneers such as Boehm (1987) and Yourdon (1998). We encountered many firms that used the basic model as a starting point, but then adopted more structured commercialized methodologies, or invented their own. By far the most common of these more elaborate models was the Rational Unified Process (RUP), generally referred to as 'Rational'.[12]

Rational/RUP

Rational's prevalence is perhaps not surprising given Yourdon's (1997) description of it as 'the Microsoft of methodologies'. Moreover, although some firms did not utilize Rational, the formal methodologies developed and practiced were often derivatives of Rational. In its current form, Rational comes from the amalgamation of several companies, most importantly Rational Approach and Object Process which merged in 1995

(*RUP Whitepaper*, 1998). From Rational Approach came iterative development and architecturing practices and from Object Process came process structure and use cases, which are functional descriptions written in non-mechanical language that describe how specific pieces of functionality work. Basically, Rational refines the requirements and development stages and communicates the results through visual models called UMLs that allow people to 'see' more easily how complex systems are to be built. These visual models become graphical representations or maps of the interrelationships between those building the product, the product's pieces, and the artifacts[13] to be produced in the process. These maps are also useful for communicating with clients as they do not require in-depth technical knowledge to read.

Rational's goal, the company asserts, 'is to ensure the production of high-quality software that meets the needs of its end-users, within a predictable schedule and budget', which it purports to do by capturing 'many of the best practices' used in software development (*RUP Whitepaper*, 1998). In short, RUP is a pragmatic combination of practices that allow firms to predict more accurately the time and cost of developing; hence its popularity according to a senior technical manager at an applications firm:

> One of the reasons why you put a process like the Rational process in place among other reasons is for predictability, so that you can say, 'I know that in X amount of time, I'm going to be able to get this'. And it's possible that you could get the same amount [of output] in half the time, but if you don't put the process in place, it might be half the time or it might be two times the amount of time. But if you put a process in place, then you have some level of predictability.

Similar thoughts were expressed by the CEO of a large applications firm that had recently adopted the Rational process:

> My team's going to be much more effective if they know what the next step is ... predictable outcomes only come from knowing something about – you, you can't always know everything, but you try to know as much as you can about what you have to do to find out whatever the thing is in your set of problems ... and that process is where it's at.

There are many stories, real and mythical, in the IT industry about large projects that were never completed after years of work. Yourdon (1997), in his widely read book *Death March*, writes about such projects. These unfinished projects are a firm's worst nightmare. Living on the financial edge as many of them are, one such project could seriously cripple or bankrupt a firm. It is not surprising, therefore, that so many of the larger ones have turned to Rational for risk reduction. As a CEO of a large applications firm emphasized, 'Essentially the idea is to identify what the risks are on the project and to schedule the project on a risk basis, do the riskiest things first'. Reducing risks and avoiding months of coding that end in a blind alley are real everyday concerns. Rational schedules the most difficult part of the project on the front end and this helps firms successfully manage the development time frame. This practice was repeatedly mentioned by respondents in firms that used elaborate methodologies. One CEO in a large applications company spoke of the consequences of not doing this.

> [E]very project [that] has been a failure no matter how – is if people have ... put the hardest things to the end, and I've seen it over and over and over again, in spite of, in some cases, being responsible for it myself, and not doing well ... Because if you really follow RUP, you end [up] dealing with hard problems early, and the easy problems later.

Executives at other companies expressed similar points of view, emphasizing the interrelationship between time, risk, and the importance of having a process. One senior manager of a product firm explained their own strategy, which seemed like a version of Murphy's Law:

> We use what we call a 'risk mitigation strategy' or a 'net risks process'. So it's basically saying, 'What can go wrong, will go wrong, so take steps to make sure that those things don't go wrong'. And we constantly are evaluating, 'What could possibly be the next thing that's going to go wrong?' And make sure that those things get done, and they don't go wrong.

All this elaborate planning occurs up-front before any coding starts. Unlike manufacturing, where the uniformity of products is machine controlled, software production is dependent upon the skills of individuals and the synchronization of their disparate efforts. Coordinating programmers' labour becomes an inherent problem and the success, particularly of large projects, is more probable if preceded by careful planning, as one CEO at a large application firm emphasized.

> The more that you can define and lay out in terms of a structure, the less you leave to chance. And the way that you ensure repeatable success is you don't leave things to chance. And so, that enables you to take Joe over here, and he's going to be successful on the project. And Sally over here, and she's going to be successful on the project. And it's not just that Joe's a smart guy or Sally's a smart woman, it's that they're following something that says, 'Here's how you write a statement of work. Here's how you do a risk assessment. Here's how you write a status report. Here's how you write a contract'. So that the

> easy things aren't dropped. And there's still a lot of human intelligence that has to go into the process. Execution is – even when you have a process – execution is always a problem. But at least if you have a defined process in place and defined tools; people know where to start.

A major external reason for adopting an elaborate methodology was the credibility it added to a firm's development capacities in its clients' eyes. 'We needed to sell our process to our clients', one CEO of a product firm said when explaining their process, 'so they had some kind of faith in us as an organization'. Another CEO in a large application firm said:

> Clients like to see it's [i.e., their process] well-formatted. It's a big part of our selling process, to start with. And [clients will] see on every statement of work the [name of process] logo at the bottom. Whenever you get your status report, the [name of process] logo's on the bottom. So they realize this is all part of a process, not just a bunch of ad hoc stuff thrown together.

However, the diversity of the sector and its state of flux meant one size did not fit all, and not all companies adopted Rational. Reasons for not adopting elaborate processes varied, although time and cost were most frequently mentioned with programmer resistance sometimes given as a third obstacle. Newer firms were under pressure to build their first product before funds were depleted, or to generate sufficient clients to establish a viable enterprise. As one developer in a newly formed product company commented, 'At a startup, you really can't afford to [use Rational]. We're trying to produce as much functionality in as little time as possible, so that you can actually make money'. Training programmers in the use of tools can take months, time which could be spent building a product. Other firms that used an elaborate process like Rational, abandoned it at 'crunch time' near the end of projects, testimony to the time problem in these startups.

Cost was equally important as a purchase price for Rational of \$US100,000 to \$US150,000 was mentioned by one respondent whose firm had made the investment, with annual license fees of \$US10,000 to \$US15,000. In one application firm the CTO suggested that a 'group of 30, 40, 50 or more developers' was the threshold for profitably and efficiently using Rational.

Firms picked and chose only certain aspects of formal processes they saw as beneficial to their interests. The CEO of a large applications company favorable toward Rational and its benefits nevertheless said the following of their initial use of Rational.

> We probably only deployed 25 to 30 per cent of the elements of Rational, not the full tool set, at the time that we did [this project]. Now,

> subsequently after that, because of the success we had with it, that's when we added a full-time Rational person. Until then, the Client Principle had really been responsible for doing whatever was possible with Rational, and now we're really going more, more fully towards a Rational resource.

A primary example of the pick-and-choose approach to available tools was the nearly universal rejection and/or non-use of code generators. A tool which automatically generates code should be a capitalist's dream tool, but these tools did not live up to their potential, as a manager of a product firm was quick to point out.

> In theory, it's supposed to take my UML [diagram], pass it along to the system architect who then converts that to the system-based UML. And then in theory [it] then generates code. Well, somewhere between the advertising and the theory it kind of breaks down. The code it generates is nothing we actually want to use. It's much faster to actually write the code.

Thus, there was a range present in the extent of the adoption and use of these more elaborate methodologies, dependent upon firm size and resources, methodology costs, and production pressures at particular times.

The software labor process as a virtual assembly line?

Our question is how closely does the software labor process resemble that of manufacturing? Does it represent a new mode of production? Because software development is in actuality a process of producing goods with exchange value we measure the labor process against the assembly line production paradigm. The transition from craft production to large-scale manufacturing culminated in the late nineteenth and early twentieth century with the introduction of technology-mediated labor, buttressed by Taylor's Scientific Management (Taylor 1967 [1911]; Braverman 1998 [1974]). These developments, together with Ford's moving assembly line, marked the zenith of capitalist industrial development (Rubin 1996; Harvey 1990; Aglietta 2000 [1979]).

At its extreme, the assembly line required the worker to perform such standardized and simplified actions that only a sliver of his/her human capacities was exercised. Spatially fixed, workers had to respond to the pace established by the assembly line. As Aglietta (2000 [1979]: 118) noted of the assembly line's introduction, 'the individual worker thus lost all control over his work rhythm'. The narrow range of skills required could be taught in a matter of days while they were denied any role in decision making about either the nature of the product or its process of development. Taylor's goal of separating conception from execution was thereby realized. Charlie Chaplin's 1936 film, *Modern Times*, provided a vivid parody of the consequences of this historical process: stress, alienation, exploitation, and the dehumanization of workers.

Recent refinements include just-in-time and small batch production, as well as various worker involvement schemes (Colclough and Tolbert 1992; Cohen and Zysman 1988; Harvey 1990). However these and other forms of technocratic reorganization of production (Burris 1999) have not fundamentally altered the basic paradigm of large-scale capitalist manufacturing. For although not all production employs an assembly line, there is generally an attempt to streamline and/or automate the labor process in order to eliminate human error as much as possible, increase the pace of production, and increase or maintain control over workers. The principal characteristics of this mode of capitalist production can be summarized along two dimensions: the labor process and the experience of workers. For the rest of this chapter we concentrate primarily on the former rather than the latter as our findings and arguments on the experience of workers are consistent with those of Barrett (this volume).

Structure vs. standardization

The first thing that confronted us in our study of software startups was the degree of rationalization and structuration present in the industry, even in small-scale startups. This was evidenced by the practice of following stages of development described above. We believe this reflects in part the prevalence of models and methodologies being taught in computer science courses, and found in a variety of commercial books on the subject (Friedman 1989; McConnell 1996). Some fragmentation is also present in the labor process in the form of a division of the total product into functionalities or discrete sections of coding. However this is not the same as Kraft's (1977) 'modular programming', but is instead an acknowledgement that tasks exceed any one programmer's capabilities. Some ordering of the labor process is a minimal condition for production efficiency and worker coordination. This structuration was already present in some types of craft work (Braverman 1974: 147–8), and a division of labor appeared in the earliest stage of manufacturing, long before the assembly line's appearance (Marx 1978 [1867]). Structuration by itself is therefore not the hallmark of assembly line production. Rather it is the dimension of standardization, added by the assembly line that distinguishes large-scale manufacturing production from other modes.

However, while some form of structuration was part of the software labor process, we found that standardization was not. The introduction by formalized firms of more elaborate methodologies such as Rational might be interpreted as standardization attempts since there tends to be more discrete steps within each stage. Moreover elaborate methodologies lead to the creation of more documents and more detailed documents. In one firm, 11 documents accompanied their software development efforts, while in another, where elements of Rational were combined, three distinct and specific forms of requirements documents were used. In yet another firm a 63-page requirements document had been created.

Friedman (1989) has argued that documentation increases control over the labor process by allowing managers and non-technical persons to better 'see' the development process, or at least its paper trail. If Friedman is correct, then the firms using formal methodologies are better positioned to control workers than those using the basic model. Although Friedman's thesis has merit, it cannot be pushed too far – at least not in our software startups. For example, while some programmers disliked commenting on their code because of the time it took away from actual coding, they also acknowledged the benefits of coding standards and complained about its absence. One developer in a small application firm using only the basic model commented, when asked if her company had any standards in place: 'No, I think there should be, but, we don't'.

Notwithstanding the number and length of documents used, cumulatively they did not add up to a technologically mediated labor process. Most documents exist at the pre-coding stages of requirements and design and were consulted in the course of development: a bit like a motorist checking a map rather than driving on autopilot. Rational is used for the 'predictability' it engenders by sequencing work and from using 'best practices' that obviate blind alleys or missed deadlines. But elaborate methodologies like Rational do not standardize the labor process to resemble an assembly line as their use is mediated by continuous decision making by managers, and some programmers, rather than by technology. Although elaborate methodologies introduce a greater measure of management control over the labor process, they fall far short of the control present in manufacturing and are unable at present to standardize the development process in startups.

Other tools introduced into the labor process, including those for version control, builds, debugging, and code generation, that are usually called 'case tools',[14] fill the function of *specialized tools* that enhance the work of programmers rather than deskilling them.[15] They are more like craft work tools or those used in the transition from craft to manufacturing to the technology of the assembly line.

Best practices: coding standards

In the absence of a technology to standardize the development process, coding standards and commenting serve as best practices aiding code production and creating transparency. Although considered important, their implementation and enforcement varied widely. One programmer in a small, new product firm said, 'There's no code Nazi that goes around and is like, "Oh, you didn't put a parenthesis in the second line. You fail."' Instead he said enforcement was 'just kind of like an honor thing'.

Firms with formalized methodologies were more likely to adopt and enforce coding standards. In some firms there was active review of standards prior to development beginning, while other firms used peer review of code to enforce standards. One programmer in a large applications firm noted:

> We have developed a derivative of Microsoft and other [industry] standards for us. So, like, our active server pages, we expect you to name a variable a certain way. And that you close your objects, and you use error handling in a certain way. So, yeah, we try to follow those standards. And those standards are published, and they were reviewed before we began development.

On the other hand, the CEO of one of our largest applications firms said that they 'haven't gotten that far yet', when asked if they had coding standards in place. This was despite their recent adoption of Rational and the hiring of a full-time RUP person, and his recognition that implementing standards is 'what the Rational Unified Process does'.

Standards can mitigate situations like the one where a developer on a summer internship creatively named every object, a practice that wreaked havoc on the other developers' ability to understand his programs. In the end, a programmer explained, '... we probably spent a day going through and kind of giving him a little bit of like religion on, "You need to give it meaningful names". And things like that'. This example shows how the software development labor process functions through constant human interventions and decisions, rather than through the use of technology.

Pacing work

As will be discussed by Voss-Dahm (later this volume) the pacing of the development work is problematic. Although builds act as markers on the journey to the finish line their timing varies across firms, depending on the firm and project's size, the number of programmers involved, and the project lead's style. Peer reviews of code, debugging, scheduled and unscheduled meetings punctuate the development process in a qualitative and often unstandardized fashion. Work is evaluated and problems discussed and resolved, all through a process of human decision-making rather than the predetermined programming of a machine.

In the absence of technologically mediated pacing, the rate and intensity of work depends on factors external to the production process itself. In applications firms, the pace of work is often influenced by client requirements. Budget and the delivery date – established and specified during the requirements stage – dictate the pulse of work. There is an incentive to finish within the deadline as firms face absorbing the cost of labor and materials if they fail to do so. Moreover, missing deadlines or release dates can lead to a negative firm image and the loss of potential clients.

In the deadline-driven world of software startups, as firms moved into 'crunch time' near the end of a project, programmers were typically required to log in the long hours for which the startup segment of the industry is infamous. This was because the actual amount of time needed to complete a project was at best an educated guess. When asked how managers decided on the time needed for an individual task or set of functionalities, a manager of a large product firm replied:

> We call 'em WAGs. Wild ass guesses. [A]t a high level, define the capability that we're looking for, okay? And then . . . we break it down even further into requirements. And then based on the requirements, we come up with tasks, and based on how long we think each one of those tasks takes, we can come up with a schedule. Now, early on . . . you don't have all that information. It takes time to develop. You know, keep breaking it down further and further. So, in the beginning, you really have a rough estimate on what you kind of think it's going to take, and a lot of that's just based on task experience, which is based on your – how . . . complicated or difficult you think that's going to be. It's based on how many different pieces of the product you're gonna have to touch in order to make that happen.

Product firms also extended the working day and intensify labor efforts in order to meet deadlines, although they did not have the same pressure from clients. Other external forces – industry competitors, technological innovation, and available capital – pressed firms to develop quickly in order to avoid obsolescence or loss of market to competitors.[16] During these frantic crunch times formal methodologies can be abandoned to expedite development. Such times made it clear that the pacing of work was driven more by deadlines than by methodologies, no matter how elaborately conceived.

Shortcuts

With limited technology to aid development, firms adopt shortcuts, such as code libraries and Commercial-Off-The-Shelf software (COTS). Source code can be preserved in code libraries then retrieved and plugged into new developments. But the utility of this appeared to depend on the active memory of existing programmers, as few firms had organized these 'libraries'. COTS are shrink-wrap commercial products that firms can purchase and insert into a development. While some firms did this it was difficult to ascertain the degree to which COTS impacted the time needed for a project.

From the standpoint of the labor process itself, it becomes difficult to equate the practices and processes in software startups with an industrial assembly line. At every stage human rather than machine intervention predominates. Whether a firm uses an elaborate methodology or not, coding is a mental rather than a manual process which depends on developers' active creativity and decision making. Primary and second-level designs give direction, but as one CEO in a large application firm said, 'coding is always a problem' because there is no one way to code a functionality and because each project requires fresh planning and decisions. This reality stands in sharp contrast to the 'one-best-way' of Taylorized work settings.

The experiences of workers in software startups

The introduction of the assembly line in large-scale manufacturing made it possible for the labor process to be fragmented and the pace of work controlled. Furthermore, Taylor argued that by separating conception and execution and placing all decisions in management's hands in a system of technologically mediated production, maximum production could be achieved. In software development, the absence of a technologically mediated process limits the degree of control that managers can exercise over workers. In office settings, Edwards (1979) has shown that managers introduce titles, promotions, and financial incentives to motivate workers, a process he labeled 'bureaucratic control'. Since the software industry combines aspects of both the production of goods and an office environment, what is the experience of workers in these firms? How are managers controlling workers, how much agency do workers maintain, and what are the factors that influence both?

Conception, execution, and control

In spite of the vaunted informality of software startups, the lines of authority remained clear. In larger firms we found that management, staff, marketing, and production all had clearly demarcated sections of existing office space. Smaller firms often lacked space for such divisions. Yet even in these firms CEOs and/or founders were clearly in charge. In one such firm the founder and CEO, himself a programmer, worked alongside other programmers in a single room and, when necessary, moved about and looked over shoulders as the following exchange illustrates.

> *Interviewer:* So you are in the same space?
> *CEO:* Yeah, back in the engineering room. One big room.
> *Interviewer:* So you can just turn around and [watch them]?
> *CEO:* Absolutely, all day long, all day long. Yeah, all day long. I like to be in there . . . no matter who it is. I like to be in there.

We also found that programmers had limited say about their particular assignments on projects which, we were repeatedly told, were made according to their skill sets. Second-level designs, likewise, had to be approved by programming leads or a management representative before work began. Managerial authority and structure, therefore, were the taken-for-granted aspects of life in a firm. There remains, nevertheless, the question of how management achieved its goals in software startups and the programmers' degree of participation in decision making.

Worker agency

As knowledge workers, programmers are valued for their creativity, decision-making and active problem-solving skills, skills that are inherently resistant to standardization. Levy and Murmane (1996) have demonstrated that automating work proves problematic when all the possible decisions and actions cannot be pre-programmed and/or ascertained. To fully standardize computer programming, therefore, would require the seemingly omniscient knowledge of both the emergent problems and the associated solutions. The ability to creatively innovate and solve problems appears still to be the sole province of active developers.

While programmers often work on separate functionalities and components of software, they do so with considerable discretion and creative freedom, which Barrett (this volume; 2001) terms technical autonomy. This contrasts sharply with Kraft's (1977) image of structured programming. Peer reviews and code standards, while suggesting some element of direct control to coordinate labor, reflect a craft rather than technical-oriented image of software development. Commenting and guidelines as other forms of direct control allow other programmers to read and interpret code, while peer reviews establish a level of quality assurance. Contrary to Kraft and Dubnoff's 1986 study, in 2001 we found little evidence of worker fragmentation in software production beyond the distribution of work by functionalities: software work was inclusive and collaborative, evidencing itself in the form of team development.

The creative nature of software development enabled our programmers to maintain a relatively high degree of agency. This was manifest in their second-level design work and frequently in the participation of at least senior developers in the requirement and design stages. Their insights were needed at these stages to ensure the firm's commitment to feasible projects. Without the technical department's input, a firm could conceivably commit to an impossible task spelling financial disaster to a small startup, as the following remarks by a lead developer at a small product firm indicated.

> Requirements is an iterative process. That is, first [marketing personnel] create the requirement document, which is a pipe dream. And

> they hand it over to us. And after that, we have a series of meetings, saying that, 'Hey, guys, you are drunk. This is not the case. You cannot do this, blah, blah, blah'. Or, 'You can do this, but it's very expensive'. And so on. And when we go through this series of meetings, finally a document emerges. So you have here the combination of technical expertise and the marketing expertise.

Conception, therefore, remains a necessary part of software development and the technical knowledge involved remains the province of developers, forcing managers to rely a great deal upon their opinions and judgments. Even in those firms where the CEO or founder was a programmer, they still relied upon the programmers' knowledge in the development process. Rarely if ever could it be said that a manager, who is him or herself a developer, had the depth of knowledge required in all aspects of programming needed for a project. Even in small firms, the specialist was valued over the generalist, as a co-founder/CTO of a small product firm emphasized:

> [S]ee, in software you can never get, or rather you can, but you don't want in a product company a jack-of-all-trades person. For example, 'How do I do encryption?'.... You can't expect everyone to know encryption thoroughly. Similarly, there could be one person who's really good at databases. You know, they're very good at writing queries to a database, extracting data, making sure performance is quick in the database. You can't expect everyone to do that because software is such a vast universe.

This need for specialized labor meant firms went to great lengths to meet the sometimes idiosyncratic wishes of some developers. Several allowed a few developers to work in Colorado, California, and even France, despite managers' preference for their being on site to mentor their juniors. Other programmers worked at home on certain days. The sophisticated technology used for programming can transcend the limitations of time and space.[17] Programmers could 'build' in their updated code through secure networks and version control systems, adding pieces at 10 am, 3 pm, or 2 am, whether in the office, at home in the same city, or across the country. In assembly line work, all workers on a particular project not only have to be physically present, but must be present simultaneously, or at least as needed. Auto workers cannot attach wheels to a car from their study at home, but programmers can add code to a project from almost anywhere.

Keeping workers happy

Even in loose labor markets, capable programmers are very hard to find and so managerial control is tempered by the need to 'keep them happy'.

Opportunities for skill enhancement are primary. 'Technology people', we were told by a manager in a small product firm, 'want new skills. They want to make sure that they're marketable all the time'. Other methods included assigning work by skill sets but not locking developers into a single position. In one case programmers, anticipating work to be done on a coming project, could request a particular position. Large firms often made a point of informing incoming workers about the potential for advancement. One such manager in a large product firm detailed how she elicited the goals of prospective employees and explained how these could be achieved:

> We talk about their future goals, and where they see themselves in five years, and make sure that we provide some opportunities for them to get there. Because you clearly want to keep people happy and motivated. Moving in that direction. So if somebody comes to me and says, 'You know, I really want to be a software designer, architect'. I say, 'Okay, well then . . . we need to work on these couple things'.

Other opportunities included in-house study groups, libraries, and outside training. Rather than managers attempting to deskill workers through available technology, they generally made every effort in the opposite direction: not only keeping them happy, but making them more valuable to the firm.

In later chapters of this book the experience of software developers is further explored. On balance it appears that the experience of workers in software startups has little in common with that of workers on assembly lines and automated factories. Available technology supports and enhances programmers' creative work, rather than deskilling them. Given the inherent problem-solving nature of software production, programmers are involved in decision making at various levels. Structuration through elaborate methodologies imposes some onerous tasks on developers, but also helps to ensure their long work hours are successful. Few developers, it seems, would prefer to return to the halcyon days of the lone cowboy programmer.

Conclusion and discussion

Philipson (this volume) outlines the history of the software industry. From the 1960s to 1980s programmers mainly worked in user companies on software for mainframes or micros. Kraft (1977) and Greenbaum's (1979) research in the late 1970s gave us our first detailed and structured view of this new area of production, and were for some time our sole source of information on software development. It was a period when developers were located in distinct, technology departments of large corporations, often supervised by non-technical managers. Kraft (1977) and Greenbaum

(1979) concluded that software production was experiencing the same fate as manufacturing – control, deskilling, and fragmentation. In the late 1980s, writing from the perspective of someone who had worked in software production, Orlikowski (1988: 108) disputed their claim, arguing that '[to] date, there is no convincing evidence that programmers have had their jobs substantially narrowed, that their skills have become redundant, or that their tasks are now performed by less-skilled, lower-paid workers'.

It should also be noted that even in 1977 Kraft tempered his overall conclusion, writing:

> Programming is still primarily a mind-skill and there are few hard and fast rules of behavior which managers can compare against an efficiency expert's model in order to check performance ... [thus programmers] persist in being something of an anomaly in the modern workplace: they are employees, but they are in a position to control much of how they will go about doing their programs – the final product – and to some extent even the form the final product will take. (Kraft 1977: 62)

In the 1990s the PC was gradually transformed from a sophisticated typewriter with a memory into a machine capable of performing a variety of tasks. More powerful PCs were introduced into the market and software vendors increased the range of products available for its use. This culminated mid-decade with the availability of very powerful, multitasking PCs and Netscape as a user-friendly portal to the Internet (Lewis 1999). The *New New Thing* Lewis wrote about was not just the story of Netscape, but the story of an IT industry 'revolution', in particular the accelerated process of software innovation. Kraft (1977) and Greenbaum's (1979) questions about the software labor process increased in relevance as commercial software production boomed with thousands of new firms and millions of programmers. What exactly was the labor process in this segment of the IT industry; and what was the experience of these workers? It is on these questions that our own research has largely focused.

Recent studies of software production suggest limited use of the technical control endemic to manufacturing, and a concurrent movement to more subtle forms of cultural control (Kunda 1992) or work-day extension (Perlow 1998, 2001). Writing on changes in the labor process generally, Kraft (1999) has suggested that new trends in the labour process represent 'flexible appropriation and flexible control'.

> If Taylorism is about separating mental and manual work and then constructing a rigid hierarchy to administer and police that separation, *process-centered management systems* are about systematically appropriating ideas and knowledge from all workers through a system

> Harvey (1990) calls 'flexible accumulation.' It may just as accurately be called flexible appropriation and flexible control.
>
> (Kraft 1999: 25 [italics added])

Yet this acknowledgment of changes in management control strategies in manufacturing and other corporate settings (Hochschild 1997) leaves unanswered our fundamental questions about the labor process in the specific area of *software production*. How can the labor process in software startups be characterized?

Shadow production

We believe that the software development labor process in startups represents a new mode of capitalist production, accompanied by new forms of control and relations of production. We call this *shadow production*, because the commodity is only 'visible', as it were, through the shadows of artifacts like comments, builds, and documentation.

The method by which surplus value is extracted and accumulated holds little resemblance to nineteenth or twentieth century manufacturing. This is probably due to the unique nature of the commodity, software, which is the result of knowledge work. Unlike manufacturing material goods, no raw materials are used; and conception and execution cannot be totally separated since the production process itself depends upon the creativity of workers. In this respect, software production resembles both craft production and service provision by knowledge workers. Even if management (or their representatives) totally assumed design functions, programmers are still required to exercise judgment, make choices, and in general exercise creativity in the very act of producing. And they accomplish this with skills that are difficult to acquire and master. Proficient programmers are part engineer, part artist and this sets them apart from both production workers in manufacturing and other knowledge workers in service industries. The labor process can be controlled to some degree through commenting, documenting, builds, and other practices, but in a sense, this control is over shadows of their work: important shadows, but shadows nevertheless. Essentially the code writing process is a conversation that takes place in the programmer's mind: it is 'pretty much just in the brain'. This essential dependency on the programmer's creativity is in part the cause of their relatively high salaries, as well as the occasion of one manager's complaint about the 'whiny rock star' developer.

> *Interviewer:* You mentioned the person – the developer who's working at home. Was he a full-time employee?
>
> *Manager:* Mhmm.
>
> *Interviewer:* He always worked at home?
>
> *Manager:* Always. And that, that particular person is interesting

> because, uh ... he's like a ... a movie star. Or a rock star, for example. So picky, you know, whiny, crazy. But you know, you're not – you don't want to do anything to piss him off because he does such good work. (Laughter)

The social relations of production we described are not absolutely new in kind,[18] but we believe they are certainly new in degree. We see a production process of intangible commodities dependent on the unique skills of a type of knowledge worker who is relatively new on the scene. It is this peculiar nature of knowledge production that characterizes what we think is a new mode of production.

Other characteristics of software production and the current competitive environment in which it operates militate against manufacturing type controls of software developers. As was noted above (and in the chapter by Voss-Dahm), the process resists exact temporal management. Elaborate methodologies introduce an element of predictability, but the actual time needed is measured in WAGs and 'crunch' periods are still endemic. Methodologies add a structural dimension by following the four stages, but variation in each stage's execution across firms defies standardization. Add to this the absence of a machine-mediated production process and we find control is more normative than technical.

Whether this new mode of production is a temporary 'deviation' of the tendencies witnessed in manufacturing is unknown. We believe that, like in manufacturing, there will remain a segment of 'periphery firms' (Edwards 1979) that differ fundamentally from the Microsofts and IBMs, and SAPs. Whether our paradigm of *shadow production* is applicable to the IBMs and SAPs we do not know. We do know that many of our respondents who previously worked in firms like these preferred working in their startups. As such we do believe that the labor process in the startup segment of small and medium-sized software firms will remain a process of shadow production into the distant future.

Notes

1 The term 'new economy' escapes precise definition, having been used in many different ways in popular media and academic journals. Here it refers to the IT industry's explosive development, particularly the expansion of computer and Internet usage throughout the economy. This usage was, of course, made possible by the software sector's development.

2 A 'service' is defined as an activity that while benefiting or useful to someone is wholly consumed in the transmission of the activity.

3 Four interviews were discarded. One was with a programmer working for a major government contractor, while another was conducted with a programmer who was unemployed when first contacted, but joined a healthcare firm by the time he was interviewed. An interview in a third firm was discarded after we found it was engaged in consulting for firms interested in adopting a process,

rather than in production itself; and a fourth was a one-person firm that was just getting started.

4 The owner of this firm was a successful software developer who hired part-time programmers as needed, but did not have any full-time workers.

5 Even the US Census does not determine 'size' of software production firms based on employee numbers. Rather, they use a proxy measure of size based on the revenue the firm generates. See: *The 1997 US Economic Census.*

6 Attempts to correlate software type with management structure failed to yield fruitful insights about these companies. Among application firms, four had formal and 11 non-formal structures; while seven formal and nine non-formal management structures prevailed among product firms.

7 By 'structuration' we mean a certain amount of ordering of the work process, whether achieved through stages or some other manner. Structuration also connotes some type of control of workers.

8 It should be emphasized that our study is a study of software startups that primarily arose during the second half of the 1990s. Although we encountered a number of managers and programmers who had worked for large firms like Apple, Hewlett-Packard, and Microsoft, these firms are not part of our sample; consequently our findings do not apply to that segment of the software industry. A word should also be said about terminology. We found a great deal of inconsistency in the terminology used among these firms. Both the name used for the commodity, software, varied as well as the name of the producers themselves. In general, we encountered three different names for the latter: 'programmers', 'developers', and 'software engineers'. Some firms used one of the three exclusively, while others used them interchangeably. Given this lack of standardization, we have adopted the latter practice.

9 'Exchange value' is a Marxian concept referring to objects (commodities) that have been made and that others would like to buy. This is in contrast to objects created for an individual's own use.

10 Although Microsoft's SourceSafe was the most commonly cited source code control software used by respondents, some firms used similar products such as Concurrent Versions System (CVS), Perforce, Integrated Development Enterprise (IDE), and Team Track.

11 There is considerable debate surrounding when the term 'bug' emerged to describe computer error or mechanical failures. Some trace it as far back as the nineteenth century, citing Thomas Edison, who is claimed to have used the term 'bug' in reference to problems with electrical circuitry. However, most associate the term with a 1947 incident when engineers found a moth stuck to a computer circuit board of a Mark II computer. For further explanation and details on the history of computer bugs, view the Smithsonian's 'Computer History Collection' at the American Museum of Natural History, available online at http://www.americanhistory.si.edu/csr/comphist/index.htm.

12 IBM recently acquired Rational Unified Process (RUP) which was formerly owned by Rational Inc.

13 'Artifact' generally refers to any document produced in the development process such as design documents and use cases.

14 Case tools include any software used to facilitate work at any of the stages of development. Within the software industry there has been a call for creating what has been called a 'case environment' (SEI no date).

15 There is a running debate about the degree of deskilling resulting from the assembly line and automation. While it is certainly true that many workers, particularly those who lost their crafts, were deskilled, others seem to have also learned new skills. Thus in automated factories, some workers have been 'upskilled' as they learned the skills necessary to operate the computers used to

maintain the automated lines (Burris 1999). Burris (1999: 41) also notes this enhancement function of technology in 'expert and professional work' in contrast to 'non-expert work'. He was however writing about skilled service rather than production work.

16 In a number of cases we were told by CEOs that work on a product had to be completed by a certain date or funds would run out. The problem of time is especially critical for small firms with limited capital and working to complete their first product. In order to obtain subsequent rounds of funding, they must demonstrate significant progress toward completion.

17 Of course today it is commonplace for various components of a commodity to be manufactured at different locations across the globe at different times, and to be assembled later at yet another location. We also interviewed a firm that had created software allowing real-time design cooperation between engineers in the US and Europe.

18 For instance, graphic designers and advertisers produce 'products', although they are tangible and tend to be ephemeral. Furthermore, the result of their labor is generally sold as a service to a client; for example, promotional ads on TV or radio.

References

Aglietta, M. (2000 [1979]) *A Theory of Capitalist Regulation: The U.S. Experience*, trans David Fernbach, London: NLB.

Babbie, E. (1999) *The Basics of Social Research*, 8th edn, Belmont, CA: Wadsworth.

Barrett. R. (2001) 'Labouring under an illusion? The labour process of software development in the Australian information industry', *New Technology Work and Employment*, 16, 1: 18–34.

Boehm, B. (1987) 'Improving Software Productivity', *Computer*, 20, 9: 43–7.

Braverman, H. (1974; 2nd edn 1998) *Labor and Monopoly Capital: The Degradation of Work in the Twentieth Century*, New York: Monthly Review Press.

Burawoy, M. (1979) *Manufacturing Consent*, Chicago: University of Chicago Press.

Burris, B. H. (1999) 'Braverman, Taylorism, and Technocracy', in M. Wardell, T. Steiger and P. Meiksins (eds) *Rethinking the Labor Process*, New York: State University of New York Press.

Cohen, S. S. and Zysman, J. (1988) *Manufacturing Matters: The Myth of the Post-Industrial Economy*, New York: Basic Books.

Colclough, G. and Tolbert, C. M. (1992) *Work in the Fast Lane: Flexibility, Divisions of Labor, and Inequality in High-Tech Industries*, New York: State University of New York Press.

Edwards, R. (1979) *Contested Terrain: The Transformation of the Workplace in the Twentieth Century*, New York: Basic Books.

Friedman, A. L. (1989) *Computer Systems Development: History Organization and Implementation*, New York: John Wiley & Sons.

Greenbaum, J. (1979) *In the Name of Efficiency: Management Theory and Shopfloor Practice in Data-Processing Work*, Philadelphia: Temple University Press.

Greenbaum, J. (1998) 'On twenty-five years with Braverman's "Labour and Monopoly Capital" (Or, How did control and coordination of labor get into software so quickly')', *Monthly Review*, 50: 8. Available HTTP: <http://www.monthlyreview.org/feb2001.htm> (Accessed 4 May 2004).

Harvey, D. (1990) *The Condition of Postmodernity*, Cambridge, MA: Blackwell Publishers.

Hochschild, A. (1997) *Time Bind: When Work Becomes Home and Home Becomes Work*, New York: Metropolitan Books.

Kraft, P. (1977) *Programmers and Managers: The Routinization of Computer Programming in the United States*, New York: Springer-Verlag.

Kraft, P. (1979) 'The industrialization of computer programming: From programming to "software production"', in A. Zimbalist (ed.) *Case Studies on the Labor Process*, New York: Monthly Review Press.

Kraft, P. (1999) 'To control and inspire: US management in the age of computer information systems and global production', in M. Wardell, T. Steiger and P. Meiksins (eds) *Rethinking the Labor Process*, New York: State University of New York Press.

Kraft, P. and Dubnoff, S. (1986) 'Job content, fragmentation, and control in computer software work', *Industrial Relations*, 25, 2: 184–96.

Kunda, G. (1992) *Engineering Culture: Control and Commitment in a High-Tech Corporation*, Philadelphia: Temple University Press.

Levy, F. and Murmane, R. (1996) 'With what skills are computers a complement?' *The American Economic Review*, 86, 2: 258–62.

Lewis, M. (1999) *The New New Thing: A Silicon Valley Story*, New York: W.W. Norton & Company.

Marx, K. (1978 [1867]) *Capital*, London: Penguin.

McConnell, S. C. (1996) *Rapid Development: Taming Wild Software Schedules*, Redmond, WA: Microsoft Press.

Mills, C. W. (1951) *White Collar*, New York: Oxford University Press.

Orlikowski, W. J. (1988) 'The data processing occupation: Professionalization or proletarianization?' *Research in the Sociology of Work*, 4: 95–124.

Perlow, L. A. (1998) 'Boundary control: The social ordering of work and family time in a high-tech corporation', *Administrative Science Quarterly*, 43, 2: 328–57.

Perlow, L. A. (2001) 'Time to coordinate: Toward an understanding of work-time standards and norms in a multicountry study of software engineers', *Work and Occupations*, 28, 1: 91–111.

Rational Unified Process Whitepaper: Best Practices for Software Development Teams (1998), Cupertino CA: Rational Software Corporation.

Rubin, B. A. (1996) *Shifts in the Social Contract*, Thousand Oaks, California: Pine Forge Press.

SEI (nd) 'What is a CASE environment?' Carnegie Mellon University, Software Engineering Institute. Available HTTP: <http://www.sei.cmu.edu/legacy/case/case_whatis.html> (Accessed 4 May 2004).

Taylor, F. W. (1967 [1911]) *The Principles of Scientific Management*, New York: Norton.

US Census Bureau (1999) *District of Columbia, 1997 Economic Census Washington, DC*, US Census Bureau.

VentureOne (2001) 'Financing'. Online. Available HTTP: <http://www.VentureOne.com/ii/Financing3Q01.xls> (Accessed June 2001).

Yourdon, E. (1997) *Death March: The Complete Software Developer's Guide to Surviving 'Mission Impossible' Projects*, Upper Saddle River, NJ: Prentice Hall.

Yourdon, E. (1998) *Rise and Resurrection of the American Programmer*, Upper Saddle River, NJ: Yourdon Press.

4 Managing the software development labour process

Direct control, time and technical autonomy

Rowena Barrett

Introduction

Software developers, those people who create software, are often viewed as typical of 'knowledge workers' (Scarbrough 1999) or 'symbolic analysts' (Reich 1991) and among those said to become the future aristocrats of the labour market (Castells 1996). Castells (1996) is one of a number of writers who argue that cooperation, teamwork, worker autonomy and responsibility are necessary to manage such informational work processes, and there are obvious echoes here of notions of responsible autonomy arising from early labour process analysis. However various writers point to problems with 'knowledge work' as a concept (see Alvesson 1993, 2000; Scarbrough 1999; Alvesson and Kärreman 2001) and there is emerging a less optimistic view about the degree of autonomy these employees may enjoy (see Hyman, Baldry and Bunzel 2001; Rubery and Grimshaw 2001; Rasmaussen and Johansen this volume). In 2002 Reich argued that stress should now be placed on creativity rather than simply analytical skills and this has been popularized by Florida's (2002) 'rise of the creative classes'.

The purpose of this chapter is to examine the development and use of the various means management uses to control the labour process of software development. Andrew Friedman (1977, 1984, 1990, 1992, 2000, 2003) argues managers have a choice of strategies, which depend on the degree of competition in labour and product markets. This choice lies between direct control and responsible autonomy 'as two directions towards which managers can move, rather than two pre-defined states between which managers can choose' (Friedman 1990: 179). However John Storey (1985a; 1985b) outlined an alternative way of conceiving management's means of control which focuses on 'layers and levels' and this was elaborated (Storey 1989) through an exchange with Friedman (1987) in *Sociology*. The purpose of this chapter is to show how Storey's ideas can be used to create a more nuanced account of Friedman's managerial strategies.

As such, in this chapter I argue that management uses a variety of means to control the software development labour process separately and simultaneously depending on the type of product being developed, the timing in the product's development lifecycle and the type or nature of the worker (see also Barrett 2004). This is illustrated through information collected in a series of interviews with management and employees in three Melbourne-based software development firms – DataHouse, Vanguard and Webboyz. However, prior to doing this, in the next section of the chapter some of the older debates in the labour process literature which led to the Friedman–Storey exchange, are revisited.

Labour process theory

The labour process under capitalism has specific characteristics, the most significant being the transformation of labour power into actual productive labour that was originally elaborated by Marx (1978 [1867]). Control is necessary for the transformation of the capacity to work into profitable production and this task falls to management as the representatives of capital at the workplace. As such exploitation and domination are characteristics of the system of capitalism rather than aspects within the control of the individual employer.

However, exploitation in this sense is a technical term rather than some form of psychological abuse. The indeterminacy of labour, the necessity to change potential into actual labour, is driven by the labour theory of value. In essence this holds that exploitation of labour is necessary and indeed appears as an externally imposed condition on individual capitals and capitalists, as labour, through the extraction of surplus value, is the source of all profit. However, as we will see in this chapter there are a number of conditions that complicate this equation. The first is that people do not arrive at workplaces as either *tabula rasa* or as instantly antagonistic members of an oppositional class. Without having to go into the deepest recesses of the post-structuralist debate, questions of identity and the attitudes and expectations that people bring to work, formed outside work, are important in determining what happens at work. Indeed, as we will see in this chapter, in the case of software developers this is crucial. The second point is that although the labour theory of value tends to focus attention on managerial control and the extraction of surplus value, other moments in the circuit of capital, for example the necessity of selling profitably what is produced, can interact in a complex and contradictory way with questions of the management of labour.

Hyman (1987) made clear that not all changes in the labour process are driven simply by management's need for control when he wrote 'Capital confronts labour not merely within the workplace but in commodity markets, in political life, in the sphere of culture and ideology. Men and women become wage-labour before they enter the gates of factory or office' (Hyman 1987: 49). Achieving control within the organization, then, depends as much on factors outside as inside the organization, however, it is beyond the scope of this chapter to detail the mechanisms by which men and women are constituted as wage labour prior to becoming wage labourers. This is despite ample evidence that, for example, firms seek to shape both public attitudes and state policies in ways which can sustain a social and economic order which is conducive to their interests (Hyman 1987). Obvious examples are reflected in efforts to ensure that industrial relations legislation enshrines the dominance of capital over labour and that the educational system produces a labour force with appropriate skills and attitudes towards work. Indeed the recognition of different groups as 'professionals' is yet another means of exercising control.

The degree to which employees accept the legitimacy of management can vary enormously both between different workers and workplaces and over time. This only serves to emphasize the tightrope management walk between autonomy and control. Thus as Littler and Salaman (1984) argue,

> All forms of control contain, in different degree, two dimensions of control: the specification of levels of performance (and this may vary from highly specified to highly autonomous) and some effort to develop some level of consent, or acceptance of the legitimacy of the employment relationship. Both dimensions are necessary for any work relationship. The utility of the specification of levels of performance depends absolutely on some minimal levels of compliance.
>
> (Littler and Salaman 1984: 57)

This leaves management with two potential contradictory needs: simultaneously to successfully make a profit from the efforts of their workforce and to create the conditions under which this is possible involving as little coercion as possible. Successive labour process theorists have developed this idea to create typologies of control strategies. Braverman (1998 [1974]), building upon Marx, focused on the emergence of new methods of management control in the context of monopoly capitalism. He argued that the logic of capitalist production was deskilling through the subdivision of tasks and separation conception and execution through the application of new technology. Deskilling provided for increased capitalist control over production because opposed centres of knowledge were destroyed and the labour process fragmented. Although there are many critiques of this work (see Thompson and McHugh (1995) for an overview of critiques following the first edition and more recently Spencer (2000) and Tinker (2002) following the release of the 25th anniversary edition), it served to focus attention on relations at the workplace and particularly managerial strategies.

For example, Friedman points to the use of two broad strategies of control, the choice of which would be dependent upon variations in the stability of labour and product markets, mediated by the interplay of worker resistance and managerial pressure. The first strategy, direct control, is similar to that originally expounded by Braverman (1998

[1974]). The second strategy of control, responsible autonomy, attempted 'to harness the adaptability of labour power by giving workers leeway and encouraging them to adapt to changing situations in a manner beneficial to the firm' (Friedman 1977: 78).

The progressive model of simple, technical and bureaucratic management strategies developed by Edwards (1979) was based upon his study of American companies. He suggested that each strategy tended to be predominant at different stages of development of American business and as such 'reflected worker resistance and changing socio-economic conditions' (Thompson and McHugh 1995: 116). The first strategy, simple control by employers or supervisors and relatively unsophisticated piecework systems, was said to prevail during the competitive capitalism of the late nineteenth and early twentieth centuries. The second, technical control, involved 'designing machinery and planning the flow of work to maximize the problem of transforming labour power into labour as well as maximize the purely physical-based possibilities for achieving efficiencies' (Edwards 1979: 112). However, although technical control kept worker discretion to a minimum, it also set up the potential for worker opposition and militancy by ensuring a common experience of work. In contrast, the third strategy of bureaucratic control, 'established the impersonal force of company rules or company policy as the basis for control' (Edwards 1979: 152). Worker loyalty, gained through positive rewards and a graded hierarchy, was returned as a result of personnel policies for secure, long-term employment opportunities.

Burawoy (1979) also pointed to different strategies of management control distinguished by the stage of capitalism's development. He argued that employers were able to obscure their fundamental imperative and as a result diffuse worker resistance by developing internal labour markets and internal states within organizations. Despotic and hegemonic were the initial modes of control identified by Burawoy (1979) – the former being similar to Edward's (1979) simple control or Friedman's (1977) direct control, the latter having parallels with bureaucratic control referring to more sophisticated means of winning consent. Subsequently Burawoy (1985) elaborated on these types of management strategies adding a third – hegemonic despotism, which basically refers to the new balance of economic forces arising from the greater mobility of capital (Bray and Littler 1988).

It is argued that Braverman (1998 [1974]), Edwards (1979), and Burawoy (1979, 1985) largely assume a linearity in their management strategies of control, with each strategy being linked to successive phases of capitalism. However, Friedman focused more on the nature of choice and argued that managers had a choice of strategies which, in turn, depended upon the degree of competition in labour and product markets. The problem nevertheless was the identification of a simple dichotomy of strategies, although in 1984 Friedman did (and continues to do so – see

Friedman 1990, 1992, 2000, 2003) argue that direct control and responsible autonomy should be conceived as 'two directions towards which managers can move . . . therefore a wide range of possible positions between extreme forms of responsible autonomy and direct control as well as different paths leading in each direction' (Friedman 1977: 3). Writers investigating questions of managerial style, strategy and employment relations have implicitly or explicitly drawn upon Friedman's later, more sophisticated analysis.

In something of a break from this way of thinking Storey (1985a, 1985b) referred to levels and circuits of control rather than a 'single track search for definitive and comprehensive modes of work control' (Storey 1985b: 194). In other words, he suggested that there may be a collection of devices, structures and practices forming control configurations that may be understood as the temporary outcomes of dialectical processes of attempting to, or actually achieving, control. Levels refer to points in the organizational hierarchy at which control might be exercised, so there are, 'interpenetrating "layers" of control which reinforce and substitute for each other as one or more becomes weak, decayed or fully untenable' (Storey, 1985b: 198).

Rather than being able to determine that, for example, simple or technological control of the type proposed by Edwards (1979) prevailed in a given organization, Storey (1985b) finds instead clusters of 'devices, structures and practices'. Fluidity exists between these controls and they are shaped by managerial and worker action. As Storey wrote,

> [M]anagers are not faced with a strategic choice between types of control – partly because the choice is not entirely in their hands and partly because rarely is it a question of using only the rules *or* targets, socialisation *or* technology, participation *or* hierarchy, selection screening *or* communication, individual *or* collective labour control. A whole multiplicity of these – with some certainly given emphasis for a time – seem to be more typically arrayed.
>
> (Storey 1985b: 199 [italics in the original])

Storey therefore emphasizes that a variety of means of control could be used simultaneously and that a dialectical framework is needed to understand the dynamics of control. Control structures and strategies will contain their own contradictions. Managers will respond to a number of forces in formulating controls including the workforce, colleagues, competitors and their operating environments. Control becomes a continuously changing, complex process, the outcome of which is uncertain: 'to achieve and sustain managerial control, then, the levels and circuits of control are subject to continual experimentation (Storey 1985b: 199).

Nevertheless, Storey still refers to the manager's ability to 'achieve and sustain' control, albeit within a process of continual experimentation. Hyman (1987), on the other hand, emphasizes the inevitable failure of management strategy rather than the terms upon which control can be sustained. The key to Hyman's (1987) approach is an emphasis on contradiction: 'Strategic choice exists, not because of the absence or weakness of structural determinations, but because these determinations are themselves contradictory ... it is necessary to stress the impossibility of "harmonising" the different functions of capital' (Hyman 1987: 30).

Consequently there is 'no "one best way" of managing these contradictions, only different routes to partial failure. It is on that basis that managerial strategy can best be conceptualized as the programmatic choice among alternatives none of which can prove satisfactory' (Hyman 1987: 30). Together the approaches taken by Storey and Hyman emphasize a dialectical rather than deterministic process of reciprocal interaction between structure and agency enabling us to develop a way of understanding the diversity of practice in the operation of management control systems. In doing this Friedman's responsible autonomy and direct control strategies can be used as a starting point. However, in more recent times there has been a rift in labour process theory reflecting a wider tension in the social sciences between structure or agency in the achievement of control. This has constrained the development of a universally accepted and coherent theory. It is not necessary to trace the paths this debate has taken in recent years (see Jaros (2000–2001), Spencer (2000) or Tinker (2002) for a review) but it is important to acknowledge the questions of identity, self and the internalization of modes of control that numerous writers have examined. These issues were insufficiently developed at the time Friedman was writing, although Hyman did point to their importance. In the following section I look at what this might mean in terms of the means of control of the software development labour process.

Means of control over the labour process of software development

Software development is not a uniform activity, the task can be organized in different ways. Developments such as software language evolution where it more closely resembles natural language and structured programming techniques (see Philipson this volume) could be seen as being consistent with the linear trend of deskilling proposed by labour process theorists such as Braverman (1998 [1974]), Edwards (1979) and Burawoy (1979; 1985). However linearity cannot be taken as an absolute because of the interactions between the dynamics of technological innovation and changing patterns of use (Morgan and Sayer 1988; Beirne, Ramsay and Panteli 1998; Quintas 1994). From a technical perspective the 2003 special issue of *IEEE Software* edited by Robert Glass shows the diversity in software development practice and clearly shows 'no one best way' of developing software. Andrews *et al.* (this volume) amply demonstrate the issue of autonomy when they argue

> Even if management (or their representatives) totally assumed design functions, programmers are still required to exercise judgment, make choices, and in general exercise creativity in the very act of producing. And they accomplish this with skills that are difficult to acquire and master. Proficient programmers are part engineer, part artist and this sets them apart from both production workers in manufacturing and other knowledge workers in service industries.
>
> (Andrews *et al.* this volume, page 71)

Autonomy in terms of the responsible autonomy type was conceptualized quite broadly as 'responsibility, status, light supervision' (Friedman 1984: 179). However, such responsible autonomy could apply at a number of levels: where individuals have the freedom to set goals and the means to pursue them it could be exercised at the level of the organization (strategic) or the task (technical). Such an argument utilizes the study of industrial R&D labs by Bailyn (1985) where she distinguishes between 'strategic autonomy' (the freedom to set one's own research agenda) and 'operational autonomy' (the freedom, once a problem has been set, to attack it by means determined by oneself, within given resource constraints). Scarbrough's (1999: 11) view that 'knowledge workers derive their power and values from occupationally-based knowledge communities' suggests that technical autonomy is a more apt description than responsible autonomy, where employees with high levels of skill or technical knowledge possess some degree of control and discretion over the software development process. Rather than lying at some point in the continuum between Friedman's responsible autonomy and direct control, technical autonomy and strategic autonomy can instead be seen as variants of responsible autonomy, operating at different points in Storey's (1985b) 'levels of control'. Technical autonomy can be evidenced by management allowing software developers autonomy to develop the 'best' program using their skills and expertise. In order to facilitate this management recruits and selects employees with the technical competence as well as the necessary 'drive' and passion for the task.

Another variant of responsible autonomy can be identified in Voss-Dahm's (2001; this volume) study of IT workers in German companies, where she shows that autonomous time management (time autonomy) is a management strategy for deepening employee commitment through practices that 'feed' and 'serve' the demand for autonomy and by creating a work environment in which individual development is fostered and encouraged. Flexible work hours and a work environment reflecting the high tech creative nature of the work being performed are part of the process of engendering commitment from developers. Time autonomy may be seen to be operating in another layer as with technical autonomy.

It is therefore possible to argue that autonomy, where employees have the freedom to set goals and the means to pursue them, can therefore be exercised at the level of the organization (strategic autonomy), over the task (technical autonomy) and at the individual level (time autonomy). Braverman (1998 [1974]) and Scarbrough's (1999) argument that management can afford to use particular strategies of control that give autonomy to those employees who occupy a privileged position in the product lifecycle suggests that these strategies can be used at different times in the production process or simultaneously: for example, the strategies of time and technical autonomy can be used together as employees are disciplined by their own sense of self (see O'Doherty and Willmott 2001a, 2001b).

At the same time, however, management can also use Friedman's strategy of direct control. This can be done for example by setting of deadlines for project completion. The necessity of completing development work within a set deadline can act as a form of direct control, but employees are still able to manage their time autonomously within the context of that deadline (to work as long or whenever is necessary) and use their technical autonomy to create the 'best product' within that timeframe. Indeed, software development project specifications also act as a form of direct control and this is exerted by the market more so than management although it is enforced by management. Software developers must work within the parameters of the project specification and they do so with technical autonomy to decide the 'best' method to achieve the desired outcome.

Implications

Three implications are drawn from Friedman's (1984: 181) contention that a firm's position on the continuum will change as 'competitive conditions in product and labour markets and worker reactions' force managers to change their strategy. First, different means of control can be used for the development of different types of software products. Software products can be broadly divided into two types. Primary, packaged software is developed by a software firm for sale to market (Brady 1992; Carmel and Sawyer 1998). Such products include operating systems (for example DOS), word-processing packages, development tools, and accounting suites. Essentially these are 'new' products that are the result of innovation, research and development or creative juices of an individual or team of developers. Primary products are then used as the basis for the second type of software products, which are either bespoke applications or modified standardized packages (Sharpe 1998). Secondary software products are those used by organizations for their information systems (IS) applications. Utility billing systems, HRM applications and airline reservation systems are all types of IS typically developed either by the organization's own IT department or by a consulting/service firm who build custom software on a contract basis for specific clients (Brady 1992; Carmel and Sawyer 1998). By and large the types of software products being developed in firms reported in this book are secondary products.

The second implication is that different means of control can be used at different stages of development of software product development. For example the daily (or weekly or monthly) build is a form of direct control exercised during the development phase of a project. A build is a regular assembly and test run of all the software produced in the project and is an iterative process of building more functions into a growing base of software. This works both as a production target and a focus for commercial development and can be likened to a total quality approach where the aim is to discover defects along the way rather than at the end: testing is incorporated into development. Cusumano and Selby (1996) call this 'synch and stabilize' which they describe as, 'continually synchronis[ing] what people are doing as individuals and as members of different teams, and periodically stabiliz[ing] the product in increments' (Cusumano and Selby 1996: 49).

Similarly client needs or 'wish lists' for secondary software product functionality or user expectations with primary products are a means of direct control at the requirements phase as they become the parameters within which the software product is developed. However, at the design phase developers enjoy technical autonomy as they must determine how best to operationalize the requirements. Once again though, at the development phase, the requirement to use structured programming techniques, software standards, code inspections, code libraries or CASE tools is a means by which direct control can be exercised over the development of both primary and secondary software products.

The third implication is that managers can use different means of control for different types of workers engaged in the software development process. For example, the issue of whether or not software developers are professionals, in the traditional sense, has importance for the way in which management treats these workers. The mobility of software workers and their lack of organizational commitment (see Baldry *et al.* this volume; Marks and Lockyer this volume) means that direct control is counterproductive: employees will only leave for other organizations where they can use their technical skill and expertise. However, maintaining divisions between software development and software testing processes enables the former group to enjoy technical autonomy and the latter direct control.

These implications are explored in three case studies of software development firms in Australia and have also been reported in a more detailed case study of two of these firms elsewhere (Barrett 1999, 2001, 2004).

Illustrating the analysis: DataHouse, Vanguard and Webboyz

To explore the means of control in the software development labour process I conducted 31 'semi-structured' interviews (Lee 1999; Fontana and Frey 2000) with managers and employees in three Melbourne-based software firms: DataHouse, Vanguard and Webboyz. These interviews were conducted in 1998 when the technology sector was beginning to emerge in Australia and firms within it were becoming a focus for media attention as part of the development of the so-called 'new economy'.

DataHouse was established in 1981 by two partners and specialized in 'connectivity' solutions and the provision of secure communications systems for client organizations. These security and connectivity solutions encompassed policy development through to high-level needs assessment, product selection and implementation, training, ongoing management and support and could include products which enabled secure remote access, authentication and authorization solutions, protection from external (and internal) network attacks and access to information systems across disparate platforms. The firm was described as having a 'fairly relaxed' management style. At DataHouse small teams worked on different software projects for clients and the requirements, design, development and testing phases were applied to creating their software products, albeit sometimes loosely. Through email updates employees were kept aware of new projects and encouraged to nominate themselves for upcoming projects. With 80 staff the firm had more formalized HR procedures in place such as a six-monthly performance reviews and annual pay reviews. Training was available if it related to the project the individual was working on, but actually doing the training depended on financial resources and time constraints. Flexible working time arrangements were in place and while there were standard forms of leave (long service, annual, sick leave) available, other forms were available at management's discretion. A dress code applied to all staff – business attire was seen as necessary to maintain DataHouse's professional image.

Vanguard Software Pty Ltd was established in early 1993 to exploit a niche opportunity in the retail banking industry. The nature of work and employment at Vanguard has been reported elsewhere in more detail (Barrett 1999, 2001). Essentially Vanguard was a small firm with a very flat management structure and few formal management practices in place. Employees were relatively young and inexperienced and the development work was undertaken in very small project teams. Vanguard specialized in addressing technology-related problems with business-based software and hardware. Vanguard's Retail Banking System was made specifically for institutions faced with the need to modernize their systems by either the replacement of obsolete banking system hardware or the development of new transactions and applications.

Webboyz, a small, publicly listed Australian company developing Internet tools and e-commerce software and solutions, was created at the CEO's kitchen table in June 1994. The product that launched Webboyz was a web-authoring tool marketed under the brand name 'CoolCat'. In another paper (Barrett 2004) the nature of work and employment at Webboyz is examined in more detail. Mainly young, male software developers were employed and although there was an employee share plan in place, most management practices were in development or on paper and left there.

Table 4.1 lists the similarities and differences between the three firms as well as the interviews conducted in each firm. Interviews sought to understand working in the firm from the interviewee's perspective (Lee, Mitchell and Sablynski 1999) and 'to understand how and why he or she comes to have this particular perspective' (King 1994: 14). Interviewees were therefore chosen 'not necessarily [for] representativeness . . . [but for] . . . the opportunity to learn' (Stake 2000: 447). Where interviewees held specific knowledge and/or role (i.e. Finance Manager, General Manager (GM) or Project Manager), then more specific, in-depth questions were asked about that area. In order to triangulate data and to improve 'measurement' through the use of diverse indicators (Neuman 2000), company documents and other information in the public domain (largely company websites and media reports) were also used.

Table 4.1 Similarities and differences between DataHouse, Vanguard and Webboyz

Criteria	*DataHouse*	*Vanguard*	*Webboyz*
Software type	Secondary, IS	Secondary, IS	Primary, packaged
Firm size	80 (65 at main site)	14	23
Legal ownership	Private, unlisted	Private, unlisted	Private, listed
Location	Main site in Melbourne outer suburb with sales offices in Sydney, Brisbane and Perth	Single office in outer suburb of Melbourne	Single office in inner city Melbourne
Year established	1981	1993	1995
Customers	Large corporates and government departments	2 (corporate) customers	600,000 registered webmasters
Management Interviews	CEO Finance Manager, HR Manager[a]	Managing Director General Manager	CEO Managing Director, General Manager, Finance Manager
Employee Interviews	2 × Project Managers,[a] 3 × Software developers	2 × Project Managers,[b] 2 × Admin,[a] 6 × Software developers, 2 × Software testers	Project Manager[b] 6 × Software developers

Notes
a Female.
b Also software developers.

Software products and production processes

Although the majority of employees in all three firms developed software, the type of software differed, as did the production processes. Data-House's 'connectivity' solutions and secure communications systems and Vanguard's retail banking system were secondary software products, while Webboyz' CoolCat web-authoring tool was a primary software product. The software development process at DataHouse and Vanguard could be said to follow a 'waterfall' model.[1] The waterfall model describes different stages in the software development process, which follow the fixed process of requirements analysis, systems specifications, design of the system architecture, implementation (programming), testing (or 'debugging'), and maintenance to correct and improve the systems functionality (Brady 1992). Carmel and Sawyer (1998) argue that such a view is consistent with IS development where there is a greater concern for process and the roles of developers in implementing appropriate methods and techniques. Certainly Andrews *et al.* (this volume) suggests this is the case, although they and others acknowledge that this is not always, or even very often, a linear development process. As one of the developers at DataHouse explains

> In practice [software development] doesn't happen that way. There's an ongoing feedback between users and developers, even while you're writing a program they may be ringing up saying 'do it slightly different'. Now that's not how they want to manage things here. They want to say 'O.K. you've signed off on this document, we're going to develop to this document so that we don't get scope creep, we don't get changes and we don't get our budget blown out', but in the name of customer relations you end up changing it for them anyway. It isn't as simple as saying the user will tell us what they want, we'll build it for them and then they'll say 'Yes, you built it right', because in the time from A to B what the user wants has changed.
>
> (DataHouse Employee 1)

At Vanguard it could take 12 months to develop a project's specifications as they first had to document their client's current banking system and then confirm the client's preference for host software and hardware and requirements for functionality. In this type of secondary software development process creativity occurred when proposing solutions to determine the project's specifications. Once determined the specifications drove the project and set very clear parameters within which all coding took place: 'When you've got very tight specifications you know what you have to do. That's when it gets down to the boring side of the job' (Vanguard Employee 2). As one of the testers at Vanguard made clear, this placed responsibility for quality and reliability on the testers.

> I'm the last person in the line; if I miss it I'm the one that bears it. The programmers make it, they do what they think is right. Some people believe that it's the tester's responsibility to test it and make sure it is right, which is my job. But when they [the programmers] fix it, they might think, 'well it might not work, let's see if [employee's name] finds it'. If I don't find it I get in trouble and I don't agree with that totally.
>
> (Vanguard Employee 5)

Unlike Vanguard and DataHouse, the Internet inspired the creation, continual development and sales and distribution of the majority of the Webboyz' products. Webboyz' core product – CoolCat – started out as a primary software product and its development process was creative, and consistent with the 'agilist' (Austin and Devin 2003) or 'pragmatist' (Quintas 1994) software development paradigm. Essentially the concern is that formalists – those who follow a waterfall model – are not open to change and therefore 'by the time you finish a system, the problem it solves has changed' (Austin and Devin 2003: 93). Agilists question time spent analysing requirements when they are going to change (Austin and Devin 2003). This is consistent with the development of packaged software, which is more likely to be motivated by the technology push and therefore puts firms under pressure to innovate and beat competitors in delivering products to market (Carmel and Sawyer 1998; Dubè 1998).

At Webboyz, although users expected to see certain features and functionality in the CoolCat program, developers 'got on with the job' and engaged in an iterative process of feedback and testing with a core user group who were sent beta versions of the software and returned suggestions for improvements and modifications to increase functionality. One of the developers described working in the CoolCat team as follows.

> It's almost like I know what I'm supposed to do and I know what [project manager name] wants me to do and usually it's only when something comes up that we get to formally discuss it. It's such a small working team, that we just discuss it from day to day what's going on and we're all aware of it, so we just sort of do it.
>
> (Webboyz Employee 3)

Webboyz showed a different way of thinking about software once the CoolCat product was out in the market. Then there was limited scope for blue sky developing – some new features and extras could be developed separate to user requirements – but by and large the development process fell back into the formalist tradition where instead of carefully analysed requirements document setting the parameters, it was the features of the software product itself and the user base who demanded certain aspects exist in their software. Whether agilist or formalist thinking underpinned the software development process, the same tools could be used.

Means of controlling the labour process

In the production of software products management used different means of control, albeit at different stages. For example, Webboyz employees were given technical autonomy (in a team) to create the product they thought would work, but management's commitment to incorporating user's suggestions became the point at which direct control over the software development process occurred. However, at the same time, employees were able to choose how to incorporate suggestions and as such enjoyed technical autonomy. At DataHouse and Vanguard, employees had technical autonomy when a project's specifications were being developed, but when finalized those specifications acted as a form of direct control over the development process. The effect of this can be seen in the following quote from a developer at DataHouse.

> The support work that we were doing for [client name] for a long time, it just kept coming in drips and drabs and you'd do one thing and they'd ask for a slightly different thing and you'd do that and then they'd ask for something slightly different and that was just no fun whatsoever. It was highly repetitive and didn't require a lot of thinking and it was old hack by then as well, it was very old hack. The most fun thing to do in terms of work here I still find is developing new things. I'm actually doing something new at the moment so it's good.
>
> (DataHouse Employee 5)

Vanguard and DataHouse employees were able to manage their time autonomously when creating the project's specifications and at all three locations employees worked when they wanted as long as they got the job done within the deadline. As one DataHouse employee explained: 'they expect people to do their work on time or whatever and they don't keep on your back and say where is this or have you done that so they give you a lot of responsibility' (DataHouse Employee 1). However deadlines were the means by which managers could exercise direct control.

The layers of control can be seen in how employees said they worked towards meeting deadlines at each of the firms, and the comment from this DataHouse employee captured how they felt: 'Well if there are deadlines to be met I'll stay here for as long as it takes' (DataHouse Employee 5). In all three firms management expected overtime when deadlines loomed. The Webboyz CEO made this clear when he explained, 'staff are left to do their own thing and gently steered from time to time. Around deadline time, this changes. We get the whip out and start cracking it, and the company becomes a different place'. However, the use of a more formalized development process meant pressure was placed on the testers.

> You'll find that at certain periods, like when we've got a release of our software that people in the testing department ... end up doing fifty, sixty hour weeks during those times. Basically a deadline comes along and you'll find yourself working quite long hours. We don't get paid for that.
>
> (Vanguard Employee 4)

In general employees saw working long hours as being acceptable if there was some form of recognition, for example, flexible hours at other times. 'If you feel like you work too much you feel justified in saying I'm going to take a day off or something' (Webboyz Employee 2). Even at DataHouse, where a formal system of hours existed, employees felt the same way as this quote indicates.

> I don't think people really see the hours, they see you get here at 9, 9:30 or whatever and they think you're being slack but I don't think they really see what goes on. Especially where I am. I'm hidden away, people just walk past me on the way out and lock me in.
>
> (DataHouse Employee 5)

Performance appraisals were an important avenue for recognizing hours as individuals could 'bargain' over the pay and conditions in their individual contract. As one of the Vanguard employees explained: 'I try to keep in mind everyday I come into work that I'm going to have a performance appraisal and if I do well at work and I show results, my performance appraisal will be good' (Vanguard Employee 7). This was an employee who said he had been told in his last two appraisals 'you're picking up a lot ... you've done some good work but still you're not performing at your full potential'.

However this quote (above) also shows how performance appraisals were a way to exercise direct managerial control. This also occurred at Webboyz where 'we've had to cut guy's salaries and lift some up and it was a good process to maybe get some feed back from the guys that they may not have said' (Webboyz Project Manager 1) and at DataHouse: 'we've had some people here who needed to be given pretty hard messages about why they were not progressing and they're welcome to stay but ...' (DataHouse Employee 3). However, a Vanguard employee made it apparent that the work, rather than its appraisal, acted as a form of control.

> They [management] set the goals and what they want you to do and give you a set of different instructions to do and it's very hard to meet those goals, they point you in the opposite direction. Yeah, I don't

know, those goals aren't very inspiring. All I want to do is make sure my job is perfect. That's all I have to ensure. The job description says make sure what we send out is correct, 100% and that's all I'm employed to do. And any other goals they set outside of that ... I don't even remember the goals. I'll probably look at them the last four months of the year and do it.

(Vanguard Employee 5)

Commitment and identity

Employees identified with the task and technology and this acted as a form of motivation. At Webboyz, for example, where the employees' work contributed to the development and growth of the Internet, one employee explained, 'I'm proud of what I'm doing and I enjoy the result when I see people using our product' (Webboyz Employee 5). This employee had written the core of the CoolCat program and was researching a new product, about which he had this to say:

My role is quite very interesting ... The company gives me all the resource that I want. If I want to buy something for example a software component that can be used in the final product they will just say 'yes' and I can spend. In fact for the last month I've been working at home. I wake up in the morning, not in the morning, the afternoon, I turn on my computer I don't even have to get changed ... I just turn on the monitor and start doing my research ... and this is very enjoyable. And I actually work. I don't just be slack and surf the web or spend the whole day doing nothing. I actually work harder when I work at home because I feel more comfortable. I don't even have to wash my face! Think about that!

(Webboyz Employee 5)

This notion of commitment was reinforced by one of the Project Managers.

This job is our life, you know. It's a very personal commitment to what we do. Especially from a developer's point of view, the product's success is directly attributable to what you put into it and it's like a baby, you know. It's like this is our baby and we've been working for three years and we'd kill ourselves to get it done. And all of our girlfriends or ex-girlfriends or ex-communicated girlfriends are all in chorus saying 'Webboyz just screws these guys' lives because they live it'.

(Webboyz Project Manager 1)

Even at DataHouse and Vanguard, where the development is not so 'cutting edge', employees still felt the same way about their work: 'the best thing, from a programmer's point of view is to an extent you're it . . . occasionally you'll say "Yeah, hey I made this work, this is my product"' (Vanguard Employee 1). Employees were excited by the challenge of the work and access to the technology: 'When you're coming up with solutions I find that a very creative process, when you are programming you can actually get quite involved in it, it's basically just a big intellectual puzzle' (Vanguard Employee 2); or, as another put it: 'When you get the chance to get into something new . . . that's challenging and it's exciting and it's something different and it's just new technology' (DataHouse Employee 3). Another reiterated this saying, 'The project I'm working on has been a different sort of thing to what I've worked on before, so it has been interesting. Something new. I'm always looking for new challenges' (DataHouse Employee 2).

Employees' use of programming languages and applications, which they by and large taught themselves and took responsibility for updating, their youth, and that for many this was their first 'real' job, all served to reinforce their self identity. Employees in all three firms were, primarily, in their 20s, although the experience requirements of Project Managers meant they tended to be a bit older. One Webboyz employee got quite emotional when he explained how he felt about his job.

> I'm in paradise. This is what I always told my parents – I am enjoying my life so much because of Webboyz because I'm enjoying the job, I'm enjoying my work. Even Saturday or Sunday, alright, I would read work related stuff. I'm not a nerd, I also go out to watch movies and that sort of thing, but I enjoy it so much that I don't really take it as a job. I take it as part of my life and I do that anyway. Like if I'm not getting paid I would still study that sort of thing. I would read it in my leisure time anyway and making it a part of my job I make money from it. So it is a paradise. Heaven. This is exactly what I'm feeling.
>
> (Webboyz Employee 5)

Employees could be given technical and time autonomy as management knew their identification with the work would act as a form of control. Employees' identity was exploited but also pandered to (up to a point) within work but created (initially at least) outside of work. As one DataHouse employee explained:

> Every IT person wants to drive it [projects], they're all builders and they won't build someone else's design they want to build their design so you have got to make sure that the projects are structured where they have an opportunity to have some control over their own destiny.
>
> (DataHouse Employee 3)

The Webboyz' CEO made this clear when he explained his 'policy' for recruiting developers.

> When we recruit people what we look for is not so much what brains they've got or how smart they are or anything like that, it's how passionate are they about this area. Is this something that means more to them than just a job? Is this really where they want their life to be and are they smart enough to cope if we step back and say 'here's a broad picture of what we want you to do go away and fill in the details yourself', will they do it?
>
> (Webboyz CEO)

Identity, work and organization

As the employees identified with and were committed to their work, rather than the organizations *per se*, then problems could arise when the work changed, became less interesting or was no longer felt to be challenging. Any reaction tended to be individualized, rather than collective and usually meant leaving the firm. This could be seen in responses to a question about why employees would leave: 'Not being able to do the job I'm doing now' (Webboyz Employee 4); '[If] my self-development wasn't that great' (Webboyz Employee 3); '[If] you're not happy with what you're doing' (Vanguard Employee 8); 'If they can't sort of offer me these [overseas travel and work] opportunities' (Vanguard Employee 2); 'If the company moves away from the development type work' (DataHouse Employee 1); and 'If there are no new challenges' (DataHouse Employee 2). It can also be seen in the reasons why employees would stay: 'There is too much variety, I mean work wise it is stimulating enough for me to stay here, there are still avenues for me to expand into' (DataHouse Employee 3).

The idea of resistance was summarized by a DataHouse employee as:

> IT is not like, say well, most other positions in that you do what you do for that company and that's not going to change in that the job will stay the same. IT is forever changing, technologies are changing, projects are changing, the work you do is changing and if you don't like it there is enough demand in the IT industry to get a job anywhere else.
>
> (DataHouse Employee 2)

For some of the younger (and more inexperienced) employees, mobility as a form of resistance was dependent on getting more experience. Employees knew potential employers wanted experience and that experience attracted higher pay. This was evident in the following quotes: 'I basically just want experience in the IT industry. . . . That's pretty much all I wanted. I wasn't looking for any big money thing or anything, I just wanted the experience and the knowledge of it' (Vanguard Employee 3); 'Since I came here, I've done so many different things. It gives you a lot of experience for different things' (Webboyz Employee 4); and 'experience and just money, that's the most important. The most important thing I think is just to gain experience to prepare myself for probably, I don't know, if I was to move, with the experience you have a better opportunity' (Vanguard Employee 1).

The buoyant conditions in the labour market meant employees could not see themselves taking any forms of collective resistance, such as joining a union. A Vanguard employee explained it in the following terms.

> If I were trying to work out how much I should be getting paid I'd probably talk around other people that I know are doing it. But given the industry, rather than getting into a huge drawn out fight about my pay, which I'd have a good chance of losing, I'd probably say 'oh stuff this' and go and find another job. That's just the way things seem to work, whether it is a good view to have or not I don't know, it just how I see it.
>
> (Vanguard Employee 8)

Employees at Webboyz and DataHouse confirmed this view. One said 'I think if you don't like a place you just find somewhere else. There is plenty of opportunity in the industry. Like, in fact I never think about being unemployed. There are always places around'. (Webboyz Employee 5). Another said,

> If I want more money I'll go elsewhere, if I'm unhappy with my job conditions I'll just go elsewhere . . . the level of job security within the industry as a whole [means] you know that you're going to pick up work somewhere else.
>
> (DataHouse Employee 1)

Union availability was also an issue. The Association of Professional Engineers, Scientists and Managers of Australia (APESMA) had been attempting to recruit employees in this industry, however their membership was limited to professional scientists or engineers (i.e. employees with recognized tertiary science or engineering qualifications). Many employees were unaware of APESMA despite some having the qualifications to join.

Premium wages were not paid at Vanguard because of the inexperienced nature of the employees and at Webboyz the Employee Share Ownership Plan (ESOP) was acknowledged by management as a cover for low wages. However, in all three locations management were aware of the form any potential resistance would take. As the HR Manager at DataHouse explained:

> And to keep our staff we have to pay them properly because they can walk out the door tomorrow and have a job the next day and that is how competitive it is at the moment and tight and good people are hard to come by, so we have to make sure that we pay them correctly and that they are satisfied with it.
>
> (DataHouse HR Manager)

Discussion

Analyses of the history of software programming show it is far from being a simple or uniform activity (see for example Kraft 1979; Quintas 1994; Beirne *et al.* 1998; Barrett 2001). There is a 'fragmentation and stratification of activities and responsibilities in software development' (Beirne *et al.* 1998: 144) and the labour process cannot easily be routinized or standardized (see Andrews *et al.* this volume). As such there are contradictory trends in strategies to control the labour process of software development. The notion of 'interpenetrating "layers" of control' (Storey 1985b: 198) is drawn upon to develop a less deterministic and restrictive approach to understanding the control of the labour process. Taken with Hyman's (1987) 'no one best way' of control, the importance of contradiction and dialectics is emphasized in understanding the complexity of the relationship between structure and agency.

Interviews with software workers at DataHouse, Vanguard and Webboyz provide support for the argument that, in terms of software development, the means of control management use over the labour process is influenced by the type of product being developed and the timing in the product's development lifecycle as well as the type of workers developing the product. In other words, there is no 'one best way' of controlling the labour process. Despite the differences between the types of software products developed at DataHouse, Vanguard and Webboyz, there was evidence of direct control, of employees enjoying technical autonomy and being able to manage their time autonomously. These means of control are used separately and simultaneously. For example, at DataHouse and Vanguard, where secondary software products were developed, employees were given autonomy when specifications were being drawn up. But those specifications then acted as a means of direct control and as such the 'waterfall' software development model acted as a form of direct control, even though it enabled employees technical autonomy at different phases of the development cycle. The situation differed at Webboyz where, in the development of a primary software product employees' skills dictated what type of product was created and therefore employees enjoyed technical autonomy. However, management's requirement of incorporating user suggestions into developing a commercially viable product acted as a form of direct control, although employees still enjoyed technical autonomy to determine solutions which enable suggestions to be incorporated. In all three firms employees could manage their time autonomously and this meant employees worked when they wanted as long as their tasks were completed (in the manner required by management). This was possible because employees' commitment to the work acted as a form of control and meant management knew employees would work long hours to get their tasks done.

The case studies emphasize the dialectical relationship between the (limited) idea of autonomy and the necessity of control. In effect managers, facing the heightened indeterminacy of creative employees' labour, walk a tightrope between autonomy and getting profitable work done by the deadline. For employees, this necessity of profitability means autonomy is limited to the use of their skills and their time. There is the potential for more standardization and routinization in software development as Andrews *et al.* (this volume) pointed out and this could increase profitability, but employees would resist as this would not be the type of work to which they are committed – it would not fit their sense of self (see O'Doherty and Willmott (2001a, 2001b) for support based on their deconstruction of Sosteric's (1996) case study of nightclub workers). The social identity of software developers revolving around intrinsically interesting and challenging work is also found in a number of other studies (for example Friedman and Cornford 1989; Beirne *et al.* 1998; Baldry *et al.* this volume; Marks and Lockyer this volume). Commitment is conditional but any response is individualized and shaped by conditions in the labour market.

The case studies in this chapter tell us that the relative importance of the elements of management's different strategies to control the labour process of software development will vary over time and that there is no 'one best way'. In so doing this chapter contributes to explaining the means management use to control the labour process of software development. What we see is that software developers are workers just like the rest of us: they are subject to management control but they also have the ability to influence how that control is constructed and applied and this is a result of who they think they are, their skills, what they are developing and the specific historical and competitive circumstances of where they work.

Note

1 The waterfall model has been the most used lifecycle model of software development over the last few decades (Georgiadou 2003).

References

Alvesson, M. (1993) 'Organisations as rhetoric: Knowledge-intensive firms and the struggle with ambiguity', *Journal of Management Studies*, 30, 6: 997–1014.

Alvesson, M. (2000) 'Social identity and the problem of loyalty in knowledge intensive companies', *Journal of Management Studies*, 37, 8: 1101–23.

Alvesson, M. and Kärreman, D. (2001) 'Odd couple: Making sense of the curious concept of knowledge management', *Journal of Management Studies*, 38, 7: 995–1018.

Austin, R. and Devin, L. (2003) 'Beyond requirements: Software making as an art', *IEEE Software*, Jan/Feb: 93–5.

Bailyn, L. (1985) 'Autonomy in the industrial R&D lab', *Human Resource Management*, 24: 129–46.

Barrett, R. (1999) 'Industrial relations in small firms: The case of the Australian information industry', *Employee Relations*, 22, 3: 311–24.

Barrett, R. (2001) 'Labouring under an illusion? The labour process of software development in the Australian information industry', *New Technology Work and Employment*, 16, 1: 18–34.

Barrett, R. (2004) 'Working at Webboyz: Life in a small Australian internet firm', *Sociology*, 38, 4: 777–94.

Beirne, M., Ramsay, H. and Panteli, A. (1998) 'Developments in computing work: control and contradiction in the software labour process', in P. Thompson and C. Warhurst (eds) *Workplaces of the Future*, Houndsmill, UK: Macmillan Business.

Brady, T. (1992) 'Software activities in the UK: Who does what?' in K. Robins (ed.) *Understanding Information Business, Technology and Geography*, London: Belhaven Press.

Braverman, H. (1998 [1974]) *Labour and Monopoly Capital (25th Anniversary Edition)*, London: Monthly Review Press.

Bray, M. and Littler, C. (1988) 'The labour process and industrial relations: Review of the literature', *Labour and Industry*, 1, 3: 551–87.

Burawoy, M. (1979) *Manufacturing Consent: Changes in the Labour Process under Capitalism*, Chicago: University of Chicago Press.

Burawoy, M. (1985) *The Politics of Production*, London: Verso.

Carmel, E. and Sawyer, S. (1998) 'Packaged software development teams: What makes them different?' *Information Technology and People*, 11, 1: 7–19.

Castells, M. (1996) *The Rise of the Network Society*, Oxford: Blackwell.

Cusumano, M. and Selby, R. (1996) *Microsoft Secrets*, London: HarperCollins.

Dubè, L. (1998) 'Teams in packaged software development: The Software Corp. experience', *Information Technology and People*, 11, 1: 36–61.

Edwards, R. (1979) *Contested Terrain*, London: Heinemann.

Florida, R. (2002) *The Rise of the Creative Class*, New York: Basic Books.

Fontana, A. and Frey, J. (2000) 'The interview: From structured questions to negotiated text', in N. Denzin and Y. Lincoln (eds) *Handbook of Qualitative Research* (2nd edn), Thousand Oaks, CA: Sage.

Friedman, A. (1977) *Industry and Labour: Class Struggle at Work and Monopoly Capitalism*, London: Macmillan.

Friedman, A. (1984) 'Management strategies: Market conditions and the labour process', in F. Stephen (ed.) *Firms Organisation and Labour*, London: Macmillan.

Friedman, A. (1987) 'The means of management control and labour process theory: A critical note on Storey', *Sociology*, 21, 2: 287–94.

Friedman, A. (1990) 'Managerial strategies, activities, techniques and technology: Towards a complex theory of the labour process', in D. Knights and H. Willmott (eds) *Labour Process Theory*, London: Macmillan.

Friedman, A. (1992) 'Understanding the employment position of computer programmers: A managerial strategies approach', in F. Borum, A. L. Friedman, M. Monsted, J. St. Pedersen and M. Risberg (eds) *Social Dynamics of the IT Field: The Case of Denmark*, Berlin: de Gruyter.

Friedman, A. (2000) 'Microregulation and post-Fordism: Critique and development of regulation theory', *New Political Economy*, 5, 1: 59–76.

Friedman, A. (2003) 'Professional autonomy compared with other types of strategies for maintaining task and social control', paper presented at the *European Sociological Association Conference*, Murcia, 24–26 September.

Friedman, A. and Cornford, D. (1989) *Computer Systems Development: History, Organisation and Implementation*, London: Wiley.

Georgiadou, E. (2003) 'Software process and product improvement: A historical perspective', *Cybernetics and Systems Analysis*, 39, 1: 125–42.

Glass, R. (ed) (2003) 'The state of the practice of software engineering', *IEEE Software*, Nov/Dec.

Hyman, J., Baldry, C. and Bunzel, D. (2001) 'Balancing work and life: NOT just a matter of time flexibility', paper presented at the *Work Employment and Society Conference*, University of Nottingham, 11–13 September.

Hyman, R. (1987) 'Strategy or structure: Capital, labour and control', *Work, Employment and Society*, 1, 1: 25–55.

Jaros, S. (2000–2001) 'Labour process theory: A commentary on the debate', *International Studies and Management and Organzation*, 30, 4: 25–39.

King, N. (1994) 'The qualitative research interview', in C. Cassell and G. Symon (eds) *Qualitative Methods in Organizational Research*, London: Sage.

Kraft, P. (1979) 'The industralisation of computer programming: From programming to "software production"', in A. Zimbalist (ed.) *Case Studies on the Labour Process*, London: Monthly Review Press.

Lee, T. (1999) *Using Qualitative Methods in Organizational Research*, Thousand Oaks, CA: Sage.

Lee, T., Mitchell, T. and Sablynski, C. (1999) 'Qualitative research in organizational and vocational psychology', *Journal of Vocational Behavior*, 55: 161–87.

Littler, C. and Salaman, G. (1984) *Class at Work*, London: Batsford.

Marx, K. (1978) [1867] *Capital*, London: Penguin.

Morgan, K. and Sayer, A. (1988) *Microcircuits of Capital: 'Sunrise' Industry and Uneven Development*, UK: Polity Press.

Neuman, W. (2000) *Social Research Methods: Qualitative and Quantitative Approaches* (4th edn), Boston: Allyn and Bacon.

O'Doherty, D. and Willmott, H. (2001a) 'The question of subjectivity and the labour process', *International Studies of Management and Organization*, 30, 4: 112–32.

O'Doherty, D. and Willmott, H. (2001b) 'Debating labour process theory: The issue of subjectivity and the relevance of poststructuralism', *Sociology*, 35, 2: 457–76.

Quintas, P. (1994) 'Programmed innovation? Trajectories of change in software development', *Information Technology and People*, 7, 1: 25–47.

Reich, R. (1991) *The Work of Nations: Preparing Ourselves for 21st Century Capitalism*, New York: Alfred A Knopf.

Reich, R. (2002) *The Future of Success*, USA: Vintage Books.

Rubery, J. and Grimshaw, D. (2001) 'ICTs and employment: The problem of job quality', *International Review of Labour*, 140, 2: 165–92.

Scarbrough, H. (1999) 'Knowledge as work: Conflicts in the management of knowledge workers', *Technology Analysis and Strategic Management*, 11, 1: 5–16.

Sharpe, R. (1998) 'Globalisation: The next tactic in the 50-year struggle of labour and capital in software development', *Proceedings of the Work Difference and Social Change Conference*, Binghamton University, USA, 8–10 May.

Sosteric, M. (1996) 'Subjectivity and the labour process: A case study in the restaurant industry', *Work, Employment and Society*, 10, 2: 297–318.

Spencer, D. (2000) 'Braverman and the contribution of labour process analysis to the critique of capitalist production – Twenty-five years on', *Work, Employment and Society*, 14, 2: 223–43.

Stake, R. (2000) 'Case studies', in N. Denzin and Y. Lincoln (eds) *Handbook of Qualitative Research* (2nd edn), Thousand Oaks, CA.: Sage.

Storey, J (1985a) 'Management control as a bridging concept', *Journal of Management Studies*, 22, 3: 269–91.

Storey, J (1985b) 'The means of management control', *Sociology*, 19, 2: 193–211.

Storey, J. (1989) 'The means of management control: A reply to Friedman', *Sociology*, 23, 1: 119–24.

Thompson, P. and McHugh, D. (1995) *Work Organisations: A Critical Introduction* (2nd edn), Houndsmill: Macmillan Business.

Tinker, T. (2002) 'Spectres of Marx and Braverman in the twilight of postmodernist labour process research', *Work, Employment and Society*, 16, 2: 251–81.

Voss-Dahm, D. (2001) 'Work intensification through introduction of an autonomous time management – Lessons from IT companies in Germany', paper presented at the *Work Employment and Society Conference*, University of Nottingham, 11–13 September.

5 Trick or treat?

Autonomy as control in knowledge work

Bente Rasmussen and Birgitte Johansen[1]

Introduction

One of the most important strategic issues for the management of knowledge workers in the new economy is how to develop and sustain an expert workforce. Managers of knowledge workers have to take into account the social conditions that promote the formation of knowledge, trust and autonomy, and the economic conditions which secure its appropriation through control over the workers' effort (Scarborough 1999). Balancing autonomy and control is accomplished in different ways depending upon the context and the economic and labour market conditions of the firms as chapters in this volume demonstrate.

In this chapter we present evidence from one segment of the 'new economy', workers in new web-based information service firms. Here new entrepreneurial organizations offer workers professional autonomy as a means to increase their work effort to meet project deadlines, even if it means unpaid overtime. We argue that in managing knowledge workers in the economic interest of the firm, autonomy and control should not be understood as opposite measures taken by management. In the cases presented in this chapter, we show how control over worker effort was achieved by offering them autonomy and honouring their position as an 'expert workforce'.

In effect, in this chapter we examine how knowledge workers work hard and for very long hours without extra pay when they are treated as professionals or expert workers and given extensive autonomy over their tasks and working time. We also show in this chapter that when knowledge workers are treated as labour power that can be easily substituted, they will withhold their effort and leave as soon as they have an opportunity.

Knowledge workers in the new economy

Public relations, media, technology consultants and software development firms are among the new 'knowledge intensive' firms, as are the so-called dot.coms. Knowledge workers in these firms are different to those in traditional professions, like accountants or lawyers, who are characterized by a strong professional affiliation and educational requirements which restrict access to the profession (Freidson 1986; Marks and Lockyer this volume).

Whereas traditional professionals are guided by codes of ethics and common professional norms, the workers in the 'new' knowledge-intensive service firms are primarily driven by business and organizational needs. They are identified by the work that they do rather than occupational norms, and they are actors in the *market* dealing with customers rather than clients (Scarborough 1999). Workers in the new knowledge-intensive service firms have skills and expertise that may or may not be taught in formal education. Information technology (IT) skills in software development and web-page design are often self-taught (Newell Robertson, Scarborough and Swan 2002: 26). Therefore as Alvesson (2001) argues, knowledge intensive firms are not necessarily defined by their expertise, but may be seen as 'systems of persuasion' relying on persuading their clients that they have the expertise to satisfy their expectations.

Although hard to define, Newell *et al.* (2002) argue that the concept of knowledge worker is useful when examining the needs of knowledge workers. Like professionals, they are hired to use their knowledge and skills to produce solutions for customers. They are motivated by their interest in their subject and the tasks that they do, and they expect to have a high degree of autonomy in their work. Management's role is therefore not one of directly controlling the work process, but ensuring that conditions for creative problem solving are in place. The high degree of autonomy necessary for innovative work and the decentralized responsibility for the quality of the results, may appear contradictory to management's need to secure workers' performance as well as meeting organizational economic targets, such as staying within budget and meeting project deadlines.

Mintzberg's (1979) adhocracy based on teams, decentralized decision-making, professionalism and shared organizational values is the prototype for organizing creative knowledge work. Indeed many knowledge-intensive service firms follow these organizational principles with non-bureaucratic dynamic structures and devolved responsibilities to self-managed project teams (Kvande and Rasmussen 1990, 1995; Voss-Dahm this volume). The dot.coms, which we focus on in this chapter, are characterized by non-hierarchical and dynamic structures where individual workers and project teams are made responsible for their projects. However, these firms operate in a very competitive market where the firm's reputation for quality, price and delivery time are important factors when negotiating new projects with customers. This gives rise to conflicting tensions between the organization of creative knowledge work and ensuring the firm's financial survival in a competitive market. How management manages this tension is addressed in the following section.

Common culture or individual contracts?

The literature on corporate culture (Deal and Kennedy 1982; Peters and Waterman 1982; Schein 1985) emphasizes the importance of strong corporate cultures. Through shared cultural values and common norms, workers can be controlled by the culture to work freely in the firm's interests. However, creating a common culture by managerial will around the firm's values is not easily accomplished, if at all possible. A firm's culture may be understood as resulting from political processes where many different cultures compete for hegemony, rather than a monolithic, unified system of shared values and norms developed and promoted by management as described in the corporate culture tradition. Instead a firm's culture may be fragmented and in flux, dynamic and changing over time (Martin 1992; Kvande and Rasmussen 1994). This does not mean workers do not share norms and values motivating them to work hard in the firm's interests. Instead, in the case of knowledge workers, individuals are motivated by the work they perform, because for many, being a knowledge worker means being a hard-working individual committed to delivering high quality services (Alvesson 2000).

There are important variations in cultures and norms across different knowledge work fields. In advertising and IT firms, the subject of this chapter, there are some specific and distinct characters. For example, among computer enthusiasts we find a culture of total absorption where the line between work and play is blurred (Turkle 1984; Håpnes 1996; Kleif and Faulkner 2003). The all-encompassing interest in computers leaves little time for social activities and excludes less enthusiastic people, in particular this leads to very few women associating with this culture and becoming computer scientists (Turkle 1988; Rasmussen and Håpnes 1991; Lie 2003; Nordli 2003). However, for management in IT firms this could mean there are fewer problems in employing computer professionals, who are willing to work hard and long hours.

In the advertising industry the culture of 'the creative artist' is a common feature. The product is tied to the individual creating it, and its success not only brings rewards to the firm, but also possible fame for the creator. The quality of the product is therefore essential for the individual producer's reputation. Among advertising industry employers the image of the artist, which includes them working all hours whenever inspiration hits him or her, is prevalent (Alvesson and Köping 1993). Managers in advertising agencies could therefore expect advertising workers to work long hours in their own interest to make high quality products.

Studies of knowledge workers show that those who are offered autonomy over their work, including autonomy over their working time, are motivated by this (Bailyn 1988) and are willing to work long hours (Deetz 1995; Barrett this volume; Voss-Dahm this volume). According to the principle of reciprocity (Gouldner 1960), there must be a balance between what the organization offers and what the worker in turn owes the organization. Therefore, knowledge workers' actions are also a result of what they consider fair and reasonable expectations. The implicit or unwritten agreement between the worker and the organization, or the *psychological contract* (Schein 1965; Rousseau 1995), is constructed from the individual beliefs regarding the terms of the exchange between the individual and the employer. It is based on what the organization offers the worker and what the worker in exchange perceives as his or her duties towards the organization (Rousseau 1995). When knowledge workers are offered autonomy, opportunities to learn the trade and a chance to try their hands at challenging tasks, they will, in turn, willingly exert effort on the organization's behalf.

A *perceived* balance between efforts and rewards does not mean that the burdens are equally divided between the two parties. Tynell's (2002) study of an IT firm shows how a new strategy of extensive freedom and autonomy at work resulted in workers accepting responsibility for all aspects of their work organization. As actors in the market they had to bid for projects, taking what the market was willing to give, and in turn they were responsible for delivering the right quality on time and within budget. When they had to put in extra hours to meet deadlines, this was their problem and this was experienced as personal failure because they had not met the organization's norms. Complaints to management about a lack of resources to do their jobs were met with the argument that they were responsible for changing the situation by negotiating better deals and organizing their work more efficiently. By devolving responsibility for the market: including customer relations, contracts and results, workers were not only made responsible for their own working time and the 'boundary control' of their work–life balance (Perlow 1998), but also for the economic result of their work for the firm. Tynell (2002) argues that by accepting this responsibility that the extensive autonomy they were given entailed, they controlled themselves in the economic interest of the firm.

In Tynell's study, although individuals felt they were not able to manage their job in the time that the customers were willing to pay for, there was no collective resistance to the system. The outcome was low professional self-confidence, but workers stayed and tried hard to meet the norms instead of leaving for another job.

This chapter tells a different story where working long hours resulted in high turnover, perhaps indicating that in the tension between autonomy and control, the balance between burdens and rewards was disturbed and the psychological contract broken. In the next section of this chapter we explore the following questions: What made the workers work so hard and long for the firm? What were their reasons for leaving or considering to leave? We begin the next section of the chapter with an outline of how and where the data were collected.

Method

We use two case studies of knowledge workers in two types of dynamic knowledge-intensive firms to explore the balance between autonomy and management control. Data were collected as part of a research project on knowledge work and 'greedy' organizations (Rasmussen and Johansen 2001, 2002a, 2002b; Rasmussen 2003).

We conducted in-depth interviews with web designers in advertising agencies at the end of 1999 and beginning of 2000 and with software systems developers in an IT-services firm in 2001. Interviews lasted between one and two hours and were recorded and later transcribed (Rasmussen and Johansen 2001). Since the interviews we have followed the careers of most of the web designers and programmers and the situation of the IT-service firm. These subsequent developments have substantiated our analysis.

The first study is a collective case study of web designers constructed from interviews with six web designers and web programmers working in the web departments of different advertising agencies in Oslo, the capital of Norway (names starting with a B), and two representatives from web design agencies in a regional Norwegian city (names starting with a P). All web designers interviewed had more than three years of experience and a professional status in the field. Only two worked in the same organization at the time of interviewing, but nearly all of the designers had, at some time, worked in the (major) agencies in Norway. The web-based advertising departments were, however, continually changing names and affiliation. Web departments were started, sold and bought by large international advertising agencies, and recently also by information and communication technology consulting firms. In this turbulent situation where both small groups and large firms saw their chance at exploring the new market for web products, the turnover among web designers and programmers and managers was very high.

Table 5.1 contains information about the respondents from which the first case study is constructed. It is important to note that interviews were only conducted with experienced web designers. As such the research did not capture directly the situation in web design of new and inexperienced workers without formal education. However, in the interviews the web designers reflected on their own work history and they discussed and gave examples of their experience as novices. The accounts of the young and inexperienced web workers are therefore their retrospective accounts. As retrospective accounts they may be part of a narrative of today and therefore contain elements of rationalizations of their recent actions. However they did not differ much from the experiences of the young and inexperienced workers in our second case study of the IT-services firm and we have found no reasons not to trust what they told us. The analysis of their situation is, however, strictly ours.

Table 5.1 Profiles of respondents for Case Study 1: Web designers in advertising agencies

Name	*Age*	*Civil status, family*	*Education*	*Job and experience*
Bob	25–30	Single	Education abroad in design and animation	Graphic designer; Design manager; 5 years in total
Ben	Approx. 25	Single	Self-taught; some years of secondary ed. in arts and design	Graphic designer/ programmer; 5 yrs; Experience in film/animation
Bill	25–30	Girlfriend in web design	Self-taught	Programmer; 6 yrs in advertising
Barbara	25–30	Single with 1 child	Self-taught	Programmer/web designer; 5 yrs in web-based advertising; Experience in TV production
Betty	25–30	Cohabits with web designer	Self-taught (O Levels in arts and design)	Graphic designer; 8 yrs in advertising; Apprentice
Bridget	Approx. 25	Boyfriend web programmer	Univ. courses; Self-taught and courses in web design	Graphic designer; 3 yrs in advertising; Apprentice
Paul	Approx. 35	Married, 2 children and one on the way	Private school of advertising	Graphic designer; Art Director; Partner; 10 years in advertising
Peter	45–50	Divorced with grown up children; cohabits with advertising worker	BA in economy	Manager of web agency; 12 years in advertising

The second case study is of a web-based IT-services provider located in a regional Norwegian city. At the time of the interviews, 23 people worked at this firm (including management, administration, sales, systems development and operations), nearly half of whom were partners in the firm. The firm specialized in new web-based IT-services, such as database systems and operating systems, primarily for the small to medium-sized enterprise market, although they also landed international contracts for their systems.

Interviews were conducted with three working managers and six workers in systems development and operations covering variations in age and gender (names starting with C). Table 5.2 shows the breakdown of the interviews with workers and working managers by age, gender, education and experience in the IT-service firm. In addition we gathered information from the general manager, finance officer and human resource manager about the firm's history, market and strategy.

In the next section of the chapter the case of web design is first presented and this is followed by the case study of work in the IT-services firm.

Table 5.2 Profiles of respondents for Case Study 2: developers in an IT-services firm

Name	*Age*	*Civil status, family*	*Education*	*Job and experience*
Chris	Approx. 25	Married with 1 child and another on the way	BA in computer science	Systems development manager; 8 months in C; Partner
Charles	Approx. 25	Cohabiting	BA in computer science and music	Systems developer; 6 months; Musician
Chuck	Approx. 20	Girlfriend	Student in social sciences; self-taught in computers	Systems developer (part-time); 4 years in C
Colin	Approx. 30	Girlfriend in the firm	(Adult student) 3 yrs. computer technology	System developer; 6 months
Cedric	Approx. 25	Married with baby on the way	BA computer science	Systems developer; 6 months
Christine	Approx. 25	Boyfriend in Oslo (also in computers)	Education abroad, MA computer science	System developer; 6 months in C
Carl	Approx. 25	Single	3 yrs computer technology	Operations Manager; Partner; 18 months
Caspar	Approx. 25	Cohabit with nurse	2 yrs computer technology	Systems operator; Partner; 18 months
Carol	Approx. 30	Partner is general manager in C and they have a baby	Master of technology	Management; Partner and founder; 5 years

Web design: from nobody to somebody

> Many working in this business have in common that they see their work as a lifestyle, and they do not want a traditional 9–5 job. What they discover is that work does not become just a life*style*, but life itself, because they work so much.
>
> (Bridget [emphasis in original])

The quote above characterized the work situation in web design. 'Work becoming life' was possible because the web designers were very young: with the exception of the managers, they were between 23 and 27 years old (see Table 5.1). Still, they were all veterans in web design as they had been involved in the establishment of new web-based departments, in mostly large traditional advertising agencies. Many had started one or two firms, either on their own or with friends, and they had all worked in (several) well-established advertising agencies.

The developer's youth could be explained by their lack of formal education in design (see Table 5.1), as there were no courses available in web design. Many programmers had begun programming on the web as a hobby, and since there was a shortage of web-based developers at the time of the research, they could easily get a well paid job.

In Norway, Westerdahls private school is recognized as *the* place to get an education in advertising. Usually, without this 'right' qualification individuals could find it difficult to get a job in an organization where it was possible to build a reputation as a designer. Furthermore, in the advertising industry web design was seen to be second rate when compared with designing on paper. Talent, some contacts and a strong will, combined with a general lack of experienced web designers, enabled enthusiastic young men and women who wanted to try their hand at web design to overcome their disadvantage of no formal design education and gain an opportunity through apprentice positions in advertising agencies.

Advertising agencies are often seen as typical 'modern' non-hierarchical organizations (Blomquist 1994; Alvesson 1995). Nonetheless they have a strong cultural hierarchy with Art Directors (AD) firmly at the top, AD assistants placed below and apprentices at the bottom. A designer's status is dependent on both their education (whether they had completed 'just courses' (Peter) or a degree from Westerdahls), and their experience and reputation. Designers are recognized for the work they have done: by what they have to show in their folders. Although they started as apprentices or AD assistants, the young web designers were eager to show that they could manage and build a reputation as designer.

Web design was a new and lucrative market and the advertising agencies were eager to sell their traditional customers the new products. It was 'hype' and everybody 'had to' be on the web. When the workers had to invoice seven hours a day at £85 (sterling) an hour (end 1999), there was much to be earned for the agencies, especially when the young workers were paid around £15,500 a year.

When the young designers and programmers were offered the opportunity to work with the new technology, they grabbed it enthusiastically. Designing new programmes for interactive and animated pages was exciting and challenging:

> The job in itself is so entertaining that there is no point in going home to watch TV. That's boring compared to this. It has been turned upside-down. You relax more at work than at home in front of the TV. You look forward to go to work more than to go home, and – you go to work and stay late.
>
> (Bill)

As a result, they were willing to work hard to explore the possibilities of the new technology and learn to design and programme on the web.

Neither sales consultants nor managers in the advertising agencies had knowledge of web designing. A young female apprentice told us how she had been made responsible for a project that neither she nor anybody else in the company had any qualifications for:

> They sold a project in a programming language that hardly anybody had even heard of. They had a vague idea of what we were supposed to do. One of the sales consultants said that it was OK, because he knew a little about it. There you are, thinking that this is gonna be *some* job. Then you work late into the night to finish on time. It was very frustrating, but I learned a lot from it, and I managed in the end.
>
> (Bridget)

We found new and inexperienced web designers managing large projects. One young, inexperienced female designer, who was responsible for developing web products for two major customers (both multinationals), told us she lived in constant fear of being exposed as incompetent. Still, they took on the jobs and responsibilities.

Being young without a formal design education or experience, the web designers had no status in the organization and were therefore vulnerable. However, in their desire to show they were worthy of management's trust and that they could manage, they worked as long as it took to get the job done. Initially the web designers did not protest against unreasonable levels of responsibility or the long hours that resulted. Unpaid extra work and 'all-nighters' to finish were expected in the new web departments and they were told that 'it's just the way it is, it's a growing business' (Betty). Interestingly, although the web departments were new, they were part of, and owned by, large, established, often multinational advertising agencies.

Still, the workers thought of the organization as small and entrepreneurial, and when asked about trade unions, they argued that it would collapse if the workers went on strike.

Freedom to work a lot

With projects, the designers and programmers could organize their work as they chose. This responsibility gave workers freedom to be flexible and to plan their working time according to their individual needs and schedules. They were responsible to deliver on time as Bob explained, 'you have always a certain amount of hours to work with in a project. Then it is up to you to organize your day so as to meet the deadline that is set'.

The sales consultants who sold the projects knew traditional 'paper' design, but had little knowledge of web designing. Therefore they ended up selling unrealistic projects. The young designers were stuck with the responsibility to deliver. The result was overtime and night work for designers and programmers:

> You have to deliver on time, and the sad thing is ... You arrive at work in the morning, and you find people who have slept a few hours on the sofa in the reception to finish the job in the morning.
>
> (Betty)

Their freedom and autonomy was therefore the freedom to organize their work to meet the deadlines. When the deadlines were too tight, the designers and programmers had to work a lot. They told us that you were in the wrong business if you wanted to go home at 4 pm because working unpaid overtime was considered normal in advertising. They were paid well (when they gained some experience), while the underlying understanding was that they would work overtime when necessary. Therefore work had to be their main interest if they were to survive in this business.

Without the experience and professional self-confidence of the 'seasoned sailors' to set limits, the young workers were prone to get overworked as Betty explained. 'I have come home from work so tired that all I could do was cry. No special reason, just that you're so tired, worn out. Then you just have to get yourself together and go back to work'.

We were told of a young designer who worked day and night in his new job and had a nervous breakdown after six months. According to one of his more experienced colleagues, this young man could not see that the amount of work expected of him was unreasonable. Betty put it this way, 'the culture is something like you're supposed to be so damned lucky to have this job, and therefore you should always be ready to work nights without extra pay'.

When everybody worked a lot to meet deadlines a culture of urgency developed:

> You get caught in a way of thinking that you have to be on your toes all the time, and that your job is more important than anything else. It is difficult to change that way of thinking ... It is difficult when nobody talks about reasonable limits. It helps little if I say something when there are 20 others working just as many hours without complaining.
>
> (Betty)

Their freedom and autonomy was in reality the 'freedom' to meet the economic demands of the advertising agencies. Having no status and little experience, the web designers were grateful for the opportunity to work and learn to be web-designers at the forefront of new technology. In return they were willing to accept responsibility given to them by management, even if it meant working unreasonable hours.

Control by devolving responsibility

Inadequate planning and budgeting, especially in the agencies in Oslo,[2] was caused by poor project management and production organization. Sales consultants sold web products without checking with the web designers about what was possible to deliver and how long it would take to make, and as a result they invariably sold the projects too cheap and with deadlines that were too tight.

One web designer had tried to change her company's routines to incorporate consultation into project planning, but she met with very little success, even though everybody agreed this was a good idea. When the developers did not have any input into project planning, pricing or timing, the outcome was being responsible for a job too large to be completed in too short a timeframe. Betty described this as, 'giving someone a yarn of wool and saying: "knit a sweater of this. It is to be size XL, and if it is not enough wool, that's your problem"'.

Responsibility for on-time delivery was delegated to the web designers and programmers, which resulted in overtime and night work for them. The sales consultants who created this situation had no responsibility for meeting the deadlines once the contract was signed. This expectation of unpaid overtime in the advertising industry was a problem for workers, but not for agencies. Unpaid overtime to deliver projects on time was therefore the 'normal' situation: 'The problem is that it is always *planned* overtime, it is not just by accident. You have it all the time, every day and week' (Bridget [emphasis in original]).

Young apprentices lacked the power and resources to counter the extreme demands for overtime. This contrasted with the situation for more experienced designers who protested and left if they were not satisfied with conditions. Even though experienced web designers often worked long hours, their experience and reputation enabled them to draw a line at work, threatening to leave if they were not heard. One of the few web designers with relevant education and experience, Bob, even managed to work shorter hours.

In general, however, the long hours resulted in high turnover amongst web designers. When the young apprentices started, they would willingly work hard with long hours for low pay, but after a while they became disillusioned. They would then try for jobs in other firms thinking that it might be better somewhere else. In new businesses they had to work hard to get established, and as newcomers they worked hard to make a good impression. They worked hard because the work was new and exciting, however, the result was burnout at a young age. For firms, the supply of new workers meant there was no incentive to normalize work hours.

We're only in it for the money

In the web design field there was a contradiction: agencies wanted the best web designers to position the firm in the advertising industry but they were not really interested in producing high quality design. When web designers were given a project offering them the opportunity for quality work, they were willing to put in extra effort. As workers who strongly identified with their work, it was important for them to produce high quality products. However, they were told by management that this was not necessary and instead they should do something simple as 'the customer wouldn't know the difference' (Ben). The work then became less interesting and their motivation plummeted. For them, work was personal. They wanted to do a *good* job to earn a reputation as a designer who could then compete for jobs, status and customers.

The web designers were willing to work hard to make products that showcased their abilities, but they were not willing to work nights because of poor planning and budgeting:

> One of the reasons for me quitting was that I started to think why do I work all this extra unpaid overtime? Why am I doing all this uninteresting work, the work others should have done? I don't even get paid. Why don't I just quit?
>
> (Betty)

There was thus a conflict between the designers' interest in high quality web design and the agencies' interest in making a profit from exploiting the new technology. The firms' short-term economic horizon meant workers felt like they were being treated as 'labour power' to be exploited rather than as competent and creative web designers and programmers. That the web designers were seen as second rate and not 'real' designers in advertising, lacking the prestigious education from Westerdahls and 'only' doing designs on the web, reinforced this.

The individualization of responsibility was reinforced by the individual employment contracts and the promise of better conditions, options and stocks which were made to valuable workers who threatened to leave. These promises were also made to valuable workers to entice them to join the firm. However, changes in management personnel when web departments and firms were bought and sold meant these promises were not honoured and workers felt management was not to be trusted (Sennett 1998). When these web workers were not treated as expert workers, their reaction was individual: they left the organization for new and more promising employers.

However, they found the same short-term market orientation in the other agencies in Oslo. Moving from firm to firm by word of mouth through their networks, they tried out the opportunities in the industry. The preferred solution for the experienced web designers was typically individual; to start a business for themselves, alone or with a few friends, using the reputation they had established. As freelancers or small entrepreneurs they wanted to choose what they wanted to do and hoped to negotiate more realistic projects giving them enough time to do quality work.[3] This was, however, not an easy solution as the experience in the IT-services firm in the next section of the chapter illustrates.

IT-services: a partnership of happy amateurs

'I think that we could certainly have managed to play post-modern with a flat structure for a long time, but to get a serious business off the ground, I think that you have to get organized' (Chuck). This quote illustrates the situation of the entrepreneurial IT-services firm, which was established as a collectively owned consulting firm by four students in the mid-1990s. Their web-based IT-services grew fast and became the firm's most important line of business. Growth necessitated changes to the flat partner-based organizational structure, but the idea of collective ownership by working partners remained. Expansion was necessary to make partnership financially attractive in a five-year perspective. At the time of the research the organization consisted of working partners and waged workers.

The firm did not offer high pay, but interesting tasks, a very good social environment and opportunities for everyone to become a partner and shareholder after six months employment. Employees were known to work long hours and had a culture of socializing after work. High turnover owing to low pay and long hours among systems developers had occurred in the year prior to this research.

Recruitment of students was preferred in this IT-services provider as this enabled management to find out 'who fitted in' (Carol). It was also a way of engendering committed workers who wanted to be part of the collective enterprise. Since most of their systems developers had left in the previous 12 months, a group of systems developers who had just graduated from college or university with a bachelor's degree had been recruited.

Computers had been a hobby for many of these new workers, and they were glad to get a job where they could work with the newest web-based systems technology. Cedric described this as, 'I have always been interested in computers. I work with system development and like to make things. For me that is the most important ... It is more like a hobby, I'm only glad that I get paid, so to say.'

They had to be at the forefront of technical developments and that made their job challenging as these were good opportunities to learn. For them, work was like being a well-paid student as they worked with other young people who shared their interests in a good social environment. In the words of one of the systems developers, 'The notion of hard fun around here is just bullshit. That they *work* weekends, that's just words. They sit here having a good time playing games on the computer' (Charles [emphasis in original]).

Since work and play were mixed, the boundaries between working time and their own time became blurred, as the following quote illustrates:

> I like to work weekends because I want to, it is fun. If I have time and I like it, why not? The idea of weekend as time off is being watered out anyway nowadays. I can always take time off on a Tuesday or a Wednesday instead.
>
> (Charles)

Work and play was intermingled in their accounts. They were motivated to work a lot because they enjoyed the challenges in their job; it was also their hobby (cf Kleif and Faulkner 2003). They would come late in the morning and leave late in the evening. After work they would often go out and have a beer together or get something to eat and drink back at work. This culture was like the 'boy's culture' where work and play coincide as has been found in studies of students' hacker cultures (Håpnes 1996).

Autonomy over time and tasks

The job in the IT-service firm offered freedom and autonomy over both the working time and the work tasks. Workers were offered freedom to work when and as much as they wanted. As young and inexperienced workers they welcomed autonomy and were willing to take on the associated responsibility. They were made responsible for their projects, individually and collectively, including responsibility to deliver on time:

> You have your freedom. You can sit all day at work and install funny and interesting software and have a nice time surfing on the web. Because it is *your* responsibility to deliver on time. In November I had 290 hours unpaid overtime to manage to finish my project by the first of December.
>
> (Charles [emphasis in original])

The small entrepreneurial firm struggled hard to establish themselves in the market. Their projects were often sold too cheap to underbid their competitors. Therefore finishing on time meant working overtime. Other workers might be mobilized to help, but in the end it was their individual responsibility. The 'self-determined' overtime was illustrated by one of the systems developers who had just finished a project and was interviewed from 5 to 6 pm:

> I seldom work eight hours a day. But that is really my own fault, because nobody pressures me to work overtime, at least not yet. At the moment, it is a bit extreme. I sat till four last night, and started again at nine this morning. I am a little weak now.
>
> (Colin)

Autonomy and freedom at work thus constructed working hours as self-determined and their amount of work as something that they, individually, were responsible for. When work and play were intermingled and developers enjoyed full autonomy over their time, it was difficult to distinguish between the firm's time and their own time. As professional 'knowledge workers', who enjoyed the freedom at work, they were also responsible for their time management (cf Voss-Dahm this volume).

Responsible management?

Both the task, developing web-based IT-systems, and the opportunity to learn in the collective organization made this an attractive place to work, even if pay was relatively low. However, the firm's entrepreneurial character and lack of establishment in the marketplace meant there was an insecure financial situation and a lack of production processes and administrative routines in place. The firm was built upon the enthusiastic collective effort of workers and working partners. Problems resulting from the lack of structure and formalized systems were highlighted when nearly all systems developers left the firm because they were dissatisfied with their pay and working conditions. The result was that new and inexperienced workers had to take over the projects that their predecessors planned.

One of the new systems developers, Cedric, used the interview to vent his frustrations about lack of professional management in the firm. He was one of the workers who told us he worked with his hobby and only was glad he got paid. He used to work 50–60 hours a week, but when one of his colleagues worked 500 hours overtime in three months, to finish a project left by one of the systems developers who had quit, without extra pay or time off, Cedric stopped working more than normal hours. He became very critical of the firm and was frustrated that his salary was not paid on time because a client had not yet paid. He felt that it was degrading to have to beg for his pay when he had done his job, and he was dependent upon the money to pay the mortgage on his apartment on time. Cedric did not complain too much at work, because he felt it negatively affected his relationships with the other staff and it was the good social relations at work which made daily work a pleasure.[4] However, he wanted to quit the job as soon as he could find another where he could work with web-based systems. His relationship with the firm had changed from a free and willing professional who worked for himself *and* the company to that of a wage-labourer working for an unfaithful employer who did not honour obligations.

Collective entrepreneurs

The situation for the partners was different from that of the workers. Being owners, they constituted themselves as collective entrepreneurs who were responsible for the firm's future. They valued the influence partnership gave in terms of their own working day and on the firm's management:

> I love it here. It is just right for me, and as good as it could be. You manage your own working day, and as a partner you have insight in and control over what happens from top to bottom in the organization.
>
> (Carl)

Because they were partners and their own employers, they were willing to give the job most of their time, within certain limits posed by family obligations as Chris explained, 'You work in your own interest, and that makes you work more than you normally would have. I am aware of my responsibility as a partner'.

Being a small firm establishing itself in the market for web-based services, however, resulted in very long hours for the systems operators. They had to be available for the customers during normal working hours, but as maintaining and updating systems was done after office hours they usually worked 10–12 hours a day. In addition customers needed to be able to reach them at night and on weekends, which meant the head of operations was 'back-up' every weekend except on his vacation (usually one week). As Carl explained, even though he loved his work, he did not think he could keep going at this pace for too long: it was exciting, but not healthy.

> I have said to myself that I will work like this for 10 more years, till I am 35. That is, in the tempo that I keep today. Any longer than that I can't imagine that I would manage. Then my body would be so worn out that it wouldn't last much longer if I didn't stop in time. There are older people working in the IT-business, but they don't work in the tempo that we do.
>
> (Carl)

Despite this, the long hours and intensive work were in his interest since he was a partner and had shares in the company, and he wanted the company to succeed.

A couple, who were founders, partners and managers, acutely experienced the conflict between their interests as owners/partners and workers when they became parents. Long hours were in the interests of the firm but this conflicted with their interests as parents for shorter working hours. As Carol pointed out, reducing their working time to something near 40 hours a week was also problematic:

> We who work as managers in the firm are supposed to motivate the others. If we start to leave at four and work less, the others will also do that. The more we work, the more the others work. That effect is very obvious, so it is a problem for us to work less.
>
> (Carol)

The firm's entrepreneurial nature and the competitive product market created a situation of constant pressure. Young workers could live with this situation for a period in their lives as work was like a continuation of their student life-style. They accepted working long hours and sometimes through the night, because they saw it as being temporary: a period in the life of the organization, and a period in their life. As a prolonged student's life where they learnt the trade and got some experience, it was acceptable to work in this way, but in the long run it was not possible. The economic pressure on an entrepreneurial organization establishing itself in the market meant that the firm was characterized by a permanent 'crisis' situation that demanded everyone's full effort. The work situation this created was not compatible with responsibilities for family and children, and workers left if they could find work operating or developing web-based systems elsewhere.

The firm's strategy was to hire young people who were still in training or had just graduated, and who wanted to work with their hobby. By organizing the firm as a collective enterprise everybody had something to gain from working hard for future success, even if it meant working long hours for low pay. Expansion was necessary to secure future gains and to increase the firm's future value. This long-term strategy, however, meant hiring more workers, who were not (yet) partners. The short-term reality of long hours and low pay led to increasing dissatisfaction amongst workers and undermined the project of hard work for future rewards that motivated the partners.[5]

Contextual explanations

Web design and IT-services are typical examples of dot.coms in the so-called 'new' economy. When they are characterized as such, the illusion is given of similarity and of a unitary work situation, exhibiting the same characteristics to be explained by the same factors and mechanisms. As we have seen above, there are some similar features that distinguish these professional service firms from more traditional professional services. The workers do not need a specific formal education to take on the work, and their work is determined by market demands rather than professional norms. However, to fully understand the cases, they need to be differentiated and analysed in their specific contexts. Advertising and IT-services are from different 'fields' of the 'new economy' with different work and professional cultures. The workers occupy different places in different labour markets, and their qualifications and positions also differ.

The web designers worked with new products in a new market, but they were employed in traditional organizations, often large multinationals with a secure financial base. The advertising agencies were characterized by a strong culture and established professional hierarchies. The web designers inhabited the lowest positions in these hierarchies: young workers without formal design training were found at the bottom, while the more experienced designers moved slowly upwards. Web designers were never recognized as 'first class' in traditional advertising as they lacked the 'right' education (Westerdahls) and they did not design on (high quality) paper.

In the advertising field individuals are only as good as their last job and web designers have to deliver high quality work to earn a reputation. However, agency managers were not really interested in developing high quality web design, instead they were interested in making a fast profit out of their web design projects. As a result the needs of the web designers came into conflict with managerial policy. Web designers felt they were treated by their managers as 'labour power' and not as expert labour, and that the firms profited from the systematic use of planned and unpaid overtime. The vulnerable position of the young and inexperienced workers, who were thankful to have the opportunity to learn the trade in a situation of ample supply of such workers in the labour market in Oslo, made the extreme exploitation of the young web designers possible. The culture in advertising, and the image of design work as the work of dedicated artists, reinforced this. Their experience of trying, without much success, to find better working conditions in other agencies points to the problems of web design as an entrepreneurial sector of advertising.

The entrepreneurial aspects are important in understanding the work situation in the IT-services firm in the regional city. The 'gründer' character of the firm, the collective partner organization of enthusiasts who wanted to make their collective enterprise a success, was both the strength and the weakness of the firm. They were very conscious of the importance of mobilizing everybody in the firm, and creating a good social environment with equal treatment and opportunities for partnership. They lacked, however, a professional organization of work and a direction of where they were going professionally. The firm was oriented towards the market, going wherever the market offered opportunities in the area of web-based services.

In the IT-services firm the new developers were recruited to complete the work of the systems developers who had quit in the previous 12 months. The new systems developers worked long hours to finish their projects, and in the 'boy's computer culture' where work and play and social life was intertwined (Håpnes 1996) 'working time' was difficult to define. These developers were not exploited by the firm for huge profit like the web designers in advertising, instead their problem was a lack of organizational systems and structures, which made their long hours necessary and unpaid. They were, however, confident enough to critique this and suggest improvements. The firm wanted to keep the workers, and they tried to comply. However, the entrepreneurial nature of the firm and its insecure financial position meant wages could not always be paid on time. Managers and workers alike were therefore trapped in a situation where they had to work very long hours to get established in the market, hoping that the business would be a success so that their position might change in the future.

Conclusion: dot.coms – opportunity knocks

A common view is that responsible autonomy and direct control are different and opposite management strategies (Friedman 1977, 2003). Our cases of web designers in the web design departments of advertising agencies and the IT-services firm are cases where autonomy for individual workers and teams is used to control the workers' output. Our cases show that autonomy can be used as a strategy for increased control over the workers in the interest of the firm and as such reinforces the notion of layers of strategies of control outlined by Barrett in an earlier chapter of this book. By devolving responsibility to workers for delivering good quality products on time and *within budget*, the responsibility for the firms' economic results was shifted from management to workers.

The young and inexperienced web designers and developers valued the opportunities they were offered in advertising and IT-systems development to learn the job and explore new technologies. However, they were vulnerable because they did not know what was expected from them, although they were eager to show their managers and co-workers that they could do their job. As a result these workers willingly worked hard and long hours. Their professionally challenging jobs were attractive and exciting with their good social environment for the young and inexperienced workers.

The autonomy they were offered signalled to them that they were being treated as 'expert' workers, and this was essential for them to be motivated to take responsibility for results and work hours far beyond 'normal' hours in a work week. When they were treated as responsible professionals, they behaved as such (see also Marks and Lockyer this volume). Having taken on the responsibility to deliver on time, they were committed to meeting these deadlines. The culture of work as a lifestyle meant that the long hours of the independent artist or the computer wizard could be interpreted as dedication to work and being professional (Alvesson 2000), rather than the result of poor work organization and management. Going home 'early' could be interpreted as individuals not being committed to work and not being serious about a career, as Epstein, Seron, Oglensky and Saute (1998) found in their study of US lawyers.

When we take a closer look at the 'free' and flexible work situation of the web designers in advertising agencies and developers in the IT-services firm, a situation said to be a characteristic of the 'new' economy, we actually see it has distinct similarities with the very 'old' economy of early capitalism. Here capitalists could increase their profit by extending the working day. With ample supply of labour, workers did not have the power to resist without scarce qualifications that were in demand or a collective workers' organization (Thompson 1969; Friedman 1977).

The jobs of web design in the advertising industry and development in the IT-services firm demanded very long hours in new firms establishing themselves in the market. These jobs were not permanent places for workers, but a place for young and inexperienced workers who wanted to try and learn. The work was not healthy and workers' responsibilities could not easily be combined with a social life outside work or family responsibilities. When workers wanted to start a family, their professionally challenging and socially exciting, but time-consuming jobs, became a problem. They were faced with the choice of participating fully or finding another job with more 'normal' work hours. When their autonomy or individualized responsibility for results and working time became too much, individuals sought individual solutions: for many this meant starting for themselves as small entrepreneurs or freelancers.

The work situations we have described in this sector of the 'new economy' are special because of the entrepreneurial character of these new firms. Here we are dealing with firms or departments in firms in a very early period of their life. Workers were also very young and most of them were establishing themselves in the labour market. The work situations, as such, were therefore not typical of knowledge workers in general. The aim of this chapter was, however, not to describe the general situation of knowledge workers or software developers, but to explore how autonomy was used as a means of control. In this chapter we have shown how giving workers freedom and autonomy, and treating them as 'expert workers' was effective in securing their responsibility to work hard and for as long as it took to finish their tasks on time. The strategy was especially effective with young and inexperienced workers who were eager to get a chance to show their abilities in these new web design or web-based IT-services firms. However, as our cases show, this was only effective in the short term: autonomy turned out to be a trick as it gave workers the freedom to work very long hours to meet the obligations of an irresponsible employer, rather than acting as a treat for valuable 'expert workers'.

Notes

1 We wish to thank Bjørn Hvinden for the notion of psychological contracts as a useful one and Tove Håpnes for ideas and comments on the paper. The editor has commented on drafts and greatly improved our English.
2 The web designer labour market was different in Oslo and the regions. In Oslo there were many firms competing in the market, and job opportunities for skilled designers and programmers were ample when the research was conducted. Turnover was therefore very high in Oslo, whereas it was difficult to recruit experienced workers in the region and the agencies were keen to keep their workers.
3 All our informants in Oslo changed jobs in the period we interviewed them or in the following six months.
4 See Rasmussen (2004) for a discussion of the multiple sources of commitment in knowledge work.
5 Since the time of our interviews the firm has expanded, but in doing so experienced financial difficulties. In 2002–03 workers were in conflict with management over cuts in pay. All the workers and many partners who were present in 2001 had quit.

References

Alvesson, M. (1995) *Managing Knowledge-Intensive Companies*, Berlin/New York: de Gruyter.

Alvesson, M. (2000) 'Social identity and the problem of loyalty in knowledge-intensive companies', *Journal of Management Studies*, 37, 8: 1101–23.

Alvesson, M. (2001) 'Knowledge work: ambiguity, image and identity', *Human Relations*, 54, 7: 863–86.

Alvesson, M. and Köping, A.-S. (1993) *Med känslan som ledstjärna. En studie av reklamarbete och reklambyråer*, Lund: Studentlitteratur.

Bailyn, L. (1988) 'Autonomy in the industrial R&D lab', in R. Katz (ed.) *Managing Professionals in Innovative Organizations*, New York: Ballinger.

Blomquist, M. (1994) *Könshierarkier i gungning*, Uppsala: Acta Universitas Uppsaliensis.

Deal, T. and Kennedy, A. (1982) *Corporate Cultures*, Reading, Mass.: Addison-Wesley.

Deetz, S. (1995) *Transforming Communication, Transforming Business: Building Responsive and Responsible Workplaces*, Creskill, NJ: Hampton Press.

Epstein, C. F., Seron, C., Oglensky, B. and Saute, R. (1998) *The Part-Time Paradox*, New York: Routledge.

Freidson, E. (1986) *Professional Powers*, Chicago: The University of Chicago Press.

Friedman, A. L. (1977) *Industry and Labour*, London: Macmillan.

Friedman, A. L. (2003) 'Professional autonomy compared with other types of strategies for maintaining task and social control', paper presented at the European Sociological Association Conference, Murcia, 24–26 September.

Gouldner, A. W. (1960) 'The norms of reciprocity: A preliminary statement', *American Sociological Review*, 25: 161–78.

Håpnes, T. (1996) 'Not in their machines. How hackers transform computers into subcultural artefacts', in M. Lie. and K. H. Sørensen (eds) *Making Technology our own?* Oslo: Scandinavian University Press.

Kleif T. and Faulkner, W. (2003) '"I'm no athlete [but] I can make this thing dance" – Men's pleasure in technology', *Science, Technology and Human Values*, 28, 2: 296–325.

Kvande, E. and Rasmussen, B. (1990) *Nye Kvinneliv. Kvinner i menns organisasjoner*, Oslo: AdNotam.

Kvande, E. and Rasmussen, B. (1994) 'Men in male dominated organizations and their encounter with women intruders', *Scandinavian Journal of Management*, 10, 2: 163–73.

Kvande, E. and Rasmussen, B. (1995) 'Women's careers in static and dynamic organizations', *Acta Sociologica*, 38, 2: 115–30.

Lie, M. (ed.) (2003) *He, She and IT Revisited*, Oslo: Gyldendal Akademisk.

Martin, J. (1992) *Cultures in Organizations*, New York: Oxford University Press.

Mintzberg, H. (1979) *The Structuring of Organizations*, Englewood Cliffs: Prentice Hall.

Newell, S., Robertson, M., Scarborough, H. and Swan, J. (2002) *Managing Knowledge Work*, Basingstoke: Palgrave.

Nordli, H. (2003) 'The net is not enough: Searching for the female hacker', unpublished thesis, University of Trondheim.

Perlow, L. A. (1998) 'Boundary control – The social ordering of work and family time in a high-tech corporation', *Administrative Science Quarterly*, 43, 2: 328–57.

Peters, T. and Waterman, R. (1982) *In Search of Excellence*, New York: Harper and Row.

Rasmussen, B. (2003) 'Equal opportunity in the 'new' economy: Gendered work and individual choice', paper presented at the *3rd Conference on Gender, Work and Organization*, Keele University, 25–27 June.

Rasmussen, B. (2004) 'Organising knowledge work(ers)', in A. Carlsen, R. Klev, and G. von Krogh (eds) *Living Knowledge*, Basingstoke: Palgrave.

Rasmussen, B. and Håpnes, T. (1991) 'Excluding women from the technologies of the future?' *Futures*, 23, 10: 1107–19.

Rasmussen, B. and Johansen, B. (2001) 'New workers in a new economy? Webworkers in the labour market', paper presented at the *Work, Employment and Society conference*, Nottingham, 11–13 September.

Rasmussen, B. and Johansen, B. (2002a) 'Kunnskapsarbeidere i 'dot.com.'-økonomien', *Tidsskrift for Arbejdsliv*, 4, 2: 25–44.

Rasmussen, B. and Johansen, B. (2002b) 'Å sage over den greina man sitter på?' *Sosiologisk Tidsskrift*, 10, 4: 332–54.

Rousseau, D. M. (1995) *Psychological Contracts in Organizations*, Thousand Oaks: Sage.

Scarborough, H. (1999) 'Knowledge as work: Conflicts in the management of knowledge workers', *Technology Analysis and Strategic Management*, 11, 1: 5–16.

Schein, E. (1965) *Organizational Psychology*, Englewood Cliffs, NJ: Prentice Hall.

Schein, E. (1985) *Organizational Culture and Leadership*, San Fransisco: Jossey Bass.

Sennett, R. (1998) *The Corrosion of Character*, New York: Norton.

Thompson, E. P. (1969) *The Making of the English Working Class*, London: Penguin.

Turkle, S. (1984) *The Second Self*, New York: Simon and Schuster.

Turkle, S. (1988) 'Computational reticence: Why women fear the intimate machine', in C. Kramerae (ed.) *Technology and Women's Voices: Keeping in Touch*, London: Routledge.

Tynell, J. (2002) '"Det er min egen skyld" – nyliberale styringsrationaler inden for human resource management', *Tidsskrift for Arbejdsliv*, 4, 2: 5–24.

6 Coming and going at will?

Working time organization in German IT companies

Dorothea Voss-Dahm

Introduction

The time dimension of software development work is the primary concern of this chapter. Specifically the focus is on working time sovereignty, which is the extent to which employees are able to influence the duration, scheduling and distribution of individual working time.[1] This is important as autonomous decision-making with regard to working time can not only create the conditions for good work but can also establish the preconditions for reconciling the demands of the workplace with those of personal relationships, social life and lifelong learning.

When it comes to working time arrangement, employees' concern with their lives outside work can conflict with employers' interest in utilizing their labour (Haipeter and Lehndorff 2003). The time employees spend in the workplace is a resource which firms seek to put to productive use. Thus employers' and employees' interests constitute a potential source of conflict in any attempt to determine the utilization of working time and, in the past, were repeatedly the cause of labour disputes. The resolution of this conflict of interests in Germany led to the establishment of a standard working time arrangement enshrined within the permanent full-time model of employment that became a major institution in Germany in the post-war period (Bosch 2001).

In the early 1980s, however, new opportunities for the more flexible use of working time were opened up by the negotiation of new arrangements, which were then enshrined in collective agreements. The introduction of greater flexibility enabled employers to cut costs when facing fluctuations in demands, while employees were compensated with a reduction in working time. However, critical voices observed that flexible working times could be a 'dangerous sort of freedom' (Seifert 1995), since the declining regulatory power of fixed working time norms made it increasingly likely that working time would be determined to an even greater extent than by decisions of company or establishment level policy makers. Conversely, others stressed the opportunities that could be created for employees through the negotiation of flexible working times and they observed that such flexibility had within it the potential to create a win–win situation (Knauth 2000).

In Germany it is now taken for granted that the flexible organization of working time has become a sphere of management policy. Thus a representative survey conducted in 2000, found two-thirds of firms used some form of flexible work organization (DIHT 2000). Besides the traditional instrument of flexitime, which allows employees to vary their starting and finishing times and has been in use for a long time, particularly for white-collar workers, working time accounts are enjoying increasing popularity. Around 30 per cent of German firms have introduced such accounts (Bauer, Groß, Munz and Sayin 2002), which can be used to record fluctuations in working time over longer periods, such as a year or even the entire working life. As working time becomes more flexible, the question of working time sovereignty has moved back on to the agenda. The increasing room for manoeuvre in decisions on the duration, scheduling and distribution of working time means that the determination of working time may, in theory, be located at any point on a continuum between heteronomy and self-determination or, in other words, between a management-oriented mode of determination or one that takes greater account of employees' needs and preferences.

In this chapter the subject of 'working time sovereignty' is investigated. The extent to which a balance can be successfully struck between the individual employees' interests and the temporal demands of the labour process largely depend on the position of employees in the labour process and a labour process with room for manoeuvre enables employees to assert their own interests. In the next section of this chapter the labour process in seven German IT services firms is examined in order to investigate the degree of latitude that exists in time allocation in project-based work. This is followed by an examination of the conditions that the nature of the labour process creates for temporal coordination in the workplace. The empirical evidence from the seven firms confirms the frequently documented observation that high-skill workers in the IT industry enjoy considerable freedom in determining the start and finish of their working day (Wagner 2000; Barrett 2001; Rubery and Grimshaw 2001; Plantenga and Remery 2003; Trautwein-Kalms and Ahlers 2003). However, the question is asked as to whether employees' decisions on working time are taken in a truly independent fashion. Are software workers really autonomous in their time management? The investigation in this chapter is shaped and structured by this critical point of view.

This chapter establishes that a high degree of self-organization, multifaceted cooperative relations and individual room for manoeuvre in work organization do not necessarily go hand in hand with a high degree of influence over individual working times. Indeed, the very freedom for software workers to organize their own work may actually lead them to losing their ability to assert their own interests in respect of working time.

Clearly we are dealing here with a paradoxical situation whose causes are sought to be ascertained. The employment policy issues that emerge from this situation will be the focus of the concluding section.

Project-based work in seven IT-services firms: between clients and indicators

This study of working time sovereignty draws on evidence from 30 interviews conducted in 2000 with personnel managers, project managers, team leaders, works councillors and software developers in seven firms in the German IT industry engaged in developing software applications.[2] Although these firms differed in terms of their product range, size and corporate structure, they all used project teams to develop their software applications. See Table 6.1 for details of the firms and interviews conducted.

Project-based work enables firms to react rapidly and flexibly to markets in a permanent state of flux. For many firms, the biggest advantage of project-based working is its inherent capacity to facilitate the adaptation of work organization to unforeseen and unexpected events. For this reason, it is a form of work organization found primarily in organizations with a high innovation dynamic and subject to strong external influences.

Projects are officially defined as undertakings characterized essentially by the uniqueness of their overall circumstances (Deutsches Institut für Normung). Thus the focus of attention in the labour process is a specific product or a specific, delimitable service. As an organizational unit, in other words, a project becomes a time-limited construct with clear, shared objectives (Baukrowitz and Boes 2002). Project-based work is carried out by project teams, whose personnel can be repeatedly reconstituted depending on the task in hand. Thus cooperation between experts in various disciplines and the integration of team members into a project group are both the basis and, at the same time, the challenge of project-based working.

The extent to which employees enjoy room for manoeuvre and opportunities for cooperation and occupy a position of strength within the labour process are indicators of work humanization. These characteristics are a fundamental part of project-based working, in that individual work tasks are not determined from outside by means of functional descriptions but are generated internally, that is they arise out of the current labour process. Work organization and the sequencing of the various stages of the labour process are the responsibility of each project team. Are these not the conditions under which 'good work' can develop? And as far as working time is concerned, is it not the case that the preconditions for the establishment of a high degree of working time sovereignty are largely met in project-based working? All employees have to do is to help themselves! The empirical evidence shows that a certain degree of freedom does

Table 6.1 Case study firms and interviews conducted

Firm name	*Description*	*Interviews*
Globe	Major world player in IT services (12,000 staff in Germany). IT services division with 520 staff adapting IT products for clients	Chair local works council, Chair German works council, Sales manager, Professional development manager, Regional HR manager, 2 × Software developers
Network	Small (23 staff) firm founded in 1995 specializing in providing internal and external communication networks for SMEs	2 × Owners, 2 × Software developers
Telcomp	IT service division (300 employees) of large German telecommunication company with 20,000 staff developing software used in dealing with customer requests in service departments of a telephone company	Chair works council, Company wide HR manager, Project division manager, Project manager, Software developer
Routplan	Firm (123 employees) founded in 1980 developing electronic marketing support systems in close cooperation with one of the biggest German carmakers	Member of managing board, 2 × Software developers
Catalonien	Small (43 staff) but growing firm founded in 1990 developing Java-based catalogue and business systems as well as adapting IT products for clients	Commercial manager, 3 × Software developers, Project manager, Technology manager
Netdesign	Young (founded 1995) and small firm (35 employees) concentrating on consulting analysis and system optimization in secure business information processing	Managing director, Project manager
Init	Mid-sized firm (189 employees) founded in 1983 as spin-out from a university IT faculty. It develops customer specific IT solutions for fare rate systems in public transport	HR manager, Chair works council, Project manager

indeed exist in such work, but that this freedom comes at a price. Modern forms of work organization, such as project-based working, may offer workers greater autonomy but they also make them subject to greater contingent constraints (Moldaschl 2001).

Cooperation, authority structures and self-organization in project-based working

Any software development project can be broadly broken down into planning and realization phases. At the beginning of a project, little is known about the various stages that will actually be required or the time and personnel resources needed to deal with the workload. When a software project has been commissioned it must be interpreted and specified. Authority structures[3] and cooperation,[4] whether formally established or simply the result of custom and practice, determine whether the project team collectively undertakes the planning, distributes the resources for the individual stages and allocates responsibility for the realization of the project or whether the project is planned 'top-down', with individual team members simply allocated their tasks within a rigid division of labour.

The question of responsibility for project planning is also bound up with that of overall responsibility for the success or failure of the project. Since each project is different, there is a degree of structural uncertainty as to the course it will take and the results it will produce; indeed, it is quite possible that the project will not produce the desired outcomes, or that it will fail altogether. If the labour process is dominated by hierarchical authority structures, project managers generally undertake planning and assume overall responsibility. In this sense, traditional ways of organizing the labour process, in which planning is separated from operations, can survive even in a modern form of work organization such as project work. Thus as far as individual project members are concerned, hierarchical authority structures are associated with less room for manoeuvre in the organization of job tasks. On the other hand, they are freed of the burden of responsibility which, because of the very real risks involved in implementing a project, may be experienced as a genuine relief.

There may also be varying degrees of cooperation and hierarchical authority structures in the organization of the project itself. A project is not a rigidly sequential process; rather, external circumstances or unexpected events can cause the whole process to proceed through a series of recursive loops (Latniak Gerlmaier, Voss-Dahm and Brödner 2003). For this reason, cooperation and authority structures are repeatedly exposed to changes in the external environment as a project unfolds and must prove themselves as organizational principles.

The hierarchical and cooperative structures of the software projects investigated in this study differed in the following way. In all the projects, there was a broad distinction between project management and project team members from various disciplinary backgrounds. Project managers were responsible, first, for the decisions taken in the course of the project and, second, for external communications. This role was different from that of the other project team members, whose principal responsibility was to utilize their technical expertise in the development of IT solutions. However, only in one project (at Globe, an international player in the IT industry with a rigid division of labour) was the formal authority structure actually deployed in its pure form in the project planning phase. Project managers broke the commission down into its individual stages and did not assemble a project team until later, on the basis of the competence profile required. In all the other projects either a level of the management hierarchy (i.e. project managers) was formally called upon to undertake the planning (Telcomp, Init, Routplan and Catalonien) or, in the smaller companies without such formal structures (Netdesign, Network), experienced employees or company directors themselves shouldered the burden of project management. However, the process of project planning described in the course of our interviews tended to suggest that the actual stages of the various projects were planned in cooperation with the team members engaged in developing the IT solutions, not least in order to harness the expertise available within the company for the purposes of project planning.

In all the projects studied, the hierarchical structure was softened during the project realization phase by the multifarious cooperative relationships. Particularly when project managers were involved only to a limited extent in the labour process (Globe), agreements on the next stages of the project were reached horizontally, that is among team members themselves, with the project management being informed of the agreements. Conversely, it was observed that when project managers were closely involved in the process, they were responsible for project supervision and coordination, at least formally. In reality, however, the division of labour was determined in close collaboration with project team members responsible for dealing with the project's technical requirements. Thus the relationship between project managers and team members was not characterized by a significant difference in hierarchical level. In this sense, project managers were team members specializing in the organization and coordination of the technical tasks, often in conjunction with responsibility for customer service. The example of Telcomp shows how porous authority structures can be at the operational level. In this firm, project management positions were filled on a temporary basis. In a subsequent project, project managers could be ordinary team members again without suffering any loss of income or status.

Cooperation horizontally, that is between the team members responsible for a project's technical aspects, was identified in the interviews in all the companies as a self-evident requirement of project work, since cooperation with other team members during the entire course of the project was necessary at the interfaces between individual work packages. Team members interviewed in the course of the study even expressed the opinion that a project's success depended essentially on 'interface management'. Work packages being carried out simultaneously had to be repeatedly coordinated otherwise there was a risk that the partial solutions developed would not be compatible at the end of the project. Cooperation within the team was also necessary, it was suggested, because individual team members acquire project-specific knowledge in the course of the labour process, not all of which could be documented. In order to prevent important knowledge from being lost when a project team member was redeployed to another project or left the company, the 'back-up principle' was brought into play in order to reduce dependency on the knowledge embodied in individual team members. Each project team member was charged with finding one or more substitutes with whom to share their knowledge. A third reason why cooperation was necessary, it was suggested, was for team members to learn from each other. The interviewees repeatedly stressed that there was not enough time nowadays to puzzle over a problem for long enough to find the solution to any difficulties that might arise by themselves. Today, it was said, team members had to seek help rapidly, even at the cost of revealing their own ignorance.

And yet if these multifarious cooperative relations are a characteristic feature of project work, so also is a high share of individual work. Work tasks are designed to be 'result-oriented', that is team members use their creativity, IT skills and background knowledge to translate their job requirements into the desired results. Detailed, pre-defined specifications stipulating exactly how to implement the commission tended to be the exception, rather than the rule, in project work, although the study found exceptions in those areas where specialist work tasks include standardized elements (e.g. in system testing). However, since these areas accounted for only a small share of the full range of tasks, self-organization[5] could be described as a third characteristic of project work, alongside hierarchical authority structures and cooperation.

The influence of the client

In all seven firms corporate strategy focused on the production of custom IT solutions. The openness of project work meant that clients could be involved in activities that create added value. In this way, they became an integral part of the firm's internal work organization, putting them in a position to exert considerable influence over the labour process.

It was clear from the interviews that clients generally had a destabilizing effect on project planning and realization. In many cases, their requirements did not emerge until the initial phase of a project, or even later, and project schedules were geared to a large extent to clients' time horizons. Generally speaking, the probability of a project actually evolving in accordance with the schedule agreed between an IT company and a client at the outset was all the lower the more frequently the planning process was interrupted or modified by changes in the client's requirements. For both organizational and financial reasons, clients as the end-users of the IT solutions needed to reach agreement on the proposed solutions within their own organizations, and interviewees reported delays caused by clients as one of the commonest sources of pressure in project work. Generally speaking, the agreed project schedule was not adjusted to take account of such delays that arose, for example, because clients did not provide the information or financial resources required to complete certain tasks within the agreed time frame.

Clients' influence also extended to the spatial organization of project work. At Globe, team members were sent to work at the client's premises, frequently on a staggered basis. At Netdesign, Network and Catalonien as well, project team members were seconded to the client firm for a time in certain phases of a project and according to interviewees, the links with the employer were maintained and the seconding firm remained the reference point. The situation at Globe was different. There were only a few permanent workstations in the company's office complex but a large number of 'e-places', which could be used by different employees at various times. E-places consisted of a desk and a power outlet; the workstations were cleared again after use. Here, the flexibility offered by project work was taken to its limits: the IT specialists required for each project worked at the customer's premises in order to be able to ascertain and implement the client's IT requirements and to integrate the new IT solution into the existing IT environment on-site. The daily work rhythms of the IT company's employees were determined by those of the client firm. Project team members, who were not on-site at the same time, used modern communication technologies to maintain contact with each other. Cooperation, therefore, took place in cyberspace. At Telcomp, on the other hand, the 40 members of a project team worked in close physical proximity to each other. Three to four team members, who usually constituted a project subgroup, shared a workroom. These organizational conditions facilitated close collaboration among team members, while clients were relatively ignored: at least direct access to team members was not possible in the same way as at Globe.

In each of the companies clients played a dual role in the production of IT solutions, being both purchaser and co-producer of IT solutions. This dual role was the reason why project team members found it difficult to avoid the frequently complicated and far-reaching influence of clients on the labour process, whether exerted directly or mediated by project managers. If clients were merely purchasers, the internal planning of work tasks could be governed by purely technical criteria and could take place in part at least behind closed doors. If they were only co-producers, internal sanctions could be imposed on them should they fail to meet their obligations. By virtue of their dual role, however, clients were able to exert their influence relatively unhindered. This applied particularly to project schedules: in these case-study companies, the time constraints imposed by clients impacted more or less directly on work tasks over the course of a project.

The considerable influence exerted by customers on project scheduling and realization does not call cooperation, authority structures or self-organization in project-based working into question. Rather, clients exploited the openness of project work for their own ends by steering it in a specific direction, thus fixing the coordinates specifying a project's organization. This created tension between the room for manoeuvre that exists in the labour process itself and the scope for negotiation that exists with regard to external factors. Employees enjoyed a certain degree of latitude in adapting their mode of operation to the clients' requirements. However, the scope for negotiation on external factors was all the more limited the greater the role the client played in the labour process.

The influence of indicators

Clients did not solely determine the conditions under which project-based working took place. The way such a mode of working was embedded in corporate organizational structures also helped to determine the room for manoeuvre existing in the organization of the labour process. All of the projects were treated as independent organizational units within their company, with responsibility for their own costs and results. Thus the resources made available for project realization were directly related to the revenue that could be generated by selling services in the marketplace.

One of the characteristics of decentralized organizational structures, therefore, is the direct linking of resources to market conditions. In vertically integrated companies, risk spreading and cross-subsidies mean that the labour process can be decoupled to some extent from the market, thereby stabilizing the organization as a whole. In decentralized companies, on the other hand, such instruments are eliminated in order to increase efficiency (Moldaschl 2001). Thus decentralization is simultaneously linked to the internalization of the market (Moldaschl and Sauer 2000), which becomes the force driving management of the labour process.

However, the example of these seven companies shows that the link between organizational decentralization and market internalization can manifest itself in different ways. In the smaller companies (Network, Netdesign, Init and Catalonien), projects coexisted more or less loosely. No professional standards were laid down by company management in order to monitor the economic efficiency of projects or compliance with cost and time schedules. Management monitoring of projects tended to be more personal in nature, since managerial staff or the owner was involved in the operational side of the business (albeit to a greater or lesser extent). At

Catalonien, however, changes were being introduced at the time of the interviews. In order to obtain new financing, the company was entering into a partnership with an investment company, which requested regular reports on the structure and efficiency of individual business areas and projects. Thus the introduction of internal control in this company was due to a demand emanating from the market. In the case of Routplan, it was company management that strengthened internal control following a planned reorganization of the company's internal structures. In order to be able to react more flexibly to market changes, the plan was to establish individual business areas as independent subsidiaries operating under the umbrella of a holding company. The holding company would set performance targets for the subsidiaries and monitor them by means of value-based controlling instruments.

In the two large companies, Telcomp and Globe, the rigorous decentralization of operational units had led eventually to the 'integration dilemma', as it gradually became evident that units, which had been cut free to operate independently in the market, had to be brought more closely together in one way or another. Both companies had tried to solve the dilemma through strategic recentralization: by setting uniform business targets (Haipeter, Lehndorff, Schilling, Voss-Dahm and Wagner 2002). Value-based forms of control and monitoring (Copeland, Koller and Murrin 2002; Dörre and Röttger 2003) replaced the previous bureaucratic and hierarchical forms of control in the individual business areas and numerical performance targets were set for the individual business areas. These included, in particular, general targets for sales and rates of return to be achieved within a certain period of time. These targets, set by head office, established the broad framework within which the operational side of the business functioned. A cascade breakdown of the targets was then produced and project managers were required to reconcile them with the project specifications. This process then had to be reversed, since the project coordinates had to be brought into line with the company's general business targets. At the end of this process, detailed planning targets were produced to facilitate real-time monitoring over the course of a project. At Telcomp, these planning targets were expressed as four measurable quantities: sales targets, targets for return on capital, a target for the sales to profits ratio, and the degree of manpower utilization. This latter target was the ratio of time spent directly on work to the time spent on 'overhead tasks', such as discussions, management duties, training etc.

Thus the resources available for the IT projects at Globe and Telcomp depended to a large extent on the performance targets set by head office for each individual project. Furthermore, the resourcing of projects tended to be better the stronger the IT company's bargaining power and the more generous the conditions and prices that could be negotiated. This made it clear that a strongly competitive business environment reduced the chances of a project being well funded. Indeed, projects regarded as strategically important were often deliberately under-costed in the expectation that the profits foregone initially would be recouped in subsequent projects.

The economic environment in which a project is implemented is a major factor in determining the degree of latitude in work organization. The fewer human and material resources a project uses, the greater the profit it generates. A project's profit margin increases the fewer discussions are arranged, the fewer people are employed in support functions (e.g. secretaries), the less time is spent on training and the less overtime is recompensed monetarily. At a time at which adherence to agreed budgets has a high priority for clients and IT companies are themselves subject to high financial performance targets and ensure that the impact of such targets is felt internally, high-quality technical work is not the only thing that counts. Cost efficiency is an equally important performance criterion for project groups, and indeed one that is vital to their survival. Unprofitable projects are at least as cogent a reason for disinvestment as the delivery of sub-standard technical work.

Freedom and constraints in project-based working

Observations on work organization in project-based work and the environment in which projects are implemented produces the following picture of employees' position in the labour process. Project group members enjoy genuine room for manoeuvre. Since each project is a one-off, it is difficult, and in some cases impossible, to draw up a detailed specification of the work tasks required in advance. Consequently, cooperation and self-organization are necessary elements of project-based working. (Flat) hierarchical structures, which certainly exist, ensure there is a certain division of labour in project-based working. However, these hierarchical structures are not associated with a clear separation of planning and operations and cannot therefore be equated in functional terms to those in the Taylorist labour process.

Nevertheless, a one-dimensional understanding of cooperation and self-organization, in which the existence of both these elements is taken as evidence of the existence of genuine room for manoeuvre and hence of good, progressive working conditions, cannot give a true picture of the labour process in project-based working. It is true that, compared with a Taylorist division of labour, an increase in cooperation and self-organization can be regarded as an improvement in the quality of working life and hence as a step forward in the humanization of work that is associated with correspondingly positive effects on job satisfaction, motivation and performance (Latniak *et al.* 2003). In an open form of work organization such as project-based working, however, cooperation and self-organization can go hand in hand with new stresses and demands. This paradoxical outcome is attributable to a new utilization of the increased room for manoeuvre. In situations in which the creation of 'knowledge networks' among project group members, and in some cases between different hierarchical levels, and the use of the genuine freedom individuals enjoy to organize their own work become a basic condition of the labour process, the room for manoeuvre available to project group members can quickly turn into a constraint.

To have to cooperate and to organize one's work independently can create additional stresses and demands, particularly when targets and resources are determined externally. In project-based working, the freedom that exists within the labour process is infringed by the demands of both clients and corporate management. Clients and management decide on targets as well as on the time and financial resources to be made available and hence on the foundations on which cooperation and self-organization can develop.

The ways in which the simultaneous existence of individual room for manoeuvre within the labour process and of externally imposed constraints' impact on the organization of individual working time is the subject of the next section. In the present section the structural elements of the labour process have been outlined. We turn now to the individual working time configurations to which these various structural elements give rise.

Working time sovereignty in project-based working

Working time sovereignty refers to the extent to which employees are able to influence the duration, scheduling and distribution of their individual working time. The clearest reference to this notion was found in a working time agreement concluded at Telcomp where it stated:

> All employees are able in principle to plan their own working time in accordance with the principle of working time sovereignty. The notion of working time sovereignty is taken to mean that employees are individually responsible for drawing up their own working-time schedules, with an appropriate balance being struck between operational requirements and personal interests.

This clause concisely expresses the idea that employees are to be given individual responsibility for the organization of working time. To that extent, they enjoy 'working time sovereignty'. And yet the granting of such sovereignty is immediately made subject to a constraint since, in planning their working time, employees have to take account of operational requirements. Individual working time should be in step with the demands of day-to-day business, although personal interests can also be taken into account. The other six companies had not laid down in writing such a clear definition of the organization of working time, but the elements of 'give and take' that are so clearly laid out in the Telcomp agreement, also played a major role in the other companies' working time practices.

It is immediately evident that working time sovereignty as defined above is a concept with a certain lack of clarity deliberately built into it. Nothing remains of the rigid framework with its fixed working times. In its stead, another framework is erected, within which operational requirements and individual interests in respect of time use have to be balanced. For this reason, the next section is given over to an examination of the opportunities available to employees to assert their own interests in respect of time use. We then turn to the question of how far employers are concerned with operational requirements in determining their approach to working time.

Working time sovereignty as a motivational strategy

Interviews with IT workers confirmed that they perceived working time sovereignty as one of the major advantages and privileges of their jobs and were motivated by the degree of freedom they enjoyed at work. For example,

> It's a great relief for me that we can organize our working time as we want to. Since I have a small daughter, I don't get to work on some days until the late morning or I leave at midday if I have something else to deal with.
>
> (Software developer, Telcomp)

> I make frequent use of the opportunity to organize my own working time. For example, if I go the gym in the afternoon, I work through my units of the on-line further training programme in the evening. The freedom to organize your own working time is a real privilege in our kind of work.
>
> (Software developer, Globe)

The freedom employees enjoy to organize their own working time made it easier to establish an acceptable work/life balance and thus became one source of the 'good working conditions' that have a positive effect on employees' motivation. It is not only in the academic literature that such a positive relationship is reported between the degree of autonomy and motivation (e.g. Büssing and Glaser 1998). A representative survey of German companies also found that one-third of firms declared that they were seeking to increase workforce motivation through the use of flexible forms of working time (DIHT 2000). In addition to improved workforce motivation, if employees are encouraged by the freedom of working time sovereignty to work at those times when they are particularly productive, their interests in the organization of working time and those of the employer can be reconciled.

Interviewees reported that they often deliberately worked outside normal office hours in order not to be disturbed. 'The nice thing is that you can work into the night because everybody else is asleep and there's nobody to make appointments with or waiting for you' (Software developer, Network).

It was clear from reports on teamwork outside normal hours that even the self-organized extension of working time could be a source of motivation. Working with colleagues in the final phases of projects, in the experimental phases with new technologies or in the event of spectacular system breakdowns strengthens mutual commitment. For example,

> When we buy in a new technology, everybody's really desperate to see how it works. We try it out well into the night and then again on Saturday. We generate our own knowledge about it. These situations awaken our pioneering spirit and get us interested in new solutions.
>
> (Software developer, Network)

Individual work outside normal hours was experienced positively when it led to success and was recognized. For example, a developer at Catalonien, who had had lengthy discussions with the managing director and was unable to make his views prevail, was advised to undertake a development task in a particular way. He followed this advice but was not convinced by the solution. So outside his normal working time, in the evenings and at weekends, he set to work to find another solution. When both solutions were ready, it transpired that the module he had developed outside his normal working hours was far superior to the other one in terms of both function and user-friendliness and was therefore selected for use. This example shows that freedom to organize individual working time encouraged the mobilization of personal commitment. Without having to circumvent external constraints, employees can take on the challenges work tasks pose for their individual problem-solving potential. This in turn opens up considerable opportunities for the development of professional and personal competences. To take advantage of such opportunities is perceived as particularly liberating when the end result is also recognized.

'Working time sovereignty' affects employee motivation because autonomous time management facilitates the reconciliation of employees' and employers' interests in the organization of working time. Yet there are also examples that show working time sovereignty is too frequently used in order to adjust work patterns to operational requirements and/or to serve the employer's interests in the productive use of working time. However, when working time sovereignty causes employees to perceive the company's interests as their own, the concept of socially acceptable working time organization (Büssing and Seifert, 1995) is turned on its head. The notion of socially acceptable working time organization is (implicitly) based on the assumption that employees are able strictly to separate their own working time interests from those of their employer, that they are concerned to assert their own working time interests and that their interests generally conflict with those of the employer. In the modern labour process, however, it may well be that the clear distinction between employers' and employees' interests can no longer be maintained in its familiar form. The exploitation of working time sovereignty all too readily creates incentives for individuals to increase their own productivity and to bring it to bear on the labour process.

So, can the granting of working time sovereignty create a win–win situation? Is there, in the blurred boundaries between corporate working time interests and those of individual workers, the potential to reconcile the interests of employers with those of employees? There are some indications that this may be the case under certain conditions. Since employees organize their own work and working time and generally do not do so to the disadvantage of their company, employers do not have to stipulate when they are to work. And yet besides the examples given here in which the conditions for a satisfactory compromise on working time issues seem to be met, other situations were observed in which these conditions were not met, because the actual work tasks very severely restricted employees' ability to organize their own time.

Working time sovereignty: the lubricant in project organization

Projects are impossible to organize without some degree of cooperation and self-organization, as has already been noted above. Autonomous time management is one of the important preconditions that has to be met if the potential for self-organization and cooperation that exists in project-based working is to develop at all. For this reason, working time sovereignty can be regarded as a logical element of the organizational and management strategy in the IT projects investigated in this study. In many cases, however, this potential cannot be exploited by individuals seeking to pursue their own working time interests. Rather, working time becomes a key organizational variable that plays a major part in determining whether or not the results demanded by both company and client can be produced. There are three reasons why working time becomes the 'lubricant' in project organization.

First, there is a tendency for some degree of flexibility to be required at the interfaces between team members. A cooperative system of work organization means that each individual is to some degree dependent on the work of his or her colleagues. The labour process becomes a concatenated value-added process, in which the work of others becomes the input required to complete an individual work assignment, as the following quote suggests: 'You can always rely on somebody lumbering you with a job to do' (Local works councillor, Globe).

Individuals have to keep up-to-date with their colleagues' progress as well as with the general background of the project in order to be able to put their own efforts into a meaningful context. If team members find themselves having to deal with technical problems that they cannot resolve by themselves, they turn to colleagues for advice. In such situations, independent working also includes self-organized cooperation with other project team members. Thus cooperation and self-organization are generally linked. In larger-scale projects in particular, the changes in the skill-mix that are required lead to high staff turnover, especially among highly specialized staff. The fact that sufficient time for initial orientation is not generally scheduled in also creates additional demands on people's time. Breakdowns in technical systems are another reason for unexpected departures from the planned schedule. Technologies, which in IT companies are both essential parts of the infrastructure and work objects, are susceptible to malfunctions. System failures can lead to unexpected interruptions to the labour process and it may take a long time for a system to be restored to full operation. All these situations can occur in project-based working and make it necessary to adjust individual working time to the time constraints to which projects are subject.

Second, contact with customers in their capacity as co-producers of bespoke IT solutions requires time flexibility as well as the flexibility to extend working hours. Any changes or additions to a client's requirements can turn project realization into a race against the clock, as this comment illustrates.

> We should have trained the client earlier not to be constantly changing the specifications, so that the team could have been spared the constant time pressure. The team must be able to work in peace and not be repeatedly forced to change tack.
>
> (Project manager, Telcomp)

Project group members' working time can serve as a lubricant in the planning phase as well. For example, a client may not make the required information available on time or in sufficient detail, making it necessary to expend additional time and effort in order to be able to define the work task at all.

Third, the physical distance between IT companies and their clients affects working time. It is true that communication between clients and project group members does not always require face-to-face contact. However, particularly in the planning phase and during implementation, when the IT solution is being integrated into the client's existing IT environment, direct communication with the client is necessary. Under certain circumstances, the associated travelling time can have significant effects on working time duration, which is why the question of whether all travelling time should be counted as working time was a potential source of considerable conflict in most of the companies studied. 'We cannot pay travel time to employees when it takes five hours from their home to get to a customer and then they are only there for three hours' (Project manager, Netdesign). Travelling time is not usually included in project costing and hence is not paid for by the client, which many firms give as a reason for not including all travelling time as working time (e.g. Netdesign). On the other hand, employees argue that they are travelling solely for work purposes and that all the time thus spent should, therefore, be counted as working time.

These examples show that the flexibility and openness to the client that are characteristic of project-based working make it necessary for employees to adopt a flexible approach to their own working time. These examples suggest that efforts to be adaptable lead not only to a flexible distribution of working time but also to an increase in working time. In this regard, it makes sense to link back to our discussion of authority structures, cooperation and self-organization in project-based working. In the projects we investigated, employees were not adopting a flexible approach to their working time because they had been instructed to do so by their managers. Working time flexibility is not a rule imposed from above but is organized by employees themselves. The management hierarchy has no significant influence on the management of the resource 'time'. As part of a results-driven approach to work organization, working time organization is delegated to employees themselves. Their ability to independently adapt working time to operational requirements becomes a resource that is systematically exploited in order to optimize project scheduling. Cooperation and self-organization are the preconditions that have to be met before this resource can be accessed at all. Consequently, they become the forces driving the situation-dependent distribution and extension of working time.

The extent to which this is self-determined and is therefore decided autonomously by employees themselves is the key concern in the following section, in which the question of resources is shown to be the decisive factor in power relations within the labour process.

Working time increases despite or because of working time sovereignty?

The dominant influence of the economic and business environment on project-based working was alluded to in the earlier description of the conditions under which the labour process takes place. The interviews with project team members made it clear that the economic and business environment and working time were particularly closely related when corporate targets were formulated in an unambiguous and unequivocal way. These targets, usually expressed by means of indicators, exerted pressure on project teams and hence on individual team members.

> The targets for returns to capital put pressure on the projects. I got a real shock when I learnt of the performance targets we're supposed to meet this year. They're very challenging, but not unattainable. I'll try to do whatever I can.
>
> (Project division manager, Telcomp)

> Basically, we take the view – and management agrees with us, because they're all reasonable people – that the targets are far too high.
>
> (Chair German works council, Globe)

> The performance spiral has become tighter and tighter. The infrastructure has been improved, which has led to productivity increases there. However, the demands have also increased enormously. Think shareholder value is a slogan, but the sales targets are also being set higher and higher. It's not an issue for me, but it is for some people: balancing work and private life, being unable to switch off, being unable to get things done as quickly as is required, because your own style of working cannot keep pace with what others are doing.
>
> (Sales manager, Globe)

Interviewees clearly interpreted the performance targets as fixed parameters that were non-negotiable. Consequently, they became fixed points of reference in the labour process and served to guide the process of project realization. However, for individual team members, they also became the yardstick by which their own performance was judged. As a result, the wage–effort bargain was permanently changed. The traditional form of the bargain stipulated that a predefined workload had to be completed within a given time and that this was the measure of individual performance. In the new bargain, individual performance was defined in terms of the end-point of the process. Performance was what the market recognized as such, that was the outcome of the labour process as assessed by the market (Bahnmüller 2002).

At the level of the labour process, the effect of the performance targets was that the key elements of performance regulation, namely workload and personnel, were no longer geared to the volume of work that was actually expected but remained largely concealed (Ehlscheid 2003). Instead, the resources available for a project were defined on the basis of the performance targets, thus to some extent by working backwards from the end point. Right at the outset of a project, it was established what the financial result at the end must be. Since companies set high performance targets, it became necessary to subject each stage of the labour process to a cost–benefit analysis and to systematically identify and take advantage of every single opportunity for rationalization. However, such rationalization was not only a concern for project managers, who were responsible for adjusting resource levels to each work step. Efficient working also became an important principle for individual project team members as well and as the following quotation suggests it may even be the dominant guiding principle in project work, 'You're working against time and against money and you know you have to bring it off' (Software developer, Globe).

And yet the goal of completing work tasks within the planned time was often not achieved. Long working hours were the consequence, and they were obviously part of the agenda in project-based working, at different phases within a project or even permanently. 'The contractual working week is 40 hours. In practice, it's never 40 hours, and there are some weeks when I work 70 or 80 hours' (Software developer, Network). As another explained, 'At the moment, we don't have to work 10 to 12 hours a day. In the last 3½ years, however, there's been constant pressure to do so' (Project manager, Telcomp). At Globe the local works councillor said, 'A lot of employees rush from project to project, taking time only to catch their breath but not to relax. Some of them can sustain that over a long period, others can't' (Local works councillor, Globe).

Increased working time seems to be an inevitable consequence of the tight conditions that are a feature of project-based working. Working time is a variable dependent on the practical imperatives arising out of the economic environment in which project-based work takes place. Autonomous time management is subject to restrictive external conditions and the freedoms that certainly exist at the operational level are utilized in order to achieve the performance targets. The simultaneous existence of autonomous time management and time constraints, that is the discrepancy between objectively and subjectively perceived levels of autonomy at work (Hacker 1998), has some ambivalent consequences: 'Of course self-exploitation and self-realization are very closely connected in our company' (Sales manager, Globe).

This ambivalence is a structural characteristic of the organization and management of project-based working. Employees aspire to autonomy in their use of time but their room for manoeuvre is severely restricted by the practical constraints of their work. The more independently they create time resources for themselves, the more likely it is they will be seek to use the opportunities for development for their own ends and the more directly the restrictive conditions will impact on their work, giving rise to increased pressure and time constraints.

As far as the link between working time and freedom of action is concerned, this leads to the following paradox. Employees make use of the scope for autonomous time management within a restrictive environment in order to independently extend their own working time. Thus working time increases both despite and because of working time sovereignty, because employees exceed their contractual working time, despite the freedoms they are granted, and do so because working time sovereignty gives them the freedom to take such decisions.

Summary and prospects

As the typical form of working time organization in the seven IT companies, working time sovereignty has a secure place within project-based working. In consequence, certain liberating factors are firmly established elements of the labour process. Being able to reconcile professional responsibilities with private time requirements is not the only advantage of having the freedom to plan one's own working time. In situations in which 'the rational utilization of time is no longer ordained from outside but becomes the intrinsic principle of independent, self-responsible action' (Böhle 1999: 15), it is employees who solve the problems thrown up by the temporal coordination of work flows. For employees, there is no question of a return to standard working time with its fixed, even rigid boundaries combined with external control of working time. There is no enthusiasm for a return to the 'gilded cage' of standardized working time, which would be seen as an undesirable infringement of their autonomy. Thus working time sovereignty in project-based working seems to be a genuine milestone on the road to the humanization of work.

Management interference in the detailed planning of working time belongs to the past, along with the introduction of working time sovereignty, since the shackles of fixed working times have been thrown off. Management has sloughed off responsibility for working time planning and have voluntarily left the field of battle, their employees' applause ringing in their ears. However, the question of management access to employees' productive capacity is not a thing of the past but is actually increasing in significance. In the new mode of work organization, it is not working time that is stipulated but rather the objective that has to be achieved. Consequently, the ability to adapt individual working time to operational requirements has now become an element in employees' productive capacity, a fact that is exploited by companies in the labour process. Because of the existence of working time sovereignty, the result is not just a shift in, but an intensification of, performance requirements, since management access to employees' productive capacity is strengthened by the requirement that individuals should manage working time themselves as a resource to be deployed in the labour process.

The level at which the conflict between employees' interest in life outside work and employers' interest in exploiting their productive capacity is played out has now shifted. The dispute no longer revolves around when and for how long workers should be at their employers' disposal but under what conditions their productive capacity is to be exploited within the labour process. To put it another way, the real nub of the old question of how firms could convert their employees' productive capacities into productive labour, namely the issue of the resources available in the labour process, was completely concealed by the dispute over working time. Now, however, the question of the environment in which responsible employees deploy their productive capacities is out in the open.

Working time policy faces new challenges as a result of this reconfiguration of power relations. Working time regulation, by virtue of its enshrinement in law and of its status as an object of collective bargaining, exerts considerable influence in Germany on companies' working time practices. The issue at stake now is the extent to which it is possible, by means of such regulation, to maintain the freedom to organize individual working time that is highly valued by employees, while at the same time preventing working time from becoming a resource that can be deployed without restrictions in order to complete work tasks within a restrictive environment. Thus the criterion for judging regulation must be whether working time conflicts are concealed by the promises of working time sovereignty, which would lead inevitably to the individualization of working time problems, or whether the existing working time disputes migrate from the level of the labour process to the collective level, where they can become an object of negotiation. If appropriate regulation were to make capacity planning and hence the question of workloads and staffing levels into objects of negotiation within organizations, this would constitute a further encroachment on management's right to manage. For this reason, in an environment characterized by working time sovereignty, working time disputes are more than ever linked to political disputes.

Notes

1 Working time sovereignty has particular importance in the concept of work humanization, a comprehensive programme of which was launched in Germany 30 years ago. In the 1970s, policymakers and academics agreed that the country's democratization should be extended to the world of work. Attempts to identify the prerequisites and conditions for healthy and empowering forms of work organization which could then be put into practice chimed perfectly with the spirit of the time. As a locus of life in society, the workplace was henceforth 'to offer people opportunities to develop their talents and thus to engage in a process of self-realisation' (BFM no date: 3). Some of the key issues to be addressed on the road to the humanization of work were 'the extent to which employees should plan and take responsibility for their own work, what opportunities for cooperation work might offer and what degree of esteem workers might enjoy' (BFM no date: 13). Thus the existence of a certain freedom of manoeuvre and of opportunities for cooperation, as well as the position of employees in the labour process, became key parameters in the evaluation of the labour process and hence fixed points of reference in the emerging research disciplines of ergonomics and industrial sociology.

2 The interviews were conducted as part of the following research projects: 'New Forms of Employment and Working Time in the Service Economy (NESY)', which was carried out on behalf of DG XII of the European Commission and included research in five service industries in 10 EU countries; and 'Labour and Employment Transformation in Software Engineering', which was commissioned by the French Ministry of Education, Research and Technology to examine the IT industry in the Netherlands, France and Germany.

3 Authority structures refer to the specific vertical division of labour within

projects, specifically the extent to which planning and operations or the allocation and supervision of work are separated from each other.

4 The term cooperation denotes a form of work in which the actors focus on a shared problem to which they seek to find solutions (Wehner, Clases, Endres and Raeithel 1998).

5 The degree of self-organization reflects the extent to which workers are allocated resources to use as they see fit.

References

Bahnmüller, R. (2002) 'Wandel in der Leistungsentlohnung: Ausmaß, Ziele, Formen', in D. Sauer (ed.) *Dienst-Leistung(s)-Arbeit. Kundenorientierung und Leistung in tertiären Organisationen*, München: ISF München Forschungsberichte.

Barrett, R. (2001) 'Labouring under an illusion? The labour process of software development in the Australian information industry', *New Technology, Work and Employment*, 1: 18–34.

Bauer, F., Groß, H., Munz, E. and Sayin, S. (2002) *Arbeits- und Betriebszeiten 2001. Ergebnisse einer repräsentativen Betriebsbefragung*, Köln: ISO-Institut.

Baukrowitz, A. and Boes, A. (2002) *Arbeitsbeziehungen in der IT-Industrie*, Berlin: Edition Sigma.

BMF (no date) *Information über das Forschungsprogramm: Humanisierung des Arbeitslebens*, Bonn: Bundesdruckerei.

Böhle, F. (1999) 'Entwicklungen industrieller Arbeit und Arbeitszeit – Umbrüche in der zeitlichen Organisation von Arbeit und neue Anforderungen an den Umgang mit der Zeit', in A. Büssing and Seifert, H. (eds) *Die Stechuhr hat ausgedient*, Berlin: Edition Sigma.

Bosch, G. (2001) 'Konturen eines neuen Normalarbeitsverhältnisses', *WSI-Mitteilungen*, 4: 219–30.

Büssing, A. and Glaser, J. (1998) 'Arbeitszeit und neue Organisations- und Beschäftigungsformen: Zum Spannungsverhältnis von Flexibilität und Autonomie', *MittAB*, 3: 585–98.

Büssing, A. and Seifert, H. (1995) *Sozialverträgliche Arbeitszeitgestaltung*, München, Mehring: Hampp.

Copeland, T., Koller, T., Murrin, J., Mc Kinsey & Company Inc. (2002) *Unternehmenswert, Methoden und Strategien für eine wertorientierte Unternehmensführung*, Frankfurt, New York: Campus.

Deutsches Institut für Normung (no date) *DIN-Norm 69 901 'Projekt'*, Berlin.

DIHT (2000) *Arbeitszeitflexibilisierung zur Steigerung der Wettbewerbsfähigkeit*, Berlin: Deutscher Industrie- und Handelstag.

Dörre, K. and Röttger, R. (eds) (2003) *Das neue Marktregime*, Hamburg: VSA-Verlag.

Ehlscheid, C. (2003) 'Der Arbeit wieder ein Maß geben- aber wie?' in J. Peters and H. Schmitthenner (eds) *Gute Arbeit . . .*, Hamburg: VSA-Verlag.

Hacker, W. (1998) *Allgemeine Arbeitspsychologie*, Bern: Huber.

Haipeter, T. and Lehndorff, S. 'Neuartige Formen kollektivvertraglicher Regulierung der Arbeitszeit in ausgewählten Industrie- und Dienstleistungsbranchen', unpublished manuscript, Institut Arbeit und Technik 2003.

Haipeter, T., Lehndorff, S., Schilling, G., Voss-Dahm, D. and Wagner, A. (2002)

'Vertrauensarbeitszeit. Analyse eines neuen Rationalisierungskonzepts', *Leviathan*, 3: 360–83.

Knauth, P. (2000) 'Innovative Arbeitszeitgestaltung: Wirtschaftlichkeit und Humanität?', *Zeitschrift für Arbeitswissenschaft*, 5: 292–9.

Latniak, E., Gerlmaier, A., Voss-Dahm, D. and Brödner, P. (2004) 'Projektarbeit und Nachhaltigkeit – Intensität als Preis für mehr Autonomie?', in M. Moldaschl (ed.) *Nachhaltigkeit von Arbeit und Rationalisierung* München and Mehring: Hanpp.

Moldaschl, M. (2001) 'Herrschaft durch Autonomie – Dezentralisierung und widersprüchliche Arbeitsanforderungen', in B. Lutz (ed.) *Entwicklungsperspektiven von Arbeit*, Berlin: Akademieverlag.

Moldaschl, M. and Sauer, D. (2000) 'Internalisierung des Marktes – zur neuen Dialektik von Kooperation und Herrschaft', in H. Minssen (ed.) *Begrenzte Entgrenzungen*, Berlin: Edition Sigma.

Plantenga, J. and Remery, C. (2005) 'Work hard, play hard?' in G. Bosch and S. Lehndorff (eds) *Working in the service society*, London: Routledge.

Rubery, J. and Grimshaw, D. (2001) 'ICTs and employment: the problem of job quality', *International Review of Labour*, 2: 165–92.

Seifert, H. (1995) 'Kriterien für eine sozialverträgliche Arbeitszeitgestaltung', in A. Büssing and H. Seifert (eds) *Sozialverträgliche Arbeitszeitgestaltung*, Berlin: Edition Sigma.

Trautwein-Kalms, G. and Ahlers, E. (2003) 'High Potentials unter Druck', in M. Pohlmann, M. D. Sauer, G. Trautwein-Kalms and A. Wagner (eds) *Dienstleistungsarbeit- Auf dem Boden der Tatsachen*, Berlin: Edition Sigma.

Wagner, A. (2000) 'Arbeiten ohne Ende?', in Institut Arbeit und Technik (ed.) *Jahrbuch Institut Arbeit und Technik 1999/2000*, Gelsenkirchen.

Wehner, T., Clases, C., Endres. E. and Raeithel, A. (1998) 'Zusammenarbeit als Ereignis und Prozess', in E. Spieß (ed.) *Formen der Kooperation*, Göttingen: Hogrefe.

7 Professional identity in software work

Evidence from Scotland

Abigail Marks and Cliff Lockyer[1]

Introduction

Identity is a central concept in social psychology. Indeed, social identities in the form of social categories such as gender, ethnicity, nationality, religion and profession are internalized and constitute a potentially important part of an individual's self-concept. Self-categorization into these groups provides important and meaningful self-references through which individuals perceive themselves and their relationship with other groups. In the modern world one of the most poignant identities for individuals is their membership of a profession and it is this facet of identification that we discuss in this chapter.

There is a belief that western economies are becoming increasingly reliant on knowledge (Drucker 1993), and that new professions such as financial advisors, management consultants and software developers have emerged as a response to these demands (Scarborough 1996). Employees operating within these occupations are frequently referred to as 'knowledge workers' (Reed 1996). However, most empirical and theoretical discussion on knowledge workers tends to focus on three unified themes (Tam, Korczynski and Frenkel 2002; von Glinow 1988): the first is concerned with the nature of knowledge and learning; the second looks at the management–employee relationships for knowledge workers; and the third investigates the processes knowledge workers use to protect their expertise and related rewards.

This chapter develops the final theme identified above. Although the relationships between loyalty, commitment and identification have been extensively researched for traditional professions such as medicine and law, despite some broad discussion about the commitment and identification of knowledge-intensive workers (Alvesson 2000; Tam *et al.* 2002), we know little about the antecedents and process of identification for knowledge workers.

The purpose of this chapter is to make some attempt to resolve part of this issue. Despite Ackroyd, Glover and Currie (2000) designating software analysts as the key occupation to examine in future studies of 'knowledge workers', we know even less about the nature and experience of work for software developers than we do for knowledge workers as a whole (Beirne, Ramsey and Panteli 1998), and we know even less about the professional identity for these software developers.

In this chapter we analyse debates about the concept of professional identity in order to focus specifically on the question of whether working in either a professional or non-professional organization has implications for professional or organizational identification of software developers. Essentially we are interested in whether software developers' professional identity has greater salience than their organizational identity when they work in software (professional) firms compared with when they work in software departments of user (non-professional) firms.

In the next section we summarize the main arguments concerned with professional identification in the context of the work performed by software developers. We then examine the four key aspects of professional work (control and autonomy; cognitive demand; qualifications and career opportunities; collegiality/professional networks) along with the relationship between these four dimensions and professional and organizational identification. These issues are explored in the context of two Scottish software organizations: Omega, a medium sized independent software house and Beta, a software division of a large national communications company.

Software professionals

'Profession', 'professional' and 'professionalization' can be examined from a functionalist perspective, in terms of 'closure' or from an interactionist perspective. From a functionalist perspective a profession is a group of individuals who share a code of ethics, single qualifying entry route and certification, a strong professional association, technical, political and/or economic control of knowledge and monopolization of a particular market (Parsons 1951; Alvesson 2000). In terms of closure, the theory of closure (Collins 1979) focuses on the strategy adopted by occupational groups to achieve closure and control, and is more closely associated with managerialist perspectives. However, when professions are examined from an interactionist perspective, as they are in this chapter, it is more important to understand how professionals construct their social worlds as participants, and how they construct their careers (Abbott 1988; Crompton 1990; Fitzgerald and Ferlie 2000) than examine the traits of particular occupations. The interactionist approach focuses on the everyday actions and interactions of professions and acknowledges ambiguities in the concept of 'profession'.

Clearly 'profession' is a contested concept, but in this chapter we follow other writers on information technology (IT) where a profession is viewed as the way the occupational group fashions itself to be regarded as a profession by themselves, other professions, industry, government and the public (for example, Sonnentag 1995; Waterson, Clegg and Axtell 1997). Thus, although software development does not possess the features ascribed by functionalists to a profession, software developers can be described as professionals in so much as they have an implicit set of professional codes and common beliefs values and ceremonies (Alvesson 2000). Importantly, by this rationale, software developers are viewed as professionals by employing organizations.

Yet, many researchers within the field argue that the diversity of software development work reflects distinctions and differences in professionalization of the occupation. In the UK almost half of the personnel in the information and communication technology (ICT) industry are found in non-dedicated ICT organizations rather than the computer services industry where dedicated software development firms exist (DfES 2002). This variety of occupational settings reflects the diversity of work in which software developers engage, ranging from the routine to the cutting edge (Barrett 2001).

This difference in the complexity and nature of software development work has led to competing views of software developers' organizational position. The first is a functionalist concern with the integration of software developers into business organizations. From this perspective, software developers are classified as professionals, with perhaps an eccentric and piecemeal pattern of occupational development (Scarborough 1993), and a division of labour based on knowledge and expertise. The second is a more critical perspective, which sees the management of software expertise as part of a horizontal division between managers and software developers (Barrett 2001). From this labour process view, the division of work into high level development work and lower level 'dirty work' of data inputting and operations, is seen as evidence of work specialization and occupational fragmentation, including job de-skilling and the extension of bureaucratic control (Kraft and Dubnoff 1979; Scarborough 1993).

Despite the diversity in day-to-day software development work, the qualifications of those doing the work and the employment policies in the firms where software developers work, this group of employees have a collective notion of professionalism through conscious schemas learned either in formal education or on-the-job socialization which occurs by working with other software developers (Bloor and Dawson 1994). Consistent with the interactionist perspective this group is viewed as a professional group and in doing so organizations tend to isolate software developers from the broader management of knowledge within the company (Waterson *et al.* 1997). However it also raises the question that if employing organizations view software developers as a separate occupational (and professional) group, is there really a difference between software developers' professional identity when they work in professional or non-professional organizations?

Professional identification

In order to understand how this collective notion of professionalism is formed it is useful to look at social identity theory (SIT) (for example, Turner 1982, 1984; Ashforth and Mael 1989). An individual's work identity refers to an employment-based self-representation, which is composed of organizational, occupational/professional, team and other identities that affect the way individuals think about themselves in the context of their work. Identities are important as they 'suggest what to do, think and even feel' (Ashforth and Kreiner 1999: 417).

SIT is used to describe the degree to which individuals define themselves in terms of their membership of a collective, and how individuals' feelings of self-worth are reflected in the status of the collective. SIT suggests that the key function served by membership of a collective is not the provision of resources, but the provision of social identity information to members which aids in their efforts to develop and maintain a favourable self-concept (Tyler and Blader 2001). SIT suggests that individuals self-categorize in order to reduce uncertainty, as uncertainty reduction, specifically about matters of value that are self-conceptually relevant, is 'a core human motivation' (Hogg and Terry 2000: 124). Certainty is important, as it presents confidence in how to behave and what to expect from a particular social situation.

One method of examining social identity is to view identification as the degree to which people cognitively merge their sense of self and the collective. That is, the extent to which individuals think of themselves and the collective in similar terms or define themselves in terms of the membership of the collective (Rousseau 1998; Tyler and Blader 2001). Professional identification can, therefore, be defined as the strength of an individual's psychological link to their profession or occupation (Tyler and Blader 2001). This link may be implicit or explicit for an individual who says, for example, that being an IT manager is very important to their sense of self as a person. However, even if individuals are unaware they merge themselves and the collective, they may say, for example when asked to talk about themselves, 'I am John Smith, I am an IT manager', thereby subconsciously referring to themselves in terms of the collective.

Although early laboratory research on SIT (Tajfel 1970) suggested that placing an individual in a collective was sufficient to foster identification, the same cannot be said within an applied, and specifically an organizational, setting. Furthermore, there are degrees of identification and the extent to which identification affects behaviour and attitude depends on the degree to which the individual identifies with the profession. For example, previous research by Ashforth and Mael (1989) and Wiesenfeld, Raghuram and Garud (2001) has specified several predictors of identification including the extent of contact between the individual and the profession and the visibility of professional membership.

Organizational identification and professional organizations

As already noted, as much as professionals may be a distinct group within the organization, this group also has a relationship with the organization and therefore individuals within this group will have varying degrees of organizational identification. Ashforth and Mael (1989: 22) argue that 'organizational identification is a specific form of social identification' and it depends on the individual's perception of 'oneness' with the organization (Ashforth and Mael 1989; Mael and Ashforth 1995). Since organizational identification, in part, shapes self-concept, it is frequently associated with work-related attitudes such as affective commitment, supervisor satisfaction and legitimacy (Tyler and Blader 2001). The degree of organizational identification for professionals is important as it is associated with such behaviours as the extent to which employees are motivated to fulfil organizational needs and goals, their willingness to display organizational citizenship and their tendency to remain within the organization (Mael and Ashforth 1992; Dutton and Dukerich 1994). Subsequently, organizational identification is seen as essential for the co-operation, co-ordination and long-term effort of employees (Wiesenfeld *et al.* 2001).

We noted earlier that individuals self-categorize group membership in order to reduce uncertainty (Hogg and Abrams 1993; Hogg and Mullin 1999) and gain positive uniqueness. In terms of organizational identification, employees develop a prototype, which embodies distinct 'beliefs, attitudes, feelings and behaviours' (Hogg and Terry 2000: 123) about the organization, and it is this that helps to reduce uncertainty. The stronger an individual identifies with the self-categorization, the more likely this category will affect behaviour. However, for professional groups, members also have an identification with, and self-categorization as, a member of a profession.

Indeed, all organizations comprise multiple social groups including work teams, departments and, of course, professional groups. Each of these is a potential source of identification for the individual working within the organization (Tajfel and Turner 1979). These nested collectives have formed the basis for researchers looking at identity salience in organizations. Individuals do not express their multiple identities simultaneously. At any one time some identities are salient and others are not (Rock and Pratt 2002). Salient identities are the ones most likely to influence behaviour, and as the salience of identities varies so do associated behaviours and attitudes (Stryker 1987). Research indicates that with multiple targets of identification the core values need to be similar in order to create compatibility, and therefore self-categorization in terms of one group does not preclude self-categorization in terms of another group (Gallois, Tluchowska, and Callan 2001).

However, when different identities become inconsistent, a sense of identity dissonance is created (Elsbach and Kramer 1996) and this triggers responses aimed at establishing consistency in the different facets of identity. As a result individuals are forced to make one identity more salient than the other(s) (Cherim 2002). Gouldner (1957) recognized the potential for conflict between organizational identification and professional identification, while Sorenson (1967) argued that organizational–professional conflict resulted from the incompatibility of organizational and professional values, such as ethics and autonomy.

Professional identification in professional and non-professional organizations

The key question in this chapter is what impact does working in a professional or a non-professional organization have on software developers' professional identification? Wallace (1995) argues that professional employees work either within professional organizations or non-professional organizations. Professional organizations are those where the majority of employees are occupied with similar types of work and the content of that work is fundamental to the organization's purpose and goals. Such organizations include legal and accounting firms and medical practices. Non-professional organizations are those where professional employees are in the minority and they usually work together within a specialist department or subunit, for example, the legal department of an accounting firm. As noted earlier, over half of British software developers work in non-professional organizations (DfES 2002).

To explore the impact of where software developers work on their professional identification we can look to the proletarianization and adaptation theses. The proletarianization thesis (for example, Oppenheimer 1973; Boreham 1983) suggests that the department in which professionals work would possess the same bureaucratic characteristics as the larger non-professional organization. This means that when professionals work in non-professional organizations they would identify with the larger organization (being the same as their department within that organization) and the result would be the erosion of their professional identification. In other words organizational identification would be more salient for professionals in non-professional organizations than professional identification.

Alternatively, the adaptation thesis (Wallace 1995) suggests that professionals in non-professional organizations are isolated and they would therefore 'mimic the structural arrangements of true professional organizations' (Wallace 1995: 230), specifically in terms of discretion and control over their professional work. Hence, these professional departments in non-professional organizations actually operate as mini-professional organizations and their professional identification is preserved. In essence this thesis suggests that the professional identity of software developers in non-professional organizations would have greater salience than organizational identification.

How working in a professional or non-professional organization affects the professional identification for software developers is examined in the next part of this chapter. In the following section we examine overall variations in professional and organizational identification in two organizations employing software developers in Scotland. We also investigate the four broad dimensions that mould professional work: (1) control and autonomy; (2) cognitive demand; (3) qualifications and career opportunities; and (4) collegiality/professional networks is these two organizations. Prior to this, however we detail the research context and our research methods.

Software developers in Scotland

Research sample and methods

The research in this chapter is part of a larger three-year project looking at the nature and experience of work in the twenty-first century. For the project we examined five software organizations, however only one was a non-professional organization – Beta. Hence, in this chapter we focus on this organization and one other large professional organization of a similar size and demography – Omega.

Where possible, Yin's (1994) recommendations for case study research were followed. The data collection process involved a triangulation of methods, specifically the collection of archival records (company history, operating procedures, and employment policies and staff characteristics), semi-structured interviews, work observation, and an organizational survey. Although all of these methods inform this research, the results of the interviews and the survey only are reported here. However, when using triangulation we took into account the limitations placed by the implicit structures of organizations and we could not always examine each construct with every research tool.

Beta is a software engineering division of a former publicly owned telecommunications company. At Beta the software development ranges from bespoke systems dealing with telephone operations (voice recognition, emergency and screen-based linkages) to robotic tools for personal computers to the protection, modification and integration of databases, special complex events and financial systems. The majority of the 275 employees are based in the head office in Glasgow. The remaining employees are based at a satellite office in Edinburgh. Most employees are engaged in projects lasting several years which contained a number of related but independent projects and work programs.

Omega, established in the 1980s, is one of the largest independent Scottish-based software houses and at the time of the research operated from one main site in Scotland and one site in southern England. A total of 137 permanent employees and 111 contractors[2] are based in Scotland working on IT services and solutions predominantly for the public sector, including applications development, knowledge management, resourcing, testing and client support. The 50 employees at the satellite office focus on AS400 technology and a combination of new build and maintenance work, generally for commercial sector clients.

Much of the work at the Scottish-based Omega operations is generated from long-term links with government, health services and some financial sector organizations. A significant proportion of Omega's work is undertaken on client sites.[3] At Omega work is also based around project teams and these projects last for two to three months to several years. The projects that Omega Head Office employees work on tend to be shorter than those which developers working off-site in client organizations tend to undertake.

All available employees at Beta and Omega based permanently at their Head Office, or satellite operations or working in client sites (Omega only) received a survey as part of a more extensive data collection process. Surveys were distributed directly to all available technical employees[4] by a team of researchers over a four-week period during 2000 and 2001. A total of 333 surveys were distributed – 163 in Omega and 170 at Beta – and 245 completed surveys were returned, representing response rates of 78 per cent (Omega) and 67 per cent (Beta). These high response rates reflect the direct contact between employees and the research team.

Full details regarding the number of survey responses from each site are listed in Table 7.1. The survey data were analysed using a series of t-tests and one-way analysis of variance (ANOVAs) in order to ascertain whether there were any differences between Beta and Omega or the different work sites at Beta and Omega in terms of professional and organizational identification, control, autonomy, cognitive demand, career-related factors, and professional networks.

In order to further understand the nature of identity we also conducted

Table 7.1 Quantitative data research sites and sample profile

	Beta	*Omega*
Head office location	Glasgow	Edinburgh
Surveys distributed	150	88
Surveys returned	103	77
Satellite office location	Edinburgh	Southern England
Surveys distributed	20	50
Surveys returned	11	28
Off-site location	n/a	Edinburgh
Surveys distributed		25
Surveys returned		23

Note
All available employees were surveyed.

a series of interviews with 10 teams in both organizations. The teams were chosen on a number of criteria including that the team had been in existence for at least six months, had more than three members and that the team accurately represented the nature of the software development work being undertaken at the particular site where they were located. Sixty-seven interviews (or 75 per cent of members of the 10 teams) were conducted, each lasting between 60 and 90 minutes (see Table 7.2 for details of the interview samples). Each interview was either transcribed verbatim or produced as field notes and coded by the researchers. A qualitative data analysis software package (nVivo 1.2) was used both for data management purposes (i.e. to organize all hardcopy and electronic documents, including labour market/industry statistics and the different types of case study notes produced by researchers), and for data analysis. The data were interrogated by using a key word search within the nVivo package.

At Omega and Beta the majority of respondents were male, particularly at Beta, which had 82 per cent male employees compared with 67 per cent at Omega. Omega and Beta were similar in terms of other demographic characteristics: 70 per cent of employees were aged between 21 and 40 years; around 30 per cent were single and another third had dependants or care responsibilities; and an average of 25 per cent had some management responsibility for people or projects. Tenure was substantially longer at Beta for permanent employees (a median of eight years compared with three years in Omega), while tenure for contractors averaged 20 months at Omega and 16 months at Beta. The length of tenure for these employees confirms the generally longer-term contracts typical in non-permanent IT work. Although there were differences in tenure between the two organizations, similar patterns were present in terms of the length of employment of head office employees versus offsite employees. At Beta, head office employees had worked an average of 96 months, while satellite

Table 7.2 Qualitative data research sites and sample profile

	Beta	*Omega*
Head office location	Glasgow	Edinburgh
Number of project teams investigated	3	2
Number of individuals in each team	7, 8, 10	8, 12
Satellite office location	Edinburgh	Southern England
Number of project teams investigated	1	1
Number of individuals in each team	8	9
Off-site location	n/a	Edinburgh (2 client sites)
Number of project teams investigated		3
Number of individuals in each team		12, 7, 8

Note
Due to resource limitations only specific teams were studied in each location.

office employees had a mean of 282 months. At Omega the tenure of head office employees was 32 months on average, whereas offsite employees' mean tenure was 58 months and an average length of employment of 73 months. At Omega, 20 per cent of employees were outsourced to host organizations.

Employee constructions of identification within the organizations

Employee views about organizational and professional identification and related domains were obtained from the employee survey and interviews. Survey responses provided data on general attitudes whilst the interviews exemplified those factors determining employee orientations towards the foci of identification. As well as a broad discussion of the relative strengths and determinants of identification within Beta and Omega, we also considered four other factors which shape professional work and impact upon the relationship between organizational and professional identification: (1) control and autonomy, (2) cognitive demand, (3) qualifications and career opportunities, and (4) collegiality/professional networks.

Organizational identification was assessed quantitatively using a modified version of Mael and Ashforth's (1992) organizational identification scale. The five items (for example, 'I feel that my values and those of the company are very similar' and 'I feel that the company's problems are my own') were averaged to form a composite score representing organizational identification ($\alpha=0.80$). Three specific items, modified from Mael and Ashforth's (1992) scale, were used to measure occupational identification (for example, 'If I could, I would go into a different occupation') and were averaged for a composite score ($\alpha=0.77$).

Overall the mean scores for both professional and occupational identification were above the midpoint of the scale (Table 7.3). However, these results indicated, for employees within Beta and Omega and across all sites, that professional identification was more salient for software developers than organizational identification. Although there were no differences in professional identification ($F=0.99$; $p=0.41$) or organizational identification ($F=2.03$; $p=0.09$) across sites or for professional identification between the organizations ($t=0.43$; $p=0.76$), Omega employees had stronger organizational identification than Beta employees ($t=2.82$; $p=0.005$).

The interviews located a number of issues associated with the low levels of organizational identification. Beta employees frequently commented on the faceless bureaucratic nature of the organization. Comments such as, 'Promoting a national Beta work identity is a lost cause, people won't identify with a large national organization' (Beta, female software engineer) were common. Concerns were also voiced about the extent to which Beta was still the centre for interesting software development work,

Table 7.3 Means and standard deviations for key variables

	Omega N=126		*Beta N=108–9*		*Omega Head office N=74*		*Omega Satellite office N=28*		*Omega Off-site N=23*		*Beta Head office N=99*		*Beta Satellite office N=11*	
	Mean	*SD*	*Mean*	*SD*	*Mean*	*SD*	*Mean*	*SD*	*Mean*	*SD*	*Mean*	*SD*	*Mean*	*SD*
Professional identification	3.67	0.72	3.62	0.71	3.75	0.78	3.64	0.66	3.42	0.58	3.62	0.73	3.61	0.49
Organizational identification	3.19	0.68	2.94	0.69	3.20	0.75	3.18	0.59	3.15	0.58	2.93	0.69	2.98	0.78
Method of control	3.85	0.67	3.99	0.51	3.78	0.68	4.06	0.67	3.84	0.59	3.98	0.50	4.09	0.56
Cognitive demand	3.85	0.77	4.03	0.78	3.84	0.79	4.06	0.73	3.68	0.75	3.98	0.79	4.42	0.68
Career prospects	4.16	1.29	3.81	1.23	3.99	1.46	4.36	1.13	4.48	0.73	3.88	1.28	3.27	1.42
Importance of on the job training	2.46	1.04	2.78	0.99	2.39	1.07	2.79	0.88	2.24	1.11	2.70	0.99	3.55	0.69
Importance of college/university	2.64	0.86	2.69	0.97	2.65	0.83	2.54	0.88	2.74	0.96	2.81	0.91	1.64	0.81
Importance of colleagues	3.09	0.74	3.25	0.78	3.04	0.78	3.04	0.64	3.32	0.72	3.29	0.77	2.91	0.83
Socialize with team	2.13	0.83	2.26	1.00	2.22	0.70	2.04	0.70	1.96	9.21	2.29	1.00	2.00	0.63
Socialize with other work	2.02	0.75	2.07	0.97	2.12	0.79	1.93	0.61	1.78	0.67	2.09	0.99	1.91	0.83
Socialize with previous colleagues	1.94	0.59	1.97	0.66	1.99	0.65	1.81	0.48	1.96	0.48	2.02	0.66	1.55	0.52
Others doing similar work	1.89	0.75	1.72	0.73	2.05	0.72	1.74	0.86	1.75	0.74	1.45	0.68	1.81	0.75

and the durability of the organization in the face of outsourcing pressures. As a young head office employee noted:

> In particular, many people seem to have an identity problem. With the rate of change introduced and with people moving from one project to another, they find it difficult identifying with anything but the company as a whole. However, identifying with a company as big as Beta requires identification at a very abstract level and does not really work.
>
> (Beta, male software developer)

Omega employees responded similarly, believing that the organization was more project focused than organizationally focused. A middle-aged software developer at Omega who worked off-site said, 'I think you don't really feel part of Omega. I usually go to events like the BBQ, I see even less faces than I used to know' (Omega, female software developer).

Employees at both Omega and Beta viewed themselves as being committed to and identifying with their work, and more so than either their work team or their organization. During the interviews there were frequent references to this. For example, in an interview with a Beta head office employee he said, 'I think the priority would be to the project, then the team and then to the company and then to the local thing somehow'. He then said, 'I do feel a sense of commitment toward the company but not directly, I've never felt really committed so much to the company as to my project', and he later said, 'In practical terms, employees would think of themselves as project based; the groups have a bit of an identity' (Beta, male software engineer). Another Beta, male, software developer also referred to the role of the project in terms of the development of identity,

> In the past that would have been true that there was more of a centre identity. And it's probably still there a bit. It is just that the more time people spend on a project, then you begin to lose the organizational identity. It becomes more on a personal basis than a work basis.

However, some employees were prepared to identify with the organization rather than their profession when they believed being seen as a software developer had negative connotations, as shown in the following quote.

> By and large I am more likely to tell people that I work for Beta than I am a software engineer. People in the world view software engineers as a little bit funny. They are probably a bit like outsiders I would say.... Software engineering is viewed as a dull but well paid profession.
>
> (Beta, male software engineer)

Autonomy, control and professional work

In earlier chapters of the book the work software developers perform is addressed and a series of arguments about autonomy and control are advanced. Expanding on this, we found that software developers tend to be engaged in open-ended work conducted in a low bureaucratic working environment (Kunda 1992; Alvesson 1995). Looser forms of management, based on responsibility, personal control, and the creation of trust, have been advocated for 'knowledge work' in general, because of the intrinsic job satisfaction and commitment typical of the work and the workforce (Drucker 1993). Research targeted at engineers in high tech companies generally reports typically non-bureaucratic management styles and highly committed employees (Kunda 1992).

Beirne *et al.* (1998) and Friedman (1990) propose that software developers seek and value intrinsically interesting and challenging work, and that it is around this that the identity of the software professional is focused. Barrett (2001) also believes that autonomy, particularly in terms of time management, is used as a deliberate strategy by managers to ensure that work is completed; routinization of work would lead to employees resisting as the work would no longer fit their sense of self (Barrett 2001).

In the survey, control and autonomy were examined using five items measuring job control on a scale of 1 'not at all' to 5 'a great deal' drawn from the *Perceived Intrinsic Job Characteristics Scale* (Warr, Cook and Wall 1979). This included items on control over method of working, opportunity to use own skills, and amount of job variety ($\alpha = 0.74$). Overall levels of control were found to be high for all groups in Omega and Beta (Table 7.3), and an independent samples t-test found no significant differences between Omega and Beta ($t = -1.87$; $p = 0.63$). Again, an ANOVA did not show any differences between sites ($F = 1.93$; $p = 0.10$).

The interview data showed little evidence of a difference in terms of control between Omega and Beta. However, overall the data concurred with the arguments made earlier in this volume: specifically that those employees who performed less routinized tasks clearly viewed themselves as having greater autonomy, and this, in turn, impacted upon how they viewed both their role and their professional identification. As one Beta employee commented, 'It makes a difference how much autonomy you have within your job and how much effect you see in what you do. You are a bigger player rather than a small cog in a big wheel' (Beta, female software engineer).

Professional roles and cognitive demand

From both the academic literature and the fieldwork, there is substantial evidence that autonomy and control is linked to cognitive demand. Beirne *et al.* (1998) and Friedman (1990) propose that software developers seek and value intrinsically interesting and challenging work, and that it is around this that the identity of the software professional is focused.

Three questions on cognitive demand were drawn from a scale devised by Jackson, Wall, Martin and Davids (1993) and measure on a scale of 1 'not at all' to 5 'a great deal'. These items included monitoring demand (for example, 'the requirement to pay close and constant attention') and problem-solving demand (for example, 'the requirement to diagnose and solve problems'). Results were analysed using a one-way ANOVA and a t-test ($\alpha = 0.73$). Although there were no differences between Omega and Beta ($t = 1.71$; $p = 0.09$) and between the sites ($F = 2.81$; $p = 0.061$), the mean score for cognitive demand was high across the board.

We found considerable evidence at Omega and Beta that employees undertaking more complex tasks presented more professional behaviours, specifically in terms of self-development and working longer shifts. As a software developer at Omega noted, 'hours are part and parcel of the job. There is a great deal of professional pride' (Omega, male software developer). A young team leader at Beta signalled these inter-relationships clearly:

> [M]y work is 'state-of-the-art'. It is high-pressure work as there are constant deadlines. People working [in this field] like the buzz. I don't need to encourage people to work overtime. They often come in at the weekend to work on problems or to meet customers' demands without me knowing about it. All members of this team have a high level of control over how they structure their time and how they carry out tasks.
>
> (Beta, male team leader)

This perspective was confirmed by another Beta staff member.

> [T]hey (employees) are motivated by success and by top targets and by that kind of achievement and that is the kind of people that we recruit here and so that is part of the whole dynamic of being in software development but we have to make sure we don't abuse that.
>
> (Beta, male team leader)

Software careers and qualifications

As stated earlier, software developers often do not follow a traditional career development or knowledge acquisition routes. For professionals or knowledge workers, a traditional model of acquiring and controlling knowledge through specialist functions within business hierarchies is increasingly being displaced in favour of networking and market style arrangements (Whittington, Pettigrew, Peck, Fenton and Conyon 1999).

Although the role of occupational communities is discussed in the next section, it is important to recognize research showing that professional identification is not related to the possession of a formal entry route into software development represented by specific IT qualifications (Marks and Lockyer 2004). If there is evidence of a professional identity emerging from a traditional qualification route and non-traditional routes into software development, then this suggests an alternative conception of professional identification from the traditional, hierarchical model of socialization into professional norms. If career and skills development are based on networking arrangements, then professional organizations may provide greater opportunities for career development than non-professional organizations.

In order to investigate this quantitatively, four single items (Table 7.3) were used. The first item, career satisfaction, was measured based on items from the short form of the *Minnesota Satisfaction Questionnaire* (Weiss, Dawis, England and Lofquist 1967), using a seven-point scale from 7 'extremely dissatisfied' to 1 'extremely satisfied'. The other three items were measured on a five-point scale from 5 'very' to 1 'not at all important' and dealt with the importance of on-the-job training, college/university and colleagues to career/skill development.

No differences were found between Omega and Beta for any of these items. Colleagues were seen as the most important vehicle for knowledge acquisition, followed by formal education and then on-the-job training. The interviews further illustrated the ways in which colleagues and qualifications related to professional development. For example,

> At the moment I have not used a lot of my skills such as system design or learning new topics as there has not been much call for that in my work. The range of skills I obtained at university is diverse and probably couldn't use all of them in any project.
>
> (Beta, female software engineer)

More generally, access to training was largely seen in terms of company requirements rather than individual development. This was more evident for older employees who frequently felt that they were not given opportunities to learn new software development languages. They also felt that their career was effectively focused on a particular area of work, as this quote reveals: 'I feel that my skills have not been utilized very well. I have spent most of my time focusing on to very small areas' (Omega, female systems analyst).

Employees frequently commented on the nature of software development work – largely a series of finite projects – that necessitated them choosing between projects as part of a planned career trajectory. People tended to stay on a project for two or three years before moving, or being moved, to another project. Having to develop new skills, either to gain access to a new project or to work effectively on a project, was necessary whether the employee's aim was to further develop skills and knowledge with a particular software language, develop an expertise in a new language or application, or gain promotion to team leader or to higher-level analysis work. For some employees an internal labour market offered some opportunities to transfer between projects, or to bid to work on particular new and/or ongoing projects, but for others, the choice was either staying or leaving for another organization.

Collegiality/professional networks

As well as the importance of work colleagues for knowledge acquisition, occupations and life are closely linked and the software developer's professional identification is reinforced by socialization within the occupational community. In software development occupational communities are said to form as a result of the social processes of software development (Sawyer and Guinan 1998). As the software development production process is based around team working, this encourages both informal and intra-group co-ordination activities (Marks and Lockyer 2004). The high degree of interaction between employees leads to close relationships, which continue after the team disbands or members leave the organization (Sawyer and Guinan 1998).

The extent to which developers socialize with work colleagues was measured within a set of questions examining broader patterns of socialization. On the survey employees were asked how often they had contact, on a social basis outside work, with various groups including: people from the work team; other people from work; former colleagues; and other people doing similar work. This was measured on a five-point scale from 1 'never' to 5 'daily'.

Comparatively little regular socializing was reported with work team members (Table 7.3) and especially with other members of the workforce. Despite relatively low levels of socialization with former colleagues and other people undertaking similar work, there was some evidence, particularly from interviews, that socialization with other members of the occupational group reinforced professional identification.

The t-test results suggest that Beta employees socialized more with their work team ($t=-1.1$; $p=0.01$) and other work colleagues ($t=-0.49$; $p=0.01$) than Omega employees, but no other significant differences were located. The ANOVAs revealed few significant differences, however, those employees working at the Omega head office (the only specific software site in the organization) were more likely to socialize within the broader software community than other groups of employees ($F=3.84$; $p=0.00$).

Our interviews also found a low level of socializing with workmates, especially among the younger unmarried workers, and most of this centred on occasions such as birthdays, engagements, or someone leaving. A few had made friendships at work that were the basis for more long-term socialization patterns. One female, offsite Omega employee noted, 'there are a lot more social events for teams on their own, because we have a lot of reason – every time we win on the lottery we just go out and spend it'.

Discussion and conclusions

The purpose of this chapter was to investigate professional identification for software developers and the impact which working in a professional or non-professional organization has on professional and organizational identity. However, conclusions drawn from this study must be interpreted within the boundaries of the research methodology. First, because our quantitative data analysis strategy solely considered the comparisons of means, we cannot make any claims regarding causality. Longitudinal research using predictive models needs to be adopted if any causal linkages are to be drawn. Second, although we used a combination of qualitative and quantitative techniques, the quantitative data were gathered using one questionnaire, hence, common method variance may have affected relationships. Finally, we concentrated on only two organizations operating in Scotland and so there are limits to which our results can be viewed as generalizable.

In this chapter a number of themes emerge. Notably, the impact of the nature of the organization on identification, the effect of autonomy, control and cognitive demand on professional identity, the role of colleagues and broader occupational communities for the construction of professional identity, and the extent to which existing arguments regarding the effects of professional and non-professional organizations are applicable within this type of work

Overall there were very limited differences between our professional organization (Omega) and non-professional organization (Beta) in terms of the factors under examination. The singular area in which we found a difference was in terms of patterns of socialization. Beta employees socialized more with their work team and other work colleagues, while Omega (head office) employees were more likely to socialize with the broader software community. However, overall data indicated that socialization with the team was more common than with other employees and socialization with people doing similar work outwith the organization was relatively limited.

This can be explained in terms of broader patterns of software development and IT work. As well as numbers of individuals employed within the IT industry rising, the scope of activities and sectors of employment have also increased. Industries that were previously removed from the IT sector such as catering and manufacturing are being impacted by technology and software. Even human resource management is becoming dependent on software for recording personnel data and computer-based psychometric testing. The arrival of e-commerce and the Internet has forced many organizations to explore IT and software options for essential business use.

Software development is therefore no longer confined to dedicated IT (or professional) organizations and software developers are increasingly located either permanently or temporarily within user (or non-professional) organizations. As a consequence software developers have more customer contact than ever before, and their workplace interactions are with a wider group of workplace actors. This can be seen with our research sites. At Beta software developers worked with internal clients, whereas at Omega software developers provided services for other organizations and as a result many developers were located off-site. Omega employees were therefore more likely to have interactions with other organizations and other organizational members and hence their team and their organization became a more salient focus for these employees. Yet, despite these differences, we found no differentiation between the two organizations in terms of professional and, indeed, organizational identification.

Overall we found high levels of professional identification compared with organizational identification. Beta employees explained limited organizational identification in terms of their position in a 'faceless' bureaucracy. At Omega, the separation of developers from head office, either permanently or on a temporary basis, was the way this result was rationalized.

Although it is problematic to make generalizations on the basis of two case studies, our results suggest that neither the adaptation thesis nor the proletarianization thesis strictly apply to software developers. We found no evidence that software developers based in non-professional organizations felt their professional status was being eroded (as suggested by the proletarianization thesis). However, to suggest that this group were unique in preserving their identity as a response to isolation from similar professionals (as the adaptation thesis suggests), would be equally naïve. Yet it could be suggested that many software developers were, in one way or another, detached from both their professional community and enduring placement within a 'professional' working environment. Hence, modifying the adaptation thesis, we would suggest that software developers were, in fact, preserving their identity as a response to this isolation.

In other research in this sector (Marks and Scholarios 2001) a hierarchical system based on education and qualifications has been found to exist and that the more qualified employees are the more they take an interest in the sector, and the greater their professional identification. Similarly, what our research in this chapter suggests is that employees undertaking less repetitive work have greater autonomy and this impacts on the level of their professional identification.

However, despite qualifications having an impact upon professional identification, software development is a collaborative activity where learning and skill development takes place primarily within project structures (Walz, Elam and Curtis 1993; Engestrom, Engestrom and Vahaaho 1999). As a consequence the process of developing software enforces the extent and need for frequent interaction and collaboration and generates a potentially valuable learning environment for employees. This frequency of interaction with other team members, as a result of collaborative work, joint problem solving and information sharing, in itself, reinforces professional identification.

In conclusion, despite some methodological limitations, there are a number of interesting issues emerging from our research in this chapter. First and foremost is that an understanding of context is essential to comprehending the nature of professional identification within professional and non-professional organizations. The nature of work, particularly in terms of the importance of the team (see Marks and Lockyer 2004), and the broadening experience of work for software developers makes it problematic to locate them within existing theories and approaches. These are a group of employees with a salient professional identity that appears separate to their employing organization and any organization in which they are based. What our cases studies therefore show is that software developers have a strong sense of belonging to their profession by mechanisms that are atypical to most professionals and, as such, this warrants substantial further investigation.

Notes

1 This chapter is based on data collected as part of an ESRC research project funded under the *Future of Work* initiative (award number L212252006) 'Employment and Working Life beyond the Year 2000: Two Emerging Employment Sectors' (1999–2001). The full research team at Strathclyde, Stirling, Aberdeen and Heriot-Watt Universities is: Peter Bain, Chris Baldry, Nick Bozionelos, Dirk Bunzel, Gregor Gall, Kay Gilbert, Jeff Hyman, Cliff Lockyer, Abigail Marks, Gareth Mulvey, the late Harvie Ramsay, Dora Scholarios, Philip Taylor and Aileen Watson.

2 Not all contractors worked at any one time.

3 It should be noted that at the time of this study the satellite office in England had just undergone restructuring and about 40 employees had been made redundant. This was the only experience of redundancies within the history of the organization.

4 This included employees engaged in software programming, software testing, systems analysis, business analysis, software design and user/application support.

References

Abbott, A. (1988) *The System of Professions. An Essay on the Division of Labor*, Chicago and London: The University of Chicago Press.

Ackroyd, S., Glover, I. and Currie, W. (2000) 'The triumph of hierarchies over markets: Information system specialists in the current context', in I. A. Glover and M. D. Hughes (eds) *Professions at Bay: Control and Encouragement of Ingenuity in British Management*, Avebury: Aldershot.

Alvesson, M. (1995) 'The meaning and meaninglessness of postmodernism: Some ironic remarks', *Organization Studies*, 16, 6: 1047–57.

Alvesson, M. (2000) 'Social identity and the problem of loyalty in knowledge intensive companies', *Journal of Management Studies*, 27, 8: 1103–23.

Ashforth, B. E. and Kreiner, G. E. (1999) '"How can you do it?" Dirty work and the challenge of constructing a positive identity', *Academy of Management Review*, 24, 3: 413–34.

Ashforth, B. and Mael, F. (1989) 'Social identity theory and the organization', *Academy of Management Review*, 14: 20–39.

Barrett, R. (2001) 'Labouring under an illusion? The labour process of software development in the Australian information industry', *New Technology, Work and Employment* 16, 1: 18–34.

Beirne, M., Ramsay, H. and Panteli, A. (1998) 'Developments in computing work: Control and contradiction in the software labour process', in P. Thompson and C. Warhurst (eds) *Workplaces of the Future*, Hampshire: Macmillan Business.

Bloor, G. and Dawson, P. (1994) 'Understanding professional culture in organizational context', *Organization Studies*, 15, 2: 275–95.

Boreham, P. (1983) 'Indetermination: Professional knowledge, organisation and control', *Sociological Review*, 31, 4: 693–18.

Cherim, S. (2002) 'Reducing dissonance: Closing the gap between projected and attributed identity', in B. Moingeon and G. Soenen (eds) *Corporate and Organisational Identities: Integrating Strategy, Marketing, Communication and Organizational Perspectives*, London: Routledge.

Collins, R. (1979) 'Functional and conflict theories of educational stratification', *American Sociological Review*, 36: 1002–19.

Crompton, R. (1990) 'Professions in the current context', *Work, Employment and Society*, 4, 5: 147–66.

Department for Education and Skills (2002) *An Assessment of Skill Needs in Information and Communication Technology*, Nottingham: DfES Publications.

Drucker, P. (1993) *Post-Capitalist Society*, New York: Harper.

Dutton, J. E. and Dukerich, J. M. (1994) 'Organizational images and member identification', *Administrative Science Quarterly*, 39: 239–63.

Elsbach, K. D. and Kramer, R. M. (1996) 'Members' responses to organizational threats: Encountering and countering the Business Week rankings', *Administrative Science Quarterly*, 41: 442–76.

Engestrom, Y., Engestrom, R. and Vahaaho, T. (1999) 'When the centre does not hold: The importance of knotworking', in S. Chaiklin, M. Hedegaard and U. Jensen (eds) *Activity Theory and Social Practice: Cultural-Historical Approaches*, Aarhus: Aarhus University Press.

Fitzgerald, L. and Ferlie, E. (2000) 'Professionals: Back to the future', *Human Relations*, 53, 5: 713–39.

Friedman, A. (1990) 'Managerial strategies, activities, techniques and technology: Towards a complex theory of the labour process', in D. Knights and H. Willmott (eds) *Labour Process Theory*, London: Macmillan.

Gallois, C., Tluchowska, M. and Callan, V. J. (2001) 'Communicating in times of uncertainty: The role of nested identities in the assessment of the change process', paper presented at the *International Communication Association Conference* in Washington, DC, May.

Gouldner, A. (1957) 'Cosmopolitans and locals: Toward an analysis of latent social roles', *Administrative Science Quarterly*, 2: 281–306.

Hogg, M. A. and Abrams, D. (1993) 'Towards a single-process uncertainty reduction model of social motivation in groups', in M. A. Hogg and D. Abrams (eds.) *Group Motivation: Social Psychological Perspectives*, London: Harvester/Wheatsheaf.

Hogg, M. A., and Mullin, B. A. (1999) 'Joining groups to reduce uncertainty: Subjective uncertainty reduction and group identification', in D. Abrams and M. A. Hogg (eds) *Social Identity and Social Cognition*, Oxford: Blackwell.

Hogg, M. A. and Terry, D. J. (2000) 'Social identity and self-categorization Processes in organizational contexts', *Academy of Management Review*, 25, 1: 121–40.

Jackson, P. R., Wall, T. D., Martin, R. and Davids, K. (1993) 'New measures of job control, cognitive demand, and production responsibility', *Journal of Applied Psychology*, 78: 753–62.

Kraft, P. and Dubnoff, S. (1986) 'Job content, fragmentation, and control in computer software work', *Industrial Relations*, 25, 2: 184–96.

Kunda, G. (1992) *Engineering Culture, Control and Commitment in a High-Tech Corporation*, Philadelphia: Temple University Press.

Mael, F. and Ashforth, B. E. (1992) 'Alumni and their alma mater: A partial test of the reformulated model of organizational identification', *Journal of Organizational Behaviour*, 13: 103–23.

Mael, F. and Ashforth, B. E. (1995) 'Loyal from day one: Biodata, organizational identification, and turnover among newcomers', *Personnel Psychology*, 48: 309–33.

Marks, A. and Lockyer, C. (2004) 'Producing knowledge: The use of the project teams as a vehicle for knowledge and skill acquisition for software employees', *Economic and Industrial Democracy*, 25, 2: 219–45.

Marks, A. and Scholarios, D. (2001) 'Identifying a profession: The creation of professional identities within software work', paper presented at the *European Group on Organization Studies Colloquium* in Barcelona, 3–5 July.

Oppenheimer, M. (1973) 'The proletarianization of a profession', *Sociological Review Monograph*, 20: 213–17.

Parsons, T. (1951) *The Social System*, New York: Free Press.

Reed, M. (1996) 'Expert power and control in late modernity', *Organization Studies*, 17, 4: 573–98

Rock, K. W. and Pratt, M. (2002) 'Where do we go from here? Predicting identification among dispersed employees', in B. Moingeon and G. Soenen (eds.) *Corporate and Organisational Identities: Integrating Strategy, Marketing, Communication and Organizational Perspectives*, London: Routledge.

Rousseau, D. M. (1998) 'Why workers still identify with organizations', *Journal of Organizational Behaviour*, 19: 217–33.

Sawyer, S. and Guinan, P. (1998) 'Software development: processes and performance', *IBM Systems Journal*, 37, 4: 552–69.

Scarborough, H. (1993) 'Problem-solutions in the management of information systems expertise', *Journal of Management Studies*, 30, 6: 939–55.

Scarborough, H. (1996) 'Understanding and managing expertise', in H. Scarborough (ed.) *The Management of Expertise*, London: St Martin's Press.

Sonnentag, S. (1995) 'Excellent software professionals: experience, work activities and perception by peers', *Behaviour and Information Technology*, 14, 4: 289–99.

Sorenson, J. E. (1967) 'Professional and bureaucratic organization in the public accounting firm', *The Accounting Review*, 42: 553–65.

Stryker, S. (1987) 'Identity theory: Developments and extensions', in K. Yardly, and T. Honess (eds) *Self and Identity: Psychological Perspectives*, New York: John Wiley and Sons.

Tajfel, H. (1970) 'Experiments in inter-group discrimination', *Scientific American*, 223: 96–102.

Tajfel, H. and Turner, J. C. (1979) 'An integrative theory of intergroup conflict', in W. C. Austin and S. Worchel (eds) *The Social Psychology of Intergroup Relations*, Monterrey: Brooks/Cole.

Tam, Y. M., Korczynski, M. and Frenkel, S. J. (2002) 'Organizational and occupational commitment: Knowledge workers in large corporations', *Journal of Management Studies*, 39, 6: 775–801.

Turner, J. C. (1982) 'Toward a cognitive redefinition of the social group', in H. Tajfel (ed.) *Social Identity and Intergroup Behaviour*, Cambridge: Cambridge University Press.

Turner, J. C. (1984) 'Social identification and psychological group formation', in H. Tajfel (ed.) *The Social Dimension, Vol. 2*, Cambridge: Cambridge University Press.

Tyler, T. R. and Blader, S. L. (2001) 'Identity and co-operative behaviour in groups', *Group Processes and Intergroup Relations*, 4, 3: 207–26.

von Glinow, H. (1988) *The New Professionals: Managing Today's High-Tech Employees*, Cambridge, Mass: Ballinger Publ. Co.

Wallace, J. E. (1995) 'Organizational and professional commitment in professional and non-professional organizations', *Administrative Science Quarterly*, 40, 2: 228–55.

Walz, D.B., Elam, J. J. and Curtis, B. (1993) 'The dual role of conflict in group software requirements and design activities', *Communications of the ACM* 36, 10: 63–76.

Warr, P. B., Cook, J. D. and Wall, T. D. (1979) 'Scales for the measurement of some work attitudes and aspects of psychological well-being', *Journal of Occupational Psychology*, 52: 129–48.

Waterson, P. E., Clegg, C. W. and Axtell, C. M. (1997) 'The dynamics of work organization, knowledge and technology during software development', *International Journal Human-Computer Studies*, 46: 79–101.

Weiss, D. J., Dawis, R. V., England, G. W. and Lofquist, L. H. (1967) *Manual for the Minnesota Satisfaction Questionnaire*, Minneapolis, MN: University of Minnesota Industrial Relations Center.

Wiesenfeld, B. M., Raghuram, S. and Garud, R. (2001) 'Organisational identification among virtual workers: The role of need for affiliation and perceived work based social support', *Journal of Management*, 27: 213–29.

Whittington, R., Pettigrew, A., Peck, S. Fenton, E. and Conyon, M. (1999) 'Change and complementarities in the new competitive landscape: A European panel study, 1992–1996', *Organization Science*, 10, 5: 583–600.

Yin, R. K. (1994) *Case Study Research: Design and Methods*, Beverly Hills: Sage Publications.

8 Organizational commitment among software developers

Chris Baldry, Dora Scholarios and Jeff Hyman[1]

Introduction

If software developers are to be taken as prototypes of the new knowledge worker, we need look no further for working hypotheses about their attachment to their work and their employing organization than those contained in the human resource management agenda. For the diffusion of information and communication technologies (ICTs) as the supposed base of the knowledge economy has been synchronous with the launch and promotion of human resource management (HRM) as the new orthodoxy in employment practice and many of the assumptions and values within each model are shared. Indeed, HRM is often portrayed as if it were in some way a reflection of the shift to non-adversarial work relationships in the new information-based service society (Baldry 2003).

This is particularly true of the core concept of employee commitment, identified by the early 1980s as the goal of the new approach to people management (Walton 1985). The assumption spelled out in Walton, and subsequent writing, is that the flexibility and quality necessary for successful competition will only come about with a transformation of employee attitudes away from a grudging compliance with the rules of the organization, monitored and regulated by command and control structures external to the individual. This attitude and behaviour set must be replaced by an internalized set of values and behaviours which are congruent with the goals of the organization and in which the goals of the organization and employees coalesce. Quality and flexibility will only be delivered through the medium of the highly committed employee.

The popular stereotype of the knowledge worker closely corresponds to the ideal subject under an HRM regime. S/he is usually portrayed as young, personally committed to the job and the organization, prepared to work long hours in an empowered job, and with an individualistic view of their career path in which they see themselves as an autonomous 'professional' rather than a conventional employee. Thus, Alvesson (2000: 1104) states, 'In many ways knowledge-intensive workers form the ideal subordinates, the employer's dream in terms of work motivation and compliance'.

Moreover, proponents of the information society such as Zuboff (1988) often portray the technology itself as a cause of heightened commitment so that, while conventional production systems could be associated with the necessity for top-down control systems, the creation of flatter post-bureaucratic and more open organizations will engender more integrated and committed employees. Castells (1996) sees the new networked organization as requiring the two major components of organizational commitment – discretionary effort and employment continuance. Much higher levels of employee involvement are needed 'so that they [employees] do not keep their tacit knowledge solely for their own benefit' (Castells 1996: 160) and there must be stability of employment 'because only then does it become rational for the individual to transfer his/her knowledge to the company and for the company to diffuse explicit knowledge among its workers' (Castells 1996: 160).

Knowledge workers may thus seem ideal recipients of prescriptive commitment-raising HRM policies and we should expect to find software organizations openly espousing an HRM high commitment agenda, with software developers displaying high levels of commitment (Kunda 1992). In this chapter we explore whether software workers do, in reality, exemplify highly committed knowledge workers and in doing so we critically examine the relevance of current models of commitment.

The empirical study reported in this chapter is based on five Scottish software development organizations and combines case study, interview and survey data. We begin with a consideration of the dominant perspectives on commitment followed by the presentation of predictions based on these models. These predictions are then examined using a combination of survey data and qualitative data from employee interviews.

The goal of high commitment

Recent management literature has been dominated by attempts to identify those people management practices, which in combination, may serve to enhance some measure of performance through a raised level of employee commitment to the organization. Such bundles of practices are termed either high commitment work practices (HCWP) or high performance work systems (HPWS), the former tending to be UK nomenclature and the latter US derived (see Legge 2001: 25). Whilst management texts remain vague about what is meant by 'commitment' and about the causal mechanics which link it to performance, this gap has been more than filled by the other main perspective studying commitment, that of organizational psychology.

The psychological perspective has focused on construct validation, measurement and identification of causes and consequences of organizational commitment. This has led to what some have called a taxonomic or componential model of commitment. At least three psychological states have been identified to be encompassed by the term organizational commitment, more usually expressed as affective commitment (an emotional identification with the organization), normative commitment (a sense of obligation towards the organization and willingness to exert effort on its behalf), and continuance commitment (an exchange based concept based on a perceived need to stay with the organization due to the high costs of leaving) (Mowday, Steers and Porter 1979; Allen and Meyer 1990).

Within this componential framework, commitment is regarded as a positive employee response to progressive employment practices, such as team working, training provision or employee share schemes. Studies show the affective dimension of commitment to be related to generally positive employee perceptions of the organization and management; for instance, perceived organizational support (Eisenberger, Fasolo and Davis-Lamastro 1990; Rhoades and Eisenberger 2002); management trust (Pearce 1993; Gopinath and Becker 2000); procedural fairness or fair treatment (Folger and Konovsky 1989; Podsakoff, MacKenzie and Bomer 1996); and particularly to 'climate' factors such as being kept informed, equal opportunities and family-friendly practices (Guest 2002).

Affective commitment, in turn, is expected to result in elevated job performance. However, while research evidence shows that affective commitment leads to greater willingness to stay with an organization, lower absenteeism, greater effort and productivity, and greater organizational citizenship behaviour (Meyer, Allen and Smith 1993; Meyer and Allen 1997), the identification of which particular employment practices result in heightened affective commitment, and thus performance outcomes, is beset with difficulties. First, the number and type of individual practices vary widely: for example, the UK Workplace Employee Relations Survey (WERS) identifies 15 practices (Cully, Woodland, O'Reilly and Dix 1999: 285), although other studies are more restrictive in their selection and few practices are common across different studies. In addition, there is uncertainty about whether individual practices such as performance-related pay are associated with positive or negative effects. Moreover, the effectiveness or competence with which the practice is exercised is seldom assessed (Legge 2001: 25–6); in an analysis of the WERS data, a poor level of managerial competence was felt to be a potential explanatory factor for the ambiguity in the effects of the HCWP model (Ramsay, Scholarios and Harley 2000: 522). Further, measurements of practice effects differ because of the diverse ways of measuring performance. Huselid (1995) provides an influential approach to designing and examining performance and claims to demonstrate positive links between a cluster of designated HCWP and broad organizational indicators such as financial performance or productivity, although questions persist concerning the mechanisms by which employee-focused initiatives can impact upon organizational level outcomes. From an empirical perspective, therefore, there are considerable doubts about the extent and depth, either of the coverage of purported commitment-inducing practices or the depth of employee response to these practices. Some of these reservations are of particular relevance to the study of software professionals as non-union workplaces in particular have been conspicuous by their lack of coverage of such practices (Kessler and Purcell 2003: 331).

The above discussion is underpinned by what we call a 'direct commitment' model which has three underlying assumptions. First, commitment is a unitary set of attitudes, with a single focus – the organization; second, commitment is voluntary; and third, high commitment to the organization will be directly reflected in enhanced performance (through the exercise of discretionary effort) and long service. We identify two sub-models of this direct commitment model.

1 The *Right Stuff* model, where the attitudes and behaviours congruent with organizational commitment are detected through appropriate recruitment and selection practices. This places the locus of commitment with the individual's attributes (including, personality, age and gender).
2 The *HCWP* model, where commitment can be imbued, developed and rewarded through adoption of appropriate people management and culture change policies. This places the responsibility for commitment on applying the correct policies and instituting an appropriate combination of organizational structures.

Management practice itself seems to be unclear about its own conceptual underpinnings and utilizes a confused mixture of both. Both direct models tend to be either static models in which individual traits, once discovered, are taken as given, or equilibrium models in which the mind-set of the employee moves from a state of un-committedness, via the application of high commitment work practices and culture change, to a new state of committedness.

An indirect process model of commitment

One goal of HCWP models is to maximize internalization of values through the development of a unitary and 'strong' culture (Peters and Waterman 1982) so that the organization becomes a unitary organization (Fox 1974) with a uniform and widely diffused culture and no rival bond objects. In such a strong culture individuals may satisfy their personal values through striving to meet those of the organization. Guest (2002) realistically points out that this narrow unitarist view of the merging of corporate and individual goals may make some limited sense in a US context but does not really resonate in more pluralist employment systems such as Europe, Australia or even the unionized parts of the US labour market. More usually the organization is going to be a pluralist entity in which individuals can simultaneously be members of a team or workgroup, a department, a trade union and an organization.

Recognizing this, Reichers (1985) proposes a multiple constituencies model of organizational commitment which accepts the possibility of multiple foci of commitment (such as work-team, project group, union, supervisor, colleagues, customers) which may be reinforcing or competing (see also Becker 1992; Becker and Billings 1993). There is after all no reason to believe that these multiple loyalties will always be complementary: the 'discovery' that launched the whole human relations movement in the late 1920s was that commitment to the norms of the workgroup could be more immediate and influencing on behaviour than the values of the wider organization.

Social identity theory (SIT) defines the self-concept in terms of personal identity, comprised of personal attributes (personality, dispositions), and social identity, which is defined in terms of self-categorization with a salient social group (e.g. nationality, race, political affiliation) and Van Dick (2001) indicates how this approach allows a more theoretical understanding of the different levels of attachment to the organization. Organizational identification is distinct from organizational commitment (Ashforth and Mael 1989; Mael and Tetrick 1992) as the latter, as usually described, implies an internalization of values. Thus you can identify yourself with an organization in the sense that this identification provides a label for a significant part of who you are ('I work for Beta') but this does not necessarily mean you take its values as your own. Employees will most strongly identify with the unit with the greatest salience for them and this in turn will result in affective commitment directed to that unit. Mueller and Lawler (1999) specified three key conditions which will result in commitment to a particular unit: a unit's 'distance' from an employee, whether proximate units produce positive emotions, and whether this positive emotion is perceived to be caused by that unit. Hunt and Morgan (1994) further suggest that commitment to a subgroup can also facilitate a more global commitment to the organization generally, which implies the existence of nested identities within an organization (Ashforth and Mael 1989) and nested levels of commitment.

Sociological perspectives have a longer tradition of extending the parameters beyond the confines of the workplace and identifying additional external foci of employee commitment, for example to occupation or profession. An external occupational community in the sense of 'software professionals' can function as a psychological group in just the same way as the organization: i.e. as a collection of people who share the same social identification but with whom the individual does not necessarily have to interact personally. Alvesson (2000) suggests, in a discussion of IT professionals, that the possibility of a professional identity makes it likely that ties to the organization may be weaker, as belonging to the latter is less essential for one's self-identity (see also Marks and Lockyer this volume).

The above discussion implies that organizational commitment can be mediated or filtered through a stronger sense of commitment to other more salient groups of which the employee is a member. Capelli (1999, 2000) argues that the economic turbulence at the end of the 1990s has resulted in a shift towards this indirect form of commitment, as employers broke the long-term commitment understanding they had previously held with their employees. Downsizing, flatter organizations and corporate relocations negatively affected employment continuity and internal promotion prospects, causing firms to construct a new contract with employees no longer based on long-term commitment, but on offering employees the means and opportunities to develop their own skills in ways that enhance their professional and occupational careers, external to the organization if need be. Organizations do not expect employees to stay with them for lifelong employment but aim to become 'employers of choice' by offering professional development and training. This changing psychological contract can be seen as a 'new deal' in which high commitment and trust can only be generated through a negotiated process of reciprocity.

The importance of reciprocity in these arguments suggests that, rather than employees' sense of commitment reflecting a steady state or equilibrium, there is a constant process of re-evaluation on their part, based on such variables as perceived reciprocity and the salience of other groups within and outside the organization for feelings of loyalty. If the employee stays late, works beyond contract and remains with the organization, this may be for attitudinal reasons or alternatively it may be for what Becker (1960) termed 'side bets', a calculation of what might be lost if these behaviours were not adhered to (enhanced career potential, chances of promotion, pension scheme, holiday entitlement, company savings plan or share option). From this perspective commitment is generated through a process of social exchange, whereby being involved in an organization also comes to involve other interests of the employee in such a way that his or her behaviour is constrained to some extent. These can include cultural expectations which involve a penalty for their violation (software workers will be expected to work the extra hours) and the organization's bureaucratic arrangements such as pensions and promotion structures. Here we are clearly focusing on the employee as a social actor within an institutional context which can include organizational structures and policies, the state of the labour market and family and household circumstances. This calculative dimension of commitment displays far less distance from the supposedly traditional attitude set of compliance than the direct high commitment model outlined earlier.

Two alternative models summarized

How do general theories of commitment apply to software workers? The discussion above identifies two possibilities concerning the employment relationship and commitment of software workers and these are contrasted in Table 8.1.

Table 8.1 Predictions of direct and indirect commitment models

Direct High Commitment Model	*Indirect Process Model of Commitment*
1 Software workers have high affective commitment and low continuance commitment	1 Software workers have higher occupational commitment than affective commitment, and low continuance commitment
2 Software organizations are exemplars of HCWP	2 Software organizations are exemplars of practices which enhance professional development (e.g. training, skill acquisition)
3 There is a positive relationship between HCWP and employee attitudes (affective commitment) and outcomes (intention to remain with the organization)	3 There is a positive relationship between practices which enhance professional development (e.g., training, career structure) employee attitudes (affective and continuance commitment) and outcomes (intention to remain with the organization)
4 Affective commitment and intention to remain with the company are most strongly influenced by HCWP rather than other variables	4 Affective commitment and intention to remain with the organization are more strongly influenced by tenure, employees' technical skill level and occupational commitment
	5 Maintenance of affective commitment over time emphasizes reciprocity – 'fair treatment' and recognition of discretionary effort

The direct high commitment model views software workers as a prototype of the new knowledge worker engaged in high-trust employment relationships where the job and the organizations in which they are employed provide high intrinsic satisfaction and autonomy. If this is the case, then software organizations will be exemplars of the high commitment management organization and will show: (1) high levels of affective commitment amongst software workers; continuance commitment will be low because employees wish to stay with the organization even if there are other opportunities elsewhere; (2) high perceived levels of job control, decision influence, fair treatment, satisfaction with pay, skills, training and career prospects, which are commonly associated with HCWP; and (3) a relationship between HCWP and affective commitment which is (4) stronger than any other potential predictor (e.g. tenure).

The indirect commitment model also portrays software workers as a prototype of the new knowledge worker but whose primary identification is with their profession. Therefore the employment relationship is likely to be viewed as more short-term and based on a reciprocal relationship which provides the benefits expected by software professionals, such as the accumulation of skills which may take them to other organizations. If this model applies, then software organizations will be exemplars of a different type of organization where the emphasis is on certain types of management practices which reinforce professional values and enhance professional development.

Thus, in terms of the predictions represented in Table 8.1: (1) affective organizational commitment will be lower than occupational commitment, and continuance commitment will again be low as software workers are likely to have options for other employment; (2) the practices which matter most will be those perceived to enhance professional development or reciprocate for employees' effort (e.g. fair treatment, satisfaction with pay, training, employability enhancement), but the model does not necessarily predict that HCWP will be absent; (3) only that these practices will have a direct relationship with affective commitment, continuance commitment and intention to remain with the organization; and (4) other key factors may be stronger predictors of these attitudes and outcomes; i.e. tenure with the organization, technical complexity of the job (indicating higher skilled software developers), and the degree of occupational commitment. The fourth prediction is based on the expectation that the importance of professional advancement (which this model sees as the main basis of organizational commitment) is likely to decline with longer tenure, but increase for more technically skilled and occupationally committed software workers. Finally, the indirect model also suggests (5) that affective commitment to these groups will be strongly related to perceptions of reciprocity and this may vary over time. Low affective organizational commitment will not necessarily result in low discretionary effort but the latter may be driven by the norms and mores of the (external) professional group.

The case studies and study design

All five organizations were located in Scotland's central belt, almost equally distributed between the greater Glasgow and greater Edinburgh areas. Four of the organizations (Lambda, Pi, Omega and Gamma) were Scottish-owned start-ups, still run by the founder or founders while the fifth, Beta, was part of an ex-public sector utility. Table 8.2 illustrates the differences between the case study organizations with respect to size, year established, current and expected business orientation and development of HRM practices and policies. Beta, a software division within a large telecommunications organization, can be distinguished from the other four smaller start-ups in all respects, particularly in its size, more conventional bureaucratic structure, the apparent sophistication of HRM policies, such as provision of training, formal performance appraisals, formal communication

Table 8.2 Description of case studies

	Beta	*Omega*	*Gamma*	*Pi*	*Lambda*
No. employees	275	248	150	50	20
Year established	Former public sector utility; restructuring of software centre 1999	1985	1986	1977/1999	1996
Product/service	Bespoke telephone operations; robotic tools; database integration; financial systems	Applications development, resourcing, testing, client support; AS400 technology	Systems integration of front and end operations; bespoke CRM systems; subcontractor linking major platforms for clients	Legal and business software development, testing, support, training and maintenance	Health and safety recording software
Primary market	Telecommunications; internal clients	Public sector, health services, financial services	Database users, initially manufacturing but recently financial and business services	Law firms	Insurance; IT multinationals
Major business direction	Providing a range of business solutions for external clients	Largely public sector; developing into English market	New release of software; shift from C++ to Java	Client server and web server versions of software	Client server and web server versions of software
Union presence	Yes	No	No	No	No

Development of HRM policies and practices	Sophisticated and highly centralized. Formal training, appraisal linked to promotion/pay, profit-sharing, communication schemes, internal recruitment and harmonization of pensions, sick leave etc. No compulsory redundancies	Informal; HRM given low priority. Inconsistent appraisal system, little formal training, profit sharing scheme in development	Informal; no formal pay structure. Little formal training, appraisal system in development, informal system of performance-related pay	Emerging. High status HR officer. Policies in development (performance related pay, appraisal, benefits)	Informal; shareholder incentives. No formal appraisal or training. Informal performance-related pay

mechanisms, recognition of a union, and harmonization of practices. Because of these corresponding differences in organization and management, it has been found useful in the following analysis to compare Beta with the other four independent organizations.

A mixed method design (Tashakkori and Teddlie 1998) was used to allow both a hypothesis testing and explorative approach. This involves the use of different methods sequentially and/or in parallel to study the same phenomenon at different levels within the organization. All data were collected over a period of four to six months in each organization between 1999 and 2002. As well as contextual case study data (such as company documents, management interviews, and observation of management meetings), data were collected from employees using three approaches.

1 A self-report questionnaire was distributed to all workers and management over a period of two to three weeks in each organization in order to capture employee perceptions and attitudes towards their job, the organization and management, as well as biographical details.
2 Non-standardized and focused interviews with key informants (managers, supervisors, software developers) provided a non-guided context for discussion about issues related to commitment.
3 In-depth semi-structured interviews were conducted with a sample of employees conducted at the workplace and in their home-community locality to explore issues of commitment and identity in and beyond the workplace.

Quantitative and qualitative data were gathered simultaneously.

The questionnaire included the following control variables: gender, age, temporary staff/contractors, tenure with the organization (measured in months), number of hours paid and unpaid overtime per week, and skill level of the job. The last was determined by six items measuring the degree of importance on a scale from 1 'Not too important' to 4 'Absolutely essential' of software programming, systems analysis, business analysis, testing, software design and user/application support in employees' jobs. The mean of these items formed a measure of technical skill complexity of respondents' jobs ($\alpha=0.83$).

Commitment was measured in respect to the organization, the occupation of software development, and to colleagues. Organizational commitment was measured using two of the components identified by Allen and Meyer (1990). Five items adapted from Allen and Meyer's original scale (e.g. 'I feel a strong sense of belonging to my company', 'I would turn down a job with more pay in order to stay with this company') measured affective commitment and formed a scale calculated from the item means ($\alpha=0.80$). Continuance commitment was measured by the mean of two items ('I believe that I have too few options to consider leaving X' and

'Too much of my life would be disrupted if I decided I wanted to leave X right now') (α=0.60). Commitment to the occupation was measured using three items capturing different aspects of professional identification: the affective dimension was measured using a single item from Blau's (1985) career commitment scale ('If I could, I would go into a different occupation'); perceptions of behavioural identification were measured using a single item ('I take an interest in current developments in the software sector') based on questions from 'The Use of Profession as Major Referent Scale' (Hall, 1968); and the normative dimension was examined using a single item ('I am proud to tell others that I am employed in the software sector') from Vandenberg and Scarpello's (1994) modification of the *Occupational Commitment Questionnaire* (Mowday *et al.* 1979). The mean of these items formed a single composite score (α=0.55). Commitment to colleagues was measured with a single item – 'I feel a strong sense of loyalty to my fellow employees'.

Intention to remain with the organization was measured by a closed question asking how respondents viewed their current job in the company. The measure was coded 1 if this was a long-term job they would stay in or if they saw the job as an opportunity for career advancement in the present company. If the job was not part of a career in this organization, or part of a career in other organizations the measure was coded 0.

Finally, the questionnaire was also used to measure employee perceptions of HRM practices usually associated with greater employee satisfaction and commitment. Drawing from the HCWP/HPWS literature referred to earlier, we measured employee perceptions of: decision influence over issues such as job allocation, shifts, training, recruitment, or incentives (10 items), job control (four items), adequate training for current job and career advancement (two items), organizational/supervisor support for non-work commitments (two items), satisfaction with pay (two items), and satisfaction with overall treatment, including performance assessment, career prospects and job security (five items). Exploratory factor analysis of all 25 items supported these six different dimensions and measures were created using the mean of the relevant items. All composite measures had high Cronbach alpha reliability ranging from 0.60 to 0.90. An additional single item measure, 'the extent to which the current job provided skills which enhanced employability externally', was used to examine support for the indirect commitment model.

A representative group of employees in each organization (according to gender, age, job type and job/organizational level) were selected for the semi-structured work interviews. These explored three themes in greater depth: (a) previous work and educational history and how it led to their present job; (b) experiences of working in the present organization (including commitment to company/peers/job/customers); and (c) work–life linkages and the future (perceptions of job risk/uncertainty, relative importance of work, perceptions of society/class/status). A total of 75 semi-structured employee interviews were obtained from the five cases, distributed in proportion to organizational size. A smaller subsection of these employees was contacted again for interviews in their home or community to explore commitment more broadly beyond the workplace.

The contours of commitment

The questionnaire respondents were predominantly male with Omega and Pi having the largest proportions of females (approximately one-third) (see Table 8.3). Half the sample was under 30 years of age and a sizeable proportion had less than two years tenure – tenure was longer only in the former public sector utility Beta. There was a relatively low proportion of contractors (only 17 and 13 per cent in Beta and Omega, respectively) and low levels of paid overtime, although, as will be shown, there was a significant amount of unpaid overtime worked in all case studies, particularly in the independent organizations.

The technical complexity score for each organization ranged from 2.82 and 2.77 for Gamma and Beta, respectively, to 2.56 and 2.24 for Lambda and Pi, respectively, with Omega falling in the middle of this range (using a four-point scale). These differences between case studies were significant (F (4,295) = 3.90, $p < 0.001$), indicating a higher skill level on average of software workers in the former compared with the latter.

Discretionary effort and the willingness to stay

If one index of commitment is a willingness to expend discretionary rather than prescribed effort (Fox 1974: 16), then the fact that half the employees in the two larger organizations and sizeable majorities in the three smaller organizations claimed to work 10 or more hours per week unpaid overtime seems to suggest a high degree of commitment. The survey responses gave

Table 8.3 Sample characteristics for each case study organization

	Beta	*Omega*	*Pi*	*Lambda*	*Gamma*
N	112	121	38	14	18
Per cent of sample	37	40	12	5	6
Female (%)	18	32	34	29	6
Age <30 (%)	42	29	34	64	44
Contractor (%)	17	13	0	0	0
Tenure <2 years (%)	20	39	37	50	61
Paid overtime[a] (%)	9	14	8	0	6
Unpaid overtime[a] (%)	51	51	84	71	89
Intend to stay with company (%)	37	42	47	71	39

Note

a Represents percentage working 10 hours or more per week.

the primary reason for working extra hours as meeting project deadlines or to get work done, with a smaller percentage citing not wanting to let down clients or colleagues.

However, when we tested for the first prediction in Table 8.1 by examining the mean ratings of different foci of commitment, shown in the top half of Table 8.4, these first impressions had to be qualified. While the image of the knowledge worker identifying with the goals of their organization found more support in the independent organizations than in Beta ($t(296)=3.77$, $p<0.001$) it was clear that in both types of organizations, commitment to the occupation and to colleagues was higher than affective organizational commitment. Paired *t*-tests found all these differences to be significant at the 95 per cent level of confidence.

For many of the developers we interviewed it was the job that drove their effort, rather than the organization:

> . . . I think in development most of us are committed more to the job than to the company because we are all in it because we enjoy programming and that's the first thing, the second thing is what company you work for and what sort of work you get to do.
>
> (Pi interview 10, female software programmer)

Table 8.4 Comparison of means for Beta versus the four independent organizations

	Beta		*All independents*		*F*
	Mean	*SD*	*Mean*	*SD*	
Commitment					
Affective	2.94	0.68	3.26	0.75	13.54***
Continuance	2.70	1.01	2.64	0.94	0.32
Occupation	3.63	0.70	3.72	0.71	0.70
Colleagues	3.60	0.73	3.71	0.78	1.48
Employee perceptions (scale)					
Decision influence	2.25	0.66	2.37	0.75	1.75
Job control	3.86	0.51	3.86	0.59	0.00
Support for non-work commitments	3.63	0.56	3.55	0.69	1.05
Satisfaction with pay (1–7)	3.93	1.38	4.43	1.32	9.72**
Satisfaction with treatment (1–7)	4.37	0.96	4.64	0.96	5.57*
Training provision (1–4)	2.56	0.58	2.22	0.68	18.17***
Employability enhancement (1–4)	2.69	0.55	2.51	0.59	7.30***

Notes
Beta $N=109$–12.
All independent organizations $N=181$–7.
All measured on scale of 1 'strongly agree' to 5 'strongly disagree' unless indicated otherwise.
* $p<0.05$
** $p<0.01$
*** $p<0.001$

> So, if you like, the commitment's to Beta in as much as they are paying me to do what I like and I like to do the job to the best of my ability.
>
> (Beta interview 11, male applications project analyst)

The salience of immediate identity groups was indicated in this comment from a developer in Beta when asked about the direction of her commitment:

> To the project yes ... (since the changes) we don't actually see much about where our place is in the whole company. So I've probably got more commitment to the project than I have to the Centre or the company, if that makes any sense ... because I know what's happening with the project more than I do about anything else that is happening outside the project.
>
> (Beta interview 17, female software engineer)

From the interviews, it was clear there was a difference between the extra effort which some managers put in for the sake of the *organization* (we can call this 'discretionary organization effort') and the long hours, working nights and weekends which were seen to be part of the *job* of software – you do the hours to get the project delivered because that is part of the identity of being a software professional – (we can call this 'discretionary job effort'). This difference, between a general and a particular commitment emphasis, can be seen in the following extracts from interviews with a sales manager at Pi, a Beta developer and an Omega analyst, when asked about their commitment to their organization.

> *Director of Sales:* [Commitment] from me to the company? Absolutely, yes.
>
> *Interviewer:* How is this expressed?
>
> *Director of Sales:* Just my general attitude to work and what I'm prepared to do, when I'm prepared to do it. Whether that's working beyond standard hours or picking up on things for colleagues, getting involved in the social things we do, being involved in pretty much every element around Pi. I mean after five years that's a bit easier because I've got a lot of friends and a lot of social things revolve around Pi as well, but in general just getting involved with everything.
>
> (Pi interview 3, male Director of Sales)

> If I have to, I'll work late. I'll work late for every night for a month to get a release out but I'd rather estimate properly ... because I don't think I can do my job properly if I'm going (flat) out every night ...
>
> (Beta interview 3, female software engineer)

At the beginning of the project I would say I was working maybe 50–52 hours a week . . . Weekends, not both days, normally a Saturday or something or I would take work home and do some work at home.
(Omega interview 4, female software engineer and team leader)

The other main index of organizational commitment is a willingness to stay with the organization. In all organizations, continuance commitment was lower than affective commitment, as predicted in both models, but again the respondents indicated that this was more likely to be due to their awareness of their positive labour market position rather than a desire to stay. In terms of intentions toward their current employer, less than half viewed their current jobs as long term, and only 42 per cent across organizations felt that their jobs were part of a long term career with the organization, although the proportion was notably higher in Lambda, the smallest organization in this sample. A Beta developer was asked if he would leave for a pay increase elsewhere and he said:

I would leave. If I stayed I guess it wouldn't be through commitment to the company, it would be because I enjoyed the work, which isn't the same thing. No, I don't think I would (stay). I'll defend them, but not to that extent, not where it's causing me personal injury.
(Beta interview 19, male technical architect)

There were several indications of continuing awareness of the state of the industry external to the current employing organization:

I try to keep in touch with my peer group from University days, in fact we are still all in pretty regular contact and we generally are in fairly good knowledge of the positions that everybody else is in . . . and it's good for me because it means I can keep in touch with what is happening in the industry and where I sit in terms of what the industry average is and that kind of stuff.
(Beta interview 10, male applications support analyst)

This orientation towards the profession or occupation on the part of the developers was recognized by some of the managers who, on the whole, were more likely to state a high commitment case for themselves. A male service manager in Pi compared his own commitment to what he saw as the more freewheeling style of the developers:

I can see the young lads that come and go, the developers in the software side tend to come and go. There is very few of them will actually stay to be long term, but my approach is, if I'm happy in a job I'm not looking in the papers for jobs. I think that's a sense of commitment and basically, if people are asking me to do anything, I'll do it for the company, it doesn't matter if it's not in my remit or if it's not making [money] for the company, if it needs to be done, I'll do it.

(Pi interview 6, male technical services manager)

These questionnaire responses and interview data indicate that any commitment software workers had to the organization was filtered through a stronger allegiance to their profession and to their immediate colleagues, thus supporting the first prediction of the indirect model.[2]

The existence and perceptions of high commitment work practices

The second prediction of the direct high commitment model was that software firms, and particularly recent start-ups would, as knowledge organizations, have adopted practices consistent with the highly autonomous and intrinsically motivated nature of software jobs. Our case study evidence suggested that this was not the case, with only Beta showing evidence of such practices existing formally (see Table 8.2). It might be argued that the reason for lower affective commitment across our cases was due to this, as yet, underdeveloped nature of commitment raising HRM practices, in which case we would expect that affective commitment would be higher in Beta than the independents. Table 8.4 shows the reverse to be the case: in the one organization with formalized HRM practices, there was lower affective commitment than in the independent organizations which utilized a variety of informal paternalist and owner-manager initiatives. An examination of employee perceptions of the different organizations' practices (see Table 8.4) confirmed differences in the management styles of Beta compared with the independent organizations, but not necessarily in Beta's favour.

Decision influence and job control

Table 8.4 shows that the independent organizations allowed software employees slightly greater influence in organizational level issues, but scores for perceived job control were uniformly higher across both types of organizations. The nature of software work suggests that personal job control will be esteemed relatively highly, regardless of the organizational context and an important aspect of the job was that it was performed in a high-trust atmosphere which was only partly a consequence of management style:

> I guess the phrase I would use is that you are responsible for your own hours. There is nobody looking over your shoulder and saying what, is he leaving at 3.45 pm? So you are trusted to work your own hours and I think that is probably better.
>
> (Beta interview 4, male software engineer)

Applications project analyst: There's the conditions that we work under within Beta ... wc are allowed to get on with our job without any real interference. We are allowed to take decisions ...

Interviewer: So you've got autonomy?

Applications project analyst: Yes and I think that's important that your employer looks on you in that way, that you can be trusted to do these sort of things and take these decisions, whether they be right or wrong ...

(Beta interview 11, male applications project analyst)

Support for non-work commitments

Table 8.4 shows that organizational support for non-work commitments was also rated fairly highly and interviews provided some evidence of positive responses to such HRM practices as family-friendly policies:

> I feel the working atmosphere overall over the seven years has been pretty good. It is quite a relaxed place to work and sort of most managers I've worked with have been flexible. They understand that you've got personal commitments as well as working commitments and for me that is important...
>
> (Beta interview 4, male software engineer)

Interviewer: Why haven't you changed job?

Software developer: Well one of the things they've been good at here, I asked to go part-time and I am now part-time just now and they said that is ok.... That's a huge bonus for me, as an employer is able to do that – I think it's good to be able to give you the flexibility.

(Gamma interview 9, female software developer)

Satisfaction with pay

Satisfaction with pay was generally high (see Table 8.4), perhaps reflecting the buoyant state of the occupational labour market, with employees in the independent organizations reporting higher levels of satisfaction and Beta employees indicating that their organization's more formalized HRM practices may have had some success in generating 'side bets' of non-salary remuneration:

Interviewer: Why does Beta get away with relatively lower pay than others?

Applications support analyst: They get largely away with it because Beta has some halfway decent fringe benefits. Certainly the annual share allocations that we get, the share-save schemes, some of the discounts we receive make a difference . . .

(Beta interview 10, male applications support analyst)

Satisfaction with treatment

Overall satisfaction with the organizations' treatment of employees was generally high (see Table 8.4), particularly in the independent organizations and it is this category that seems to encompass the notion of fairness and reciprocity: 'I think if they are willing to put in the same commitment, yes then I am' (Pi interview 7, female technical author). Another said, 'So I do have that commitment – I hope it's a two-way thing. The company has invested in me and I've invested in the company and . . . the commitment's, I think, got to be there' (Gamma interview 1, male product development manager).

But where this perceived exchange breaks down, so do feelings of obligation:

> I have made a conscious decision that when I get home now that that's an end of it, because I get no reward for working when I'm at home in my own time and I think I give the company enough because I tend to work extra hours almost every day, and I've had periods working for the company when several of us have worked for months without a day off, including weekends, and worked stupidly long hours, and a few weeks ago we were in until 4 o'clock in the morning to try to complete a demo, an internal demo of all things, not even for a customer, and I don't feel that's appreciated the way it used to be. I think, when we were a small company, it was very much all hands to the wheel as it were and it was appreciated. . . . I think that core of people who were there at the start have worked very, very hard, as I think I've just described, to get the company to where it is and again, to be blunt, I don't think there has been any reward for that.
>
> (Gamma interview 11, male IT consultant and team leader)

> I regret that I have spent so much time on work in the past, because there have been times in the past when I have worked until two o'clock in the morning and so on, and it's not like you're ever going to get promoted for it.
>
> (Pi interview 8, male software programmer)

Management also identified a breakdown in reciprocity as was forcefully stated by the senior manager at Pi in an almost textbook exposition of the Capelli argument.

Interviewer: [Do you have a] commitment to Pi?

Chief operations officer: I do, yes, but then I've got reason to be committed to it. I don't expect that from anybody else. I think the company has got to earn that commitment from people and there are a lot of committed people and a lot of people who are here 9 to 5 and I've got no problem with any of that. I mean, commitment is something that's earned and it's something that's won, rather than something you give nowadays. Once upon a time, when I was in a company like Hewlett Packard or Burroughs, the commitment was expected, but there was a commitment back the way as well. It was a two way process of commitment, but when I was in Hewlett Packard, a company that was absolutely dedicated to the notion of a job for life, they themselves broke that unwritten agreement between employee and employer and subsequently every company's broken that, Burroughs, Digital, whoever you go to, they've all broken that, made people redundant, got rid of good people, so that's broken – the business world no longer has that, you can't expect commitment from anybody and I don't. If you get it, it's great ... It's a concept that's had its day, I feel.

(Pi interview 2, Chief operations officer)

Training provision and employability enhancement

Beta, as a larger organization, was a better provider of HCWP practices associated with professional development (training, employability enhancement). Although in both types of organization, these practices did not score so highly in terms of employee perceptions (see Table 8.4), it was apparent in the interviews that there was a sense of reciprocity or obligation following from professional enhancement. For example, when asked whether he has a sense of commitment, one Gamma interviewee replied:

Product consultant: Yes I do. I do feel a sense of commitment, I wouldn't say if a great opportunity came along somewhere else with the right opportunity that I wouldn't consider it, but it would have to be very good.

Interviewer: What would you miss?

Product consultant: ... the fact that you have got some sort of control over your career path here, so you can switch across different department more easily I think than most organizations ...

(Gamma interview 6, male product consultant)

Software organizations, then, did display some of the characteristics of high commitment management but are less conscientious about the 'new deal' practices which enhance professional development. The indirect model suggests that this may be a contributory factor to lower affective commitment.

The effects of high commitment work practices

Whether the presence of HCWP had either a positive or negative effect on attitudes and intentions towards the organization (predictions 3 and 4) was tested by regressing employee perceptions of practices on each of the key employee attitudes and outcomes (affective commitment, continuance commitment, intention to remain with the organization) while controlling for tenure, technical skill level of the job and occupational commitment. Table 8.5 shows these regressions for Beta and the independent organizations separately.

For Beta, fair treatment and training provision related to internal career advancement were both positively related to affective commitment, but there was no relationship between commitment and other HCWPs. The larger and more hierarchical Beta clearly had a career ladder which employees perceived as being worthwhile, which suggested that this career structure could affect identification with the organization. This supports the prediction of the direct high commitment model to some extent although the fact that these practices embody elements of reciprocity (in contrast to, for example, decision influence and job control) tends to also provide support for the indirect model. Further evidence for this is shown in the equation for intention to remain with the organization, which showed the importance of training for internal career advancement in making such decisions. This aspect of Beta, which as mentioned above was significantly better developed than in independent organizations, could influence employees to stay with the organization.

> They pay my wages, I should be defending them.... Beta has put a lot of money into my development especially over the last year or so and I do feel to slag the company off to external people is wrong. It's ok if it's internal.
>
> (Beta interview 7, male software engineer)

Table 8.5 Regressions predicting employee outcomes: Beta compared with the four independent organizations

	Affective commitment		*Continuance commitment*		*Intention to remain*[a]	
	Beta	*Indpts*	*Beta*	*Indpts*	*Beta*	*Indpts*
Tenure	0.41***	0.25***	0.36***	0.17*	0.02***	0.02*
Technical skill level				−0.18*		
Occupational commitment		0.19**				
Decision influence						
Job control		0.15*				
Support for non-work commitments						
Satisfaction with pay						
Satisfaction with treatment	0.26*	0.42***		0.17*		
Training provision	0.20*			0.21**	1.33*	0.91***
Employability enhancement						
N	87	164	87	164	87	164
Adjusted R^2	0.33	0.37	0.13	0.16		
R^2	0.31	0.36	0.12	0.14		
F	13.77***	23.77***	12.95***	7.68***		
-2LL					75.15	185.18
Chi-squared statistic					44.06***	38.18***

Notes:
a Logistic regression – coefficients are unstandardized.
*$p<0.05$
** $p<0.01$
*** $p<0.001$

In the independent organizations, fair treatment and greater job control were positively related to affective commitment, and training to intention to remain. For these organizations more than Beta, then, elements of the direct high commitment model appeared to be operating. Our qualitative data illustrated these relationships both for those directly involved in software development and other staff in supporting roles.

> I do feel committed here. I feel they have invested a lot of training, time and development in me, so I do feel that I owe that back to the company but, then, if an excellent opportunity arose elsewhere I would be inclined to take up another opportunity. . . .
>
> (Lambda interview 1, female PA to Financial Director)

Interviewer: Commitment to the company?

Senior software engineer: Yes, pretty much so . . . ideally (another job) would have to offer, in the same way as this current job offered me, the prospects of being more involved with the design, making of the designs as well as money. This company being relatively small, if you get in at this stage, as it grows the people who are in roughly senior positions are likely to be taken with it and move up through the ranks; if in two years time there is 300 employees rather than 100 employees, someone like that might find it harder because there is more people vying for that one position. So, if I get in at this early stage I think I could benefit from it.

(Gamma interview 7, male senior software engineer)

The final predictions related to the possible effects of other factors. Table 8.5 shows that tenure was a strong predictor of all outcomes in both types of organization and that for independents affective commitment was also influenced by occupational commitment.

This may show that in the independent organizations, which had a higher proportion of workers at the lower technical skill levels, identifying with the organization cultivated identification with the occupation, while in the case of the more highly skilled Beta workers the two foci of identification came from different sources (e.g. the organization versus professional qualifications).[3] This speculation is given further support by the finding that continuance commitment in the independents was inversely related to technical skill level, which means that the higher their skill level, the less likely employees were to stay with the organization because of no other choices. Thus, there is evidence to support the third prediction of the direct commitment model in both types of organizations, and some evidence for the indirect model in Beta, although the influence of training in Beta seemed to be internally orientated with respect to the organization (hence its relationship to affective commitment) rather than externally orientated towards enhancing employability in the industry.

Conclusions

We can see from this analysis that the model of the software worker as the prototypical highly committed knowledge worker lacks usefulness because it confuses commitment to the organization with commitment to the job and to the professional identity which the job bestows. It was the job itself, rather than the internalization of organizational goals, which led our software workers to expend discretionary effort and it was those management policies which offered the prospect of enhancing the career trajectory (either within or outside the current employing organization) that induced the most reciprocal affective commitment.

Similarly the assumption that knowledge-based organizations such as software houses will lead the field in developing direct high commitment management policies has been found wanting in the companies in this sample. Only the more bureaucratic former utility, Beta, had any formalized HCWPs, the other smaller, more organic, enterprises relying on the mix of paternalism and informal arrangements more typical of small and medium-sized enterprises. On a wider note, these findings from the Scottish software industry offer endorsement to the repeated observations of large scale UK studies such as the 1992 Workplace Industrial Relations Survey (WIRS), the 1998 UK WERS, and a recent ESRC study by Guest and colleagues, that the development and diffusion of high-commitment management practices in general remains extremely sparse (Cully *et al.* 1999: 295; Taylor 2002: 25). We would suggest that their absence in the very sector where it has been widely hypothesized such practices would be most appropriate does not lend support to the view that we are witnessing the gestation of a new high-trust, high commitment knowledge economy.

Thus it would seem that software developers' commitment to their organization is markedly indirect and is sustained only in so far as:

1 the organization expresses the values, such as autonomy, of the professional community;
2 the organization offers the prospect of enhancing personal development and labour market leverage; and
3 the expenditure of discretionary job effort is recognized and reciprocated by the above and by levels of pay.

In this situation the organization may be valued if it is seen to embody those values which are seen to be prototypical of the professional occupational community in which, as Alvesson suggests, being a knowledge worker might mean being seen (by others) as a hard-working person, committed to doing a good job. Thus even a positive response to the statement 'I find my values and those of the organization are similar' does not, as Ashforth and Mael (1989) point out, imply a discrete allegiance to that particular organization – it may mean rather 'to all organizations which are like this' or which 'embody my professional values and identity'.

It would seem therefore that software organizations could influence workers' attachment to the organization by providing the conditions for professional development (such as levels of pay, autonomy and skill acquisition) and these norms may promote high commitment to the work and identification with the organizational goals (Kunda 1992) because of the perceived gains of staying with that organization.

Finally we should be reminded of the contextual parameters for reciprocity. Western employers, as demonstrated elsewhere (see Sennett 1998; Thompson 2003), have only offered the prospect of long-term employment when continued growth, labour market shortages and other economic conditions favour such an approach. Their commitment to employees is, and always has been, founded on economic pragmatism. Employees are not slow to recognize the limited and conditional commitment offered to them by their employers and many vulnerable employees traditionally turn to trade unions for at least minimal protection. Those professional and highly skilled employees who enjoy specific labour market leverage may be expected to take advantage of their scarcity by seeking optimization of income and employment conditions with their current employer or by skimming the labour market to the best of what may be their short-term advantage. This is the sort of reciprocal behaviour predicted by equity theory (Adams 1963), which owes little to conceptualizations of organizational commitment, but more to the realities of fluctuating labour market dynamics and rational responses to employer behaviour.

Notes

1 This chapter is based on data collected as part of an ESRC research project funded under the *Future of Work* initiative (award number L212252006) 'Employment and Working Life beyond the Year 2000: Two Emerging Employment Sectors' (1999–2001). The full research team at Strathclyde, Stirling, Aberdeen and Heriot-Watt Universities is: Peter Bain, Chris Baldry, Nick Bozionelos, Dirk Bunzel, Gregor Gall, Kay Gilbert, Jeff Hyman, Cliff Lockyer, Abigail Marks, Gereth Mulvey, the late Harvie Ramsay, Dora Scholarios, Philip Taylor and Aileen Watson.

2 A background aspect of commitment that can also be considered is trade union identification, which can be seen as an alternative and potentially competing source of worker loyalty and values. Rejection of trade union membership might be associated with closer affiliation to the employing organization and its objectives. In our study, over two-thirds of the sample of software developers, including nearly half of the union members, did not see union membership as being appropriate to their work and labour market situation, confirming the general position on the individualistic/collectivist spectrum reported of software workers elsewhere (Barrett 2001; Hyman, Lockyer, Marks and Scholarios 2004). This view was typified by the Beta software engineer who stated 'I wouldn't trust a union to represent my views to Beta. I'd rather represent my views myself' (Beta interview 4, male software engineer).

3 Note that the regression equations conducted here do not resolve the issue of direction of causality between these two types of commitment.

References

Adams, J. S. (1963) 'Towards an understanding of inequity', *Journal of Abnormal and Social Psychology*, 67, 4: 422–36.

Allen, N. J. and Meyer, J. P. (1990) 'Organizational socialization tactics: A longitudinal analysis of links to newcomers' commitment and role orientation', *Academy of Management Journal*, 33: 847–58.

Alvesson, M. (2000) 'Social identity and the problem of loyalty in knowledge-intensive companies', *Journal of Management Studies*, 37, 8: 1101–23.

Ashforth, B. and Mael, F. (1989) 'Social identity theory and the organization', *Academy of Management Review*, 14, 1: 20–39.

Baldry, C. (2003) 'Employment relations in the information society', in B. Towers (ed.) *A Handbook of Employment Relations and Law*, London: Kogan Page.

Barrett, R. (2001) 'Labouring under an illusion? The labour process of software development in the Australian information industry', *New Technology Work and Employment*, 16, 1: 18–34.

Becker, H. (1960) 'Notes on the concept of commitment', *American Journal of Sociology*, 66, 1: 32–40.

Becker, H. (1992) 'Foci and bases of commitment: Are they distinctions worth making?' *Academy of Management Journal*, 35: 232–44.

Becker, T. E. and Billings, R. S. (1993) 'Profiles of commitment: An empirical test', *Journal of Organizational Behavior*, 14, 2: 177–90.

Blau, G. J. (1985) 'The measurement and prediction of career commitment', *Journal of Occupational Psychology*, 58: 277–88.

Capelli, P. (1999) *The New Deal at Work: Managing the Market-Driven Workforce*, Boston: Harvard Business School Press.

Capelli, P. (2000) 'Managing without commitment', *Organizational Dynamics*, 28, 4: 11–24.

Castells, M. (1996) *The Rise of the Networked Society*, Oxford: Blackwell.

Cully, M., Woodland, S., O'Reilly, A. and Dix, G. (1999) *Britain at Work: as Depicted by the 1998 Workplace Employee Relations Survey*, London: Routledge.

Eisenberger, R., Fasolo, P. M. and Davis-Lamastro, V. (1990) 'Effects of perceived organizational support on employee diligence, innovation, and commitment', *Journal of Applied Psychology*, 53: 51–9.

Folger, R. and Konovsky, M. K. (1989) 'Effects of procedural and distributive justice on reactions to pay raise decisions', *Academy of Management Journal*, 32: 115–30.

Fox, A. (1974) *Beyond Contract: Work, Power and Trust Relations*, London: Faber and Faber.

Gopinath, C. and Becker, T. E. (2000) 'Communication, procedural justice, and employee attitudes: Relationships under conditions of divestiture', *Journal of Management*, 26: 63–83.

Guest, D. (2002) 'Human resource management, corporate performance and employee wellbeing: Building the worker into HRM', *Journal of Industrial Relations*, 44, 3: 335–58.

Hall, R. H. (1968) 'Professionalization and bureaucratization', *American Sociological Review*, 33: 92–104.

Hunt, S. and Morgan, R. (1994) 'Organizational commitment: One of many commitments or key mediating construct?' *Academy of Management Journal*, 37, 6: 1568–88.

Huselid, M. A. (1995) 'The impact of human resource management practices on turnover, productivity, and corporate financial performance', *Academy of Management Journal*, 38: 635–72.

Hyman, J., Lockyer, C., Marks, A. and Scholarios, D. (2004) 'Needing a new program? Why is union membership so low among software workers?' in W.

Brown, G. Healy, E. Heery and P. Taylor (eds) *The Future of Worker Representation*, London: Palgrave.

Kessler, I. and Purcell, J. (2003) 'Individualism and collectivism in industrial relations', in P. Edwards (ed.) *Industrial Relations Theory and Practice in Britain*, 2nd edn, Oxford: Blackwell.

Kunda, G. (1992) *Engineering Culture, Control and Commitment in a High-Tech Corporation*, Philadelphia: Temple University Press.

Legge, K. (2001) 'Silver bullet or spent round? Assessing the meaning of the "high commitment management"/performance relationship', in J. Storey (ed.) *Human Resource Management: A Critical Text*, London: Thomson.

Mael, F. A. and Tetrick, L. E. (1992) 'Identifying organizational identification', *Educational and Psychological Measurement*, 52, 4: 813–25.

Meyer, J. P. and Allen, N. J. (1997) *Commitment in the Workplace: Theory, Research and Application*, Thousand Oaks, Ca.: Sage.

Meyer, J. P., Allen, N. J. and Smith, C. A. (1993) 'Commitment to organizations and occupations: Extension and test of a three-component conceptualization', *Journal of Applied Psychology*, 78: 538–51.

Mowday, R.T., Steers, R.M. and Porter, L. W. (1979) 'The measurement of organizational commitment', *Journal of Vocational Behavior*, 14: 224–47.

Mueller, C. W. and Lawler, E. D. (1999) 'Commitment to nested organizational units: Some basic principles and preliminary findings', *Social Psychology Quarterly*, 62, 4: 325–47.

Pearce, J. L. (1993) 'Toward an organizational behavior of contract laborers: Their psychological involvement and effects on employee co-workers', *Academy of Management Journal*, 36: 1082–96.

Peters, T. and Waterman, R. (1982) *In Search of Excellence: Lessons From America's Best-Run Companies*, New York: Harper and Row.

Podsakoff, P. M., MacKenzie, S. B. and Bomer, W. H. (1996) 'Transformational leader behaviours and substitutes for leadership as determinants of employee satisfaction, commitment, trust and organizational citizenship behaviours', *Journal of Management*, 22: 259–98.

Ramsay, H., Scholarios, D. and Harley, B. (2000) 'Employees and high performance work systems: Testing inside the black box', *British Journal of Industrial Relations*, 38, 4: 501–31.

Reichers, A. E. (1985) 'A review and reconceptualization of organizational commitment', *Academy of Management Review*, 10: 465–76.

Rhoades, L. and Eisenberger, R. (2002) 'Perceived organizational support: A review of the literature', *Journal of Applied Psychology*, 87, 4: 698–714.

Sennett, R. (1998) *The Corrosion of Character*, New York: Norton.

Tashakkori, A. and Teddlie, C. (1998) *Mixed Methodology: Combining Qualitative and Quantitative Approaches*, Thousand Oaks, CA: Sage.

Taylor, R. (2002) 'Britain's world of work – Myths and realities', *ESRC Future of Work Commentary Series*, Swindon: Economic and Social Research Council.

Thompson, P. (2003) 'Disconnected capitalism, or why employers can't keep their side of the bargain', *Work, Employment and Society*, 17, 2: 359–78.

Van Dick, R. (2001) 'Identification and self-categorization processes in organizational contexts: Linking theory and research from social and organizational psychology', *International Journal of Management Reviews*, 3: 265–83.

Vandenberg, R. J. and Scarpello, V. (1994) 'A longitudinal assessment of the

determinant relationship between employee commitments to occupation and the organization', *Journal of Organizational Behavior*, 15: 535–47.
Walton, R. E. (1985) 'From control to commitment in the workplace', *Harvard Business Review*, March-April: 77–84.
Zuboff, S. (1988) *In the Age of the Smart Machine: The Future of Work and Power*, New York: Basic Books.

9 The reality of software developing

Rowena Barrett

Introduction

The key issue in this book has been why and how, given different national cultures and institutional features and arrangements with respect to business and employment, different product and labour markets, firm sizes and cultural and social expectations about work and employment, do you get workers and managers in software firms around parts of the developed world thinking and behaving in a remarkably similar fashion? Why are there such similarities between what software developers and their managers say about their work? My argument, and that which the individual and collective chapters in this book seek to develop, is the need to consider the dualisms between structural forces and human agency if we are going to find any 'answers' to these questions. I explore the general conclusions reached in the first part of this chapter. In the second section I explore how fixed and eternal the conditions were that produced this apparently 'new economy'. In both parts of the chapter I draw on insights from a series of semi-structured interviews I conducted between June 2002 and May 2003 with 14 software developers around Australia.

Conclusions

If we look at the story of one software developer I interviewed in Melbourne in June 2002 we can see a number of the themes that have run throughout the chapters in this book. David had been working as a software developer since he migrated to Australia with his Australian wife in 1994. He started working in a small software house where he stayed for two years before 'reading the writing on the wall' and 'jumping ship' to a fast growth, high profile IT firm in Melbourne (IT Firm). This firm had an off-site joint venture with a large multi-national information and communication technology firm (multi-national ICT firm) and David spent the next four years (1997–2001) working off-site before he was made redundant. As far as David was concerned, he identified with the multi-national ICT firm not the one which employed him, as the following quote indicates.

> From my perspective I was treated like a [multi-national ICT firm] employee and essentially I did all my work for [multi-national ICT firm]. That was what attracted me to the job. But I was actually employed by [IT firm].
>
> (David, Melbourne June 2002)

After being made redundant in May 2001 David went to work for a small start-up software firm and, as he told it, 'I was there six weeks and then they just stopped paying us. The wages . . . I am still chasing them for the money'. It was for this reason that David joined the union – the Association of Professional Engineers Scientists and Managers of Australia (APESMA) – who were acting on his behalf to try to recover his wages. In November 2001 David 'got out of that really bad company' and in December he started with his current employer (at the time of the interview). This firm was an Australian subsidiary of a large UK software product supplier which employed some 6500 people worldwide. David worked in a division that concentrated on the finance sector with a software product that incorporated a set of trading and settlement systems. But, because this product was 'killed off' in the UK market, the company only supported the product in the Asia-Pacific market. As a result David's job revolved around maintenance while they waited for the company's release of the new, replacement product.

This story captures a number of the structural forces in the software and IT industries – growth, consolidation, decline, consolidation – but this is at best only part of the story. What is missing is how individuals behave or react or respond to these structural conditions. As Kunda (1992: 21) argues '[organisational members] create themselves within the constraints imposed on them' and in a number of chapters in this volume, notably Marks and Lockyer and Baldry *et al.* issues of software workers' identity and commitment are explored.

However these structural conditions also provide the parameters within which software development work is organized, managed and conducted. As Ray, a software engineer (his description) in Perth explained,

> I guess the biggest risk in my industry is that you lose touch. I guess that's the risk, that's the killer. And I guess it's that worry. It's that tension, the need to sort of keep up with things. Because there's been, the ground's been shifting permanently for years. Just recently I've been updating my CV . . . and the main parts of my CV, the bits that have been most impressive, looking over it again. Really it's not that impressive now because the things I was doing are so easy to do now. I was inventing the wheel whereas there are a lot of better wheels around now of doing things that have now been replaced by out of the box sort of technology. So yes it's not that impressive any more, so you have to try and keep up with things.
>
> (Ray, Perth July 2002)

David expressed a similar sentiment about the nature of the industry and what it meant for him staying in the IT industry when he said,

> You're constantly trying to keep up all the time, especially when you've got very bright colleagues and often who do have qualifications, you think 'well, it's going to be harder and harder for me to keep up', and 'am I going to be allowed to stay at a senior developer's level?'
>
> (David, Melbourne June 2002)

These examples are not given in order to agree with the Braverman deskilling thesis as these software developers and others I spoke to remain highly skilled: the tools they use to develop software keep changing and they take responsibility for ensuring their skills are up to date. The issue is the changing nature of the industry and the continual requirement to learn that is given as the responsibility of the employee. As one Melbourne-based developer said 'if you're in this industry you have to learn all the time, that's always been the way in IT' (Joe, Melbourne August 2002). Or as another said 'I subscribe to all sorts of magazines as well, so I'm forever reading at home' (Jeff, Perth October 2002). The encroachment of work learning into home life was made clear by another developer in Perth who said,

> I just read. My bedroom is full of books on one side. It's just really hard to keep up. It keeps it exciting, but then again when you just sort of want to mellow for a while it's a bit frustrating. You can just sit back for 6 months and just keep on keeping on, and then you realise you have missed a whole boatload of new stuff.
>
> (Jeff, Perth October 2002)

Cappelli (2001) pointed to the unique situation of these workers where skill requirements change quickly and often do not build on each other. He suggested the need for policy intervention arguing this explained a large part of the high turnover in IT. The crucial questions raised here are how long can individuals maintain their position within the labour market hierarchy and equally importantly how long these positions can retain their relatively privileged status.

A 'new economy'?

For me the changing nature of the industry and the effect on the identity and commitment of employees was apparent in the attitudes to working long hours (for example) that were elicited from software developers in interviews I conducted in 1998 compared with the ones conducted in 2002. A lot of the mystery and mystique of the industry, viewed from the outside, had been stripped away by the NASDAQ correction in March 2000. The 'tech wreck' and subsequent developments such as a drop in corporate investment in IT appear to have had an equally important effect on attitudes within the industry. In 1998 the software developers I spoke to worked long hours, expected to work long hours and accepted it as part of the job. In 2002 software developers had worked long hours in the past and realized there was no 'pay off' for doing so and they were not in a rush to do it again. This is consistent with Scholarios and Marks' (2004) results where they found negative work–life spillover affects work-related attitudes. For example Jeff told the story of how he had worked for a large software firm in Perth.

> At one stage there we were under a lot of pressure and we actually worked seven weeks straight without a break. And we worked about ten hours a day sort of, say about fifty days straight. We kept a tally on a white board. It was bloody awful and it's really put me off. Really, really bad stuff.
>
> (Jeff, Perth October 2002)

Another software developer in Perth also felt the same way and Mike explained, 'at the last place we worked sometimes all through the night and on weekends. But now, nup' (Mike, Perth October 2002). David's experience in several good and bad software firms led him to say,

> I don't think I'll ever be a corporate person who believes in the company as a family because. I think that is very naïve. The companies have no loyalty to their employees. They can't afford to have ... The way industry works, it's basically a jungle, it's a competition and your boss may be a nice guy and he may, you know, do his best for you and the people you work with, but the company has no loyalty to you. So ultimately I have no loyalty to the company. That is, I wouldn't sacrifice everything for the company because I know the company wouldn't do that for me.
>
> (David, Melbourne June 2002)

Another software developer who also had a bad work experience in a firm that had been at the time a 'darling' in the media said,

> There are a lot of people that I know who don't really care where they work or what they do. As long as they're just working. And they move from job to job and don't really care. And companies are getting that way as well where they don't care where their employees come from. They just cycle them through.
>
> (Jim, Melbourne Aug 2002)

A number of the software developers I spoke to in 2002 wanted to keep their work and home life separate. For example the only female software developer I have ever interviewed said 'Programming is just a means . . . I don't want to turn the computer on when I get home' (Jane, Brisbane August 2002). She was not alone, Ray in Perth said 'when you stare at your computer all day and you come home and there might be things that you want to do and I might even have the mental energy left to do it, it's just sitting in front and looking at a computer screen is just so unappealing' (Ray, Perth August 2002). Another said 'I don't even have an Internet connection at home because I do it all day. I get home I don't want to do it' (Mike, Perth October 2002). And another who had a computer at home which didn't work said 'I spend about 8 or 9 hours on the computer at work so that's enough for me during the week' (Jeff, Perth October 2002).

Perhaps it was that these people were talking to me because they had bad experiences, after all they had volunteered to participate in the research from an article published in *The Age* and *The Sydney Morning Herald* newspapers about my research (Mulcaster 23 July 2002a; 23 July 2002b). However, it is also possible to argue that what people think about their work and how they behave is a result of the reciprocal interaction of structure and agency.

The means management uses to control the software development labour process are also caused and influenced by this interaction. How software development work is organized and what means managers use to control the labour process were addressed in this book. Regardless of the geographical location in which the work was performed, the tension between autonomy and control was evident. We can quite clearly see this in David's account of what he does at work on the mature application his firm sold across the Asia-Pacific region.

> We set dates when we're going to release the next version and there's a change review committee and they decide the work that's going to go into the next release. The team leader gets the whole bunch of tracker items [tracker is the in-house systems that tracks bugs or change requests] so that's the whole list of these changes that need to be made and they then task them out to individual developers. So the developers come in the morning, they have their list of tracker items up, pick one to work on, and they'll fix it, and they look at the next one, they fix it and it goes like that. Most of the time. . . . So that's what a developer will do day to day and on top of that the team leaders they task out bugs but we also have a nightly build So the team leader has to make sure that the nightly build always works and if it doesn't, they fix those problems. And then every week or so we do a release build which then goes to test. We have a separate test team. And that goes to the test team and then they will test all those bugs that have gone in since their last release build. And eventually that goes on to the

> release date when that release build is a candidate for releasing to the customer. And it's actually not released to the customer, it's released to an operations group who are responsible for installing it on the customer site. So what happens is, you reach the release date for development and then that release build goes to testing and they should get two weeks to test it. And then it goes to the operations group and they get another two weeks to test it. That's the most stressful period of the whole thing because it goes into testing, of course they find bugs and they find bugs that have to be fixed but because that has now officially left development . . . sometimes you get a chance to do another release build, other times you have to tag up the code as though it has gone into the previous release build and then build it again. Because the way configuration management is done, all the files are tagged for the particular build they're in. So yeah, you have to do some really naughty stuff. So you might have to do something like that. Then you have got to try and keep track of all this manually. And when it goes into operation it's even more crucial that things get fixed, so this is where you start getting people asked to work weekends and evenings. Because then that's going to the customer and there are things the customer won't accept, you can't make a customer cross. We don't have an enormous number of customers, so you can't afford to be arrogant. You just can't. If they say jump, you have to jump. So there's a kind of a rhythm about the whole thing.
>
> (David, Melbourne June 2002)

In this (long) quote we can clearly see issues of the type of autonomy software developers have – the user requirements set parameters for what can be developed, but developers need to be given technical autonomy in order to come up with some solution. In terms of time we can see that deadlines act as a form of direct control but employees are still able to manage their time autonomously within the context of that deadline and use their technical autonomy to create the 'best product' within that timeframe. The influence exerted by the market is also quite apparent in how the labour process is controlled. Also evident, when David says it is 'naughty' to retag the code, is the control that the 'shadows' (Andrews *et al.* this volume) exert over the labour process.

Most importantly for me this quote quite clearly strips away any remaining 'mystery' of the software development labour process. 'Pick a bug, fix it. Pick a bug, fix it'. However, while this would appear to be a modern day assembly line, unlike the work performed on an assembly line, no two bugs are the same nor is the coding needed to fix those bugs. As one software developer in Sydney said to me in an email,

> If you stand back far enough from the actual effort needed to perform the meta-level tasks then almost anything can look like an assembly

> line – coding (and academic life) isn't really like that though. Unless you're writing the same thing over and over again, there is always some analysis to be done – and probably more so in debugging – no two bugs are the same.
>
> (George, Sydney July 2002)

The argument in this book has been that it is not a question of management using one strategy or another to control the software development labour process, it is more about how different strategies are used separately and simultaneously as Storey made clear when he wrote about 'levels and circuits of control'.

> The idea of levels is not meant to imply discrete forms of control corresponding with the hierarchical strata in bureaucratic organizations. Rather, it is intended to denote the inter-penetrating 'layers' of control which reinforce and substitute for one each other as one or more becomes weak, decayed or fully untenable. Thus, in my fieldwork, in manual and non-manual settings, I would find it very difficult to determine whether 'simple', 'technological' or 'bureaucratic' control 'types' prevailed. What seemed instead to exist was a cluster of devices, structures and practices. One particular form, such as tighter discipline, might be favored for a period and then, *without it ever being totally replaced* but merely subsumed, a supplemental form would surface. Equally, not only was there some oscillation over time – a kind of cycle of control – but even at a particular time the structure of control was typically comprised of a number of layers.
>
> (Storey, 1985: 198 [italics in original])

Storey then brings in an example from his research but goes on to make the following point.

> The fluidity between control means is the point to note. So too is the shaping of the interplay between managerial action at more than one level and worker action. Hence managers are not faced with a strategic choice between types of controls – partly because the choice is not entirely in their hands and partly because rarely is it a question of using only rules *or* targets, socialization *or* technology, participation *or* hierarchy, selection screening *or* communication, individual *or* collective labour control. A whole multiplicity of these – with some certainly given emphasis for a time – seems to be more typically arrayed.
>
> (Storey, 1985: 199 [italics in original])

With control, however it is played out, there is also compliance or consent, as well as the flip-side, resistance. While the earlier discussion about software developers wanting to keep home and work separate suggests there may not be such enthusiastic and wholehearted consent, in this industry it is primarily driven by the commitment software developers have to their task. For example, one software developer explained it as 'my primary responsibility is to use the talents that I have productively so you know I think it will be wrong of me to stay in a company that didn't have opportunities for my talents' (David, Melbourne June 2000). The point about commitment to the task was made by another developer who used the situation of a job he had been offered prior to the one he currently had where the job would involve auditing code written in India: 'I would have been auditing their code and making sure it was good. And I was going to get a decent pay packet for it and I thought "I'd rather shoot myself"' (Jim, Melbourne August 2002). The attraction of the opportunities with the technology was made apparent by Mike who had moved to his current job from one which had typified those at the height of the dot.com boom, as Mike explained, 'And it's just different. They use different tools to develop, a different style, which is all good. I learned heaps from the first day' (Mike, Perth October 2002).

The commitment to the task and technology is a constant across the countries involved in this book and it is a constant across time. As others in this book and Baldry *et al.* (this volume) in particular argue, software developers are committed to the job not the organization. Software developers recognize that the opportunity to work with new languages on challenging projects is what will enhance their career trajectory. However, once the challenge is gone so too will employees and this is why software developers take on the responsibility of their own learning – to ensure they are able to leave. They understand there will always be someone willing to make a buck out of the latest technology or use the latest tools. One software developer put it as follows.

> If you don't keep up with the technology sector you lose . . . I'm a very self-resourceful person, the only thing I considered would be of any value to helping me [find a new job] was effectively a very scary concept, but was discarding everything I'd done, forgetting about it and actually going, 'where was I before I started here and what did I want to do?' And if that meant the bleeding edge then find it. Figure it out. . . . I moved out from Brisbane to here. I waited about 6 months to get a job with these guys. I waited for it to come along and they were perfect.
>
> (Jim, Melbourne August 2002)

Another software developer, who was older and had family responsibilities, was not as positive.

> The ground is shifting underneath me so I've got to keep up and how long can I keep that up for. I don't know. . . . I guess that's on my mind at the moment, how do I keep up and you know, for example, if I take

> the full, well I'll probably have to take up a full time position where I'm working at the moment, is it almost going to be like a retirement home for me? I might slip back into oblivion. Again, I guess that's what a lot of people face, the uncertain future. I guess the whole idea at the moment is everyone needs to be insecure so in that's the most competitive and the most productive and that's what's required of you in the modern economy.
>
> (Ray, Perth August 2002)

The (real or perceived) mobility of software workers and their commitment to the task and technology rather than the firm means that there is no one best way of controlling the labour process – it is not a simple matter of saying 'management, faced by a certain labour market situation, chooses a strategy and that explains the type of work control that emerges'. For example, management strategies of direct control are counterproductive in situations where the stability of creative and expert labour is required. Managers, faced with the heightened indeterminacy of the labour of creative staff, have to walk the tightrope between autonomy and getting profitable work carried out within deadlines. For employees autonomy is constrained by the necessity of profitability. For management profitability can come from routinizing the work and creating greater divisions between software development and software testing processes, but it is clear that if work becomes too routinized employees will consider their options.

In 1998 many of the software developers I interviewed made it clear they would walk, they were certain someone else would employ them and they felt sure they enjoyed a privileged position in the labour market. The developers I interviewed then were mainly young and inexperienced and knew they had to get some experience to get on (see Barrett this volume and Barrett 2001, 2004). In 2002 this response was still evident, but the developers I interviewed made it clear that they knew they had to keep up to stay in the game. In a short amount of time their privileged position within the labour market was shown to be only relatively so. In 2004 things have changed again and the increasing enthusiasm with which firms in developed economies are outsourcing some of their software development to places like India, Latin America and states in the former Soviet bloc (see Philipson this volume) means there is greater uncertainty about the position of these workers. Whilst I would not claim that we can deduce all the trends apparent in the employment of software developers on the basis of interviews with 14 software developers around Australia in 2002, the analysis in the book, drawing on studies in the UK, Norway, Germany and the US in addition to Australia, does point in a number of similar directions.

The interaction between the dynamics of technological innovation and changing patterns of technology use (Morgan and Sayer 1988; Quintas

1994) is why positive and negative scenarios about job quality (Rubery and Grimshaw 2001) have started to develop. This is certainly the conclusion drawn by Beirne, Ramsay and Panteli (1998: 158) when they argue that the future of software work is 'unlikely to match straightforward and unambiguous images of deskilling and degradation, or enskilling and job enrichment'. With software there is still the same requirement for management to convert labour, potential into actual productive labour, but simply the processes for doing this has changed. Friedman (1984: 181) said this would happen when he contended that a firm's position on the responsible autonomy/direct control continuum would change as 'competitive conditions in product and labour markets and worker reactions' force managers to change their strategy. How managers do this and the response of workers to the means of management control were explored in this book.

The consequence of changing global economic conditions and the demise of the dot.coms is tighter labour markets for software workers. As a result 'the privileged market position which specialized and technically trained labour possess in the earlier phase of its development, at a time when the supply of such labour is catching up with the needs of capital accumulation' (Braverman 1974: 407) is changing. This highlights that the relatively privileged position of software workers within the labour market is precisely that – relative – as capitalism, and its process of uneven development is constantly creating and undermining such positions.

Accordingly we can speculate that the social identity of software developers is also changing. Evidence of a type of unionization amongst software workers in the US (Buffini 15 June 2001) supports this proposition as Working Today is a national non-profit group that agitates for portable health and pension plans, and the extension of tax incentives, discrimination and labour laws to independent workers, which describes the status of many software workers. Similarly David, one of the Melbourne-based software developers I interviewed, joined the union as he needed someone to support him in his quest for unpaid wages. While another of the software developers was not a member, she was considering it after her recent experience with pay as the following quote made clear.

> At the moment we just have to take what we get because of the whole economy. We got really bad pay rises this year, some people didn't get any, it's really very depressed everywhere. We've got hardly any new work coming in so they made 30 people redundant in Sydney, about 10 up here [Brisbane]. So everyone is frightened and I just said 'yes, where do you want me to sign?' I did let them know, right on the form, that I wasn't impressed with my pay rise and that was it, you know. There's not much you could do at all. That was why I was looking at the union site!
>
> (Jane, Brisbane August 2002)

One of the software developers in Perth put it this way.

> Until very recently I felt I've sort of worried for other people and not myself. I felt that I'm on the right path and I'm going to be okay . . . And of course for a while now I have been career wise. When you're on this trajectory upwards and when you're looking up the slope, you sort of see I'm going to have a comfortable life, a comfortable retirement and I'll be able to afford to buy reasonable cars every now and then and if I ever have kids I can be able to send them to a private school and that sort of thing. So of course that's all levelled out now. It's going downwards. It's a downwards slope and the picture suddenly changes and obviously it's a more realistic picture. It's an adjustment . . . But the thing that's really got to me was finding out that the Australian government was actually negotiating to have my career sort of taken away from me [reference to outsourcing government work to India]. You observe those sorts of things happening, that sort of behaviour towards other professions or the trades, people in more sort of labour based industries or even trade based and there's almost, contempt is a bit over the top, but there's certainly no real regard for their value. And all of a sudden I'm in the same boat.
>
> (Ray, Perth July 2002)

When we peel away the hype about the 'new economy' to carefully evaluate the work of software development we see that software developers may be in 'the belly of the beast' (Kraft 1979: 2) but their labour power still has to be converted from potential into actual work. The issue is around the nature of their work although as one developer put it,

> I'm a software engineer, and to me it's like you build things, but the exciting thing is you can build anything you want almost, as long as you can represent it in symbols.
>
> (Ray, Perth July 2002).

One developer in Melbourne made the point 'when you actually know what IT can really deliver, I mean it's useful but it's not magic' (David, Melbourne June 2002).

The prediction that software developers would become the aristocrats of the labour market has not been realized and we can see this in what one of them says.

> Maybe from outside it's sort of black magic. Maybe that's where the aristocrat or priesthood view of it came from. But we're really getting over that concept of computers are something a bit sort of cutting edge and special and magic. Really, it's not that different and it's just maybe a different sort of approach.
>
> (Ray, Perth July 2002).

His response to my comment about the type of work he does putting him right at the centre of the new economy was 'I wonder if we are. I mean, to some extent yeah, you certainly feel, I guess I've felt that I've been part of the new economy. I got picked to play, so to speak. That was the game that was in town and we were lucky (Ray, Perth July 2002).

References

Barrett, R. (2001) 'Labouring under an illusion? The labour process of software development in the Australian information industry', *New Technology Work and Employment*, 16, 1: 18–34.

Barrett, R. (2004) 'Working at Webboyz: Life in a small Australian internet firm', *Sociology*, 38, 4: 777–94.

Beirne, M., Ramsay, H. and Panteli, A. (1998) 'Developments in computing work: Control and contradiction in the software labour process', in P. Thompson and C. Warhurst (eds) *Workplaces of the Future*, Houndsmill, UK: Macmillan Business.

Braverman, H. (1974) *Labour and Monopoly Capital*, London: Monthly Review Press.

Buffini, F. (15 June 2001) 'Dot comrades of the e-lance world unite', *The Australian Financial Review*, 17.

Cappelli, P. (2001) 'Why is it so hard to find information technology workers?', *Organizational Dynamics*, 30, 2, 87–99.

Friedman, A. (1984) 'Management strategies: Market conditions and the labour process', in F. Stephen (ed.) *Firms Organisation and Labour*, London: Macmillan.

Kraft, P. (1979) 'The industralisation of computer programming: From programming to "software production"', in A. Zimbalist (ed.) *Case Studies on the Labour Process*, London: Monthly Review Press.

Kunda, G. (1992) *Engineering Culture: Control and Commitment in a High-Tech Corporation*, Philadelphia: Temple University Press.

Morgan, K. and Sayer, A. (1988) *Microcircuits of Capital: 'Sunrise' Industry and Uneven Development*, UK: Polity Press.

Mulcaster, G. (23 July 2002a) 'Hard yakka at the coding coalface', *The Age (NEXT)*, 10.

Mulcaster, G. (23 July 2002b) 'Hard yakka at the coding coalface', *The Sydney Morning Herald (NEXT)*, 10.

Quintas, P. (1994) 'Programmed innovation? Trajectories of change in software development', *Information Technology and People*, 7, 1: 25–47.

Rubery, J. and Grimshaw, D. (2001) 'ICTs and employment: The problem of job quality', *International Review of Labour*, 140, 2: 165–92.

Scholarios, D. and Marks, A. (2004) 'Work–life balance and the software worker', *Human Resource Management Journal*, 14, 2: 54–74.

Storey, J (1985) 'The means of management control', *Sociology*, 19: 193–211.

Index

Suffix n on locators indicates *notes*